JESUS, CHRIST AND SERVANT OF GOD

MEDITATIONS ON THE GOSPEL ACCORDING TO JOHN

By

David Johnson

Inner Light Books
San Francisco, California
2017

JESUS, CHRIST AND SERVANT OF GOD
MEDITATIONS ON THE GOSPEL ACCORDING TO JOHN

© 2017 David Johnson
All Rights Reserved

Except for brief quotations, no part of this publication may be reproduced, stored in a retrieval system, or transmitted, in any form or by any means, electronic, mechanical, photocopy, recorded, or otherwise, without prior written permission.

Editor: Charles Martin
Copyediting: Kathy McKay
Layout and design: Matt Kelsey

Published by Inner Light Books

San Francisco, California

www.innerlightbooks.com

editor@innerlightbooks.com

Library of Congress Control Number: 2016956015

ISBN 978-0-9970604-6-1 (hardcover)
ISBN 978-0-9970604-7-8 (paperback)
ISBN 978-0-9970604-8-5 (eBook)

Scripture quotations marked NIV are taken from The Holy Bible, New International Version eBook®, NIV®. Copyright © 1973, 1978, 1984, 2011 by Biblica Inc.™ Used by permission. All rights reserved worldwide.

Contents

PREFACE — vii
    The Quaker Gospel — x
    Approaching the Scripture — xii

1. JESUS — 1
    Jesus as a Human Being — 1
    Jesus Does Nothing without the Life and Power and Instructions and Authority of God — 2
    Jesus Embodies the Eternal Indwelling Christ, the Truth, the Word, the Light, and the Life — 4
    Jesus as Both Servant and Christ — 6

2. THE ETERNAL MYSTICAL VISION REACHING OUT TO US—THE CALL — 8
    Praying the Word — 8
    John the Baptist as the Messenger—First Sounds of the Call — 13
    The Calling—What Do You Seek? — 15

3. HOW MUCH CHANGE MIGHT WE EXPERIENCE? — 19
    Jesus Introduced to the World as an Extraordinary Being: The Wedding at Cana — 19
    Clearing Out in Preparation for the Journey — 22
        Table 1. Major Jewish Festivals — 23

4. REBIRTH—A VERITABLE LEAVING BEHIND OF THE OLD — 29
    Jesus Confirms Rebirth by the Spirit to Nicodemus — 29
    Rebirth Is a Universal Gift — 34
    John the Baptist Reminds Us That Humility Is an Essential Gift to Practise — 36
    Complete Rebirth — 38

5. JESUS INSTITUTES THE NEW WORSHIP IN SPIRIT AND TRUTH, IRRESPECTIVE OF GENDER, CLASS, OR RACE — 40
    Samaritan Woman at the Well — 40
    Healing the Nobleman's Servant — 50
    Equality — 52

6. THE DAY OF VISITATION AND HEALING — 53
- The Day of Visitation — 53
- God's Work Not Subject to Human Timetables — 55
- God Is the Source of Jesus' Life and Powers — 56
- The New Covenant — 57
- Repudiating the Lack of Love — 59

7. BREAD OF LIFE — 61
- Sign of Feeding the Multitude — 61
- Miraculous Walking on Water — 63
- John's Version of the Eucharist — 65

8. MEETING OUR RESISTANCES — 72
- Jesus in Jerusalem — 72
- Waters of Life — 73
- Our Own Resistances — 75

9. THE BALANCED LIFE OF PRAYER AND MINISTRY — 79
- Mercy and Forgiveness — 79
- The Light of Christ Within — 81
- Coming to Convincement — 87

10. OUR BLINDNESS — 93
- Restoring Sight to the Blind — 93
- Refute the Voice of the Pharisees That the Voice of the Spirit May Prevail — 95

11. DO WE FOLLOW THE VOICE OF THE SHEPHERD? — 98
- The Good Shepherd — 98
- Jesus Gives of His Own Free Will — 102
- Continuing Resistance: The Worldly Voice That Disputes the Voice of the Spirit — 103

12. CHRIST IS NOT JUST A HEALER BUT THE SOURCE OF LIFE — 106
- Raising of Lazarus from Death — 106
- Political Scapegoat — 112

13. CONFRONTING THE POWERS WITHOUT VIOLENCE — 114
- What Were the Disciples Thinking? — 114
- Jesus' Final Public Summary of His Ministry — 119

14. CHURCH OF EQUALITY, HUMILITY, SERVICE, AND LOVE   123
- The Washing of Feet   123
- Dismissing the Spirit of Betrayal   127
- Love One Another   129
- The Spectre of Fear Within   130

15. PRIESTLY INSTRUCTIONS FOR THE WAY TO LIFE AND PEACE   134
- I Am the Way   135
- If Ye Love Me, Keep My Commandments   136

16. THE SPIRITUAL COMMUNITY   140
- The Vine—Intimate Union with Jesus and God   140
- Abide in My Love   143

17. COMFORT, GUIDANCE, AND HOPE   146
- Promise of the Holy Spirit Again   146
- Pray for Courage and Hope   148

18. JESUS' OWN PRAYERS BEFORE GOD   150
- Supplication, Vows, and Intercession   150
- Vision of Unity with Jesus and God   152

19. TRIALS AND CRUCIFIXION   154
- Nonviolence, Submission, and Yielding in the Struggle between Light and Dark   154
- Suffering and Sacrifice   164

20. RESURRECTION   168
- Jesus Appears after His Death to His Disciples   168
- First Gift of the Holy Spirit and Call to Discipleship   170

21. DISCIPLESHIP—A LIFE OF FAITHFULNESS AND HOLY OBEDIENCE   174
- Jesus Confirms the Benefits of a Life of Obedience to the Spirit   174
- Reconciliation and the Call into Ministry   177

22. THE SPIRITUAL JOURNEY WITH JOHN   181
- Sequence of Teachings in the Gospel According to John   181
- Jesus Acknowledges God as Far Greater Than Himself   186
- John's Gentle Corrections of Earlier Gospels   191

The Change Required	192
Struggle between Light and Dark on the Way	193
Forgiveness, Not Condemnation	194
Jesus and the Union with God	196
Love Always	196

23. I AM — 198
"I AM" Is the Name of God; "I Am" Refers to the Presence of God — 198
Jesus and God: I Am — 201
I Am the Bread of Life — 202
I Am the Life, the Vine, and the Living Water — 203
I Am the Light — 204
The Universal Nature of the Light — 207
I Am the Truth — 209
I Am the Way and the Door — 210
I Am the Good Shepherd — 211
I Am the Resurrection, the Giver of Life — 212

EPILOGUE — 214

APPENDIX 1 — 215
Historical Background — 215

APPENDIX 2 — 219
Significant Dates in Palestine Based on the Old Testament — 219

APPENDIX 3 — 222
Brief Background of the Gospels — 222

APPENDIX 4 — 229
Significant Dates in Early Christianity Based on the New Testament — 229

ACKNOWLEDGEMENTS — 233

BIBLIOGRAPHY — 236

ENDNOTES — 240

PREFACE

It is more important to read the Gospel According to John than to read this book. If you are moved to enter this venture, please take time to read the gospel and meditate on the text each day as you read this book.

In 2007-8 I was led to read the gospel of John, verse by verse. For eight months I read nothing else. The Holy Spirit took me through the gospel and began opening its meaning for me. This experience convinced me that the gospel is not just a record of Jesus' ministry; it is also a consummate guide to the spiritual life. The reader starts at the beginning and progressively enters more and more deeply into a relationship of holy faithfulness with Jesus.

The Gospel According to John is for me a book of divinely inspired writing, a record by one who had direct experience with Jesus. John had the gifts of both a remarkably deep understanding and a mystical experience of Jesus' spirituality. The traditional view was that John wrote the gospel towards the end of his life, at the request of churches in Asia, as a summary of his teachings on the life of Jesus as the Christ.[1]

So the gospel records the experiences and teachings of a saintly man, late in life, who had practised Jesus' message for fifty to sixty years. Selected memories of Jesus' life are carefully and accurately arranged. The gospel contains the spiritual certainty of what a committed following of these teachings did for John and can do for each of us. His own experience is clear from his explanation that this book was *written, that ye might believe that Jesus is the Christ, the Son of God; and that believing ye might have life through his name* (John 20:31 KJV).

This book contains my own understandings of the Gospel According to John. I do not pretend that this is a scholarly work, although I value such works on John's gospel by others.[2]

I have come to these understandings late in life and have been through Chuck Fager's three phases[3] in my relation to the Scriptures. The first phase, 'Detoxification', involved my gradually overcoming the disenchantment and aversion I felt towards the Scripture based on my early years and on observing the aberrant ways of so many Bible users in society around me. The next stage was 'Uncovering a Resource', in which I was drawn to read and study and understand the variety of texts in the Bible. Finally I came, by grace, to the phase of 'Godwrestling' as the writings began to speak to me, to appear to me at vital times when I needed them, to challenge and reprove me, and to suffuse me with their deeper message of spiritual certainty and communion. I know now that there is both more wisdom and more comfort in the Bible than the Church had led me to believe.

I am not concerned with philosophical analyses, nor whether John's text justifies Christian doctrines of any particular church persuasion, nor with analyses of the extent to which John recast the oral traditions to suit his own theological bent, nor which heresies he may or may not have been counteracting, nor which verses have been modified or inserted by later copiers of the original manuscript. Many scholars have explored these issues.[4] I am sure that John's gospel was assembled from the teachings of the John who was a disciple of Jesus, the beloved disciple, and I am mainly interested in the lessons these gospel writings have for the individual spiritual journey.

Other commentaries explore the links of this gospel to ancient philosophical works or metaphysical theories and address the meanings of 'logos' and 'light'. For me, the terms 'Word' and 'Light' are to be encountered as spiritual experiences and realities rather than through their meaning in linguistics and philosophy.

John's gospel on Jesus opens up a new spiritual world that concentrates on our being in the here and now. Jesus demolishes religious, cultural, and gender walls to reveal a way of being that transcends these regulations. The spirituality of Jesus is eternal and universal and is of the heart, not of buildings and doctrines. This was clearly stated by the Apostle Peter speaking about Jesus' ministry in *The Inclusive Bible* (TIB): *I begin to see how true it is that God shows no partiality—rather, that any person of any nationality who fears God and does what is right is acceptable* to God (Acts 10:34–35). It is time to recover the wonderful impact of Jesus' teachings anew.

What do I mean by 'God'? As I explained in another little book:

> 'God', for me, is simply a three-letter word that refers to that extraordinary inner mystery of Divine Presence in all its manifestations: creating, sustaining, enlightening, pacifying, reproving, guiding, inspiring and energising. It carries no theological doctrine or ritual requirements. It is simply a short word to convey that huge range of inward mystical feelings and understandings, most of which cannot be put into words. Many words have been used to refer to this mystery by others, most of them longer: Universal Wisdom, Divine Presence, Eternal Presence, Supreme End, Infinite Light, Love, Truth, Creator, the NeverChanging, the Infinite, Immutable, OmniPresent One, Unnameable, Source of all Being, All that has been that is and ever will be, "that in which I live and move and have my being", Great Spirit, etc. I use the three letters 'G', 'o', 'd'. To enter into the 'Kingdom of God' is to enter into a state, in the present, of deep awareness, connectedness and responsiveness to the divine implantings of Truth and Love, so we can do no other.[5]

The Bible records an even wider range of names for the undefinable being of God, apart from the truly delivered name I AM voiced by God to Moses (Exodus 3:14). The Quaker William Shewen wrote in 1675:

> God is infinite and incomprehensible in himself, and all the words of men and angels cannot define him, as he is, being in all, through all, and above all. And the various names given him throughout the holy scriptures, were according to the manifestation or appearance and operation of his spirit in their hearts that wrote them, and according to the state it found them in, when it appeared to them; hence he is called a consuming fire. Our God is a consuming fire, and his word as a hammer, and as a fire, and a jealous and angry God, who as a

devouring fire goes through the briars and thorns, and consumes them; and the day of his appearance among these briars and thorns, thistles, and stubble, is compared to the burning of fire in an oven, in which the wicked cannot dwell. And others could call him by quite contrary names, even according to the operation of his spirit in them, and by the same could say, that God is love, and his word was as milk, and sweeter than honey or the honey-comb, and that the light of his countenance was better than the increase of corn, wine, and oil; and that he was a shield and a shadow of a rock in a weary land; and his name as a strong tower, and a safe dwelling place, and as a precious ointment poured forth; and his face or presence, glory and power, which is terrible to the worker of iniquity, is pleasant and desirable by those that witness Sion's redemption, by the spirit of judgment and burning, from iniquity. . . . He that can understand, let him.[6]

Some relate to God as a sense of mysterious 'isness' or 'being', and I will come back to that sense later in this book. To know God is more than reading and understanding theories about God, for it is about experiencing the divine presence and openings of spiritual reality. It is about developing a deep relationship, accepting that God is leading each of us, and surrendering to that leading. It involves a fundamental shift from an uncertain apprehension of God to a complete awareness and acceptance of the reality of the divine within everything at every moment and treating every moment and person and situation as if only God were present.

The Quaker Gospel

In this essay I quote the King James Version (KJV) of the Bible as the primary reference because these were the words known by George Fox and early Quakers.[7] In the seventeenth century, the KJV was the "modern" translation, though some of the English used was even then becoming outdated. I have also read much of the 2011 *New International Version Study Bible* (NIV), *The Inclusive Bible* of 2007 translated by the Priests for Equality (TIB), *The Four Gospels* 1977 translation by the Quaker classics scholar Norman Marrow (TFG), and *The Jerusalem Bible* of 1968 (TJB). The version is only specified where passages from these other translations are quoted. Many may find alternative translations to the KJV more meaningful.

For me, to be a Quaker, a member of the Religious Society of Friends, is to understand the writings of those extraordinary men and women who were the first Quakers—Fox, Fell, Barclay, Bathurst, Crisp, Howgill, Hubberthorne, Burrough, Nayler, Penn, the Peningtons, et al. To understand their writings, I need to understand the Scriptures that inspired and justified them, and the KJV was the version that was most readily available to them. The Geneva Bible and other translations were available in the seventeenth century, but the KJV was the first version in English that was widely read by common people. The words of Fox and other early Quakers recall expressions in the KJV, so it is important to get a feel for the effect that their words would have had on people who also knew the same text. I am sure that when Fox and others used just a phrase from Scripture, their listeners would have recalled the full text and understood what they were getting at.

The Gospel According to John has often been termed the 'Quaker gospel' for it contains so much that was so close to the heart of the early Quakers. John is very different to the gospels of Matthew, Mark, and Luke, which are known as the Synoptic Gospels because they tell such a similar story (see appendix 2).

What I have written may not suit many steeped in the doctrines of a particular Christian denomination. I do not emphasise that Jesus was sent to die on the cross, nor do I refer repeatedly to his shedding of blood for our sins. I believe that Jesus died because he saw no other path of love than to submit to death; anything else would have required him to retaliate. He died on the cross so that the cycle of violence would stop with him and would not be passed on. He could do this only because of his complete surrender into the love of God.

Approaching the Scripture

It is not possible to comprehend John with the mind alone. The Scriptures have many layers. Years ago I read that the stories in the Hindu epic *The Mahabharata* have three main purposes: they are to be amusing and educational for children, instructive for adults, and illuminating for the sage. The Hebrew practice of *midrash* is intended to discover the layers of meaning in a biblical text. I have found my reading of the Scriptures to be the same. Moreover, the illuminations are not limited to the first reading, nor is it mandatory to understand every word and verse. Some passages in John, or elsewhere in the Scriptures, may have a verse that is key to one reading, whereas other verses are perplexing or even obnoxious. I have learnt to let those others alone. They are not important at that time. Despite protestations by our critical minds, if we be patient, the meaning of difficult verses will be revealed by the Spirit when the time is ready.

My own method is to read the text and commonly to check any aspects of the stories where a little knowledge would be helpful—the nature of a festival, the location of the town, the season of the year. Then I allow myself to be immersed in the text, to see if I can imagine what it was like at the time. Imaginative prayer is fruitful for me. It may take half an hour or more for the scene and the individuals to become clear. I have to allow their previous attitudes to become apparent and then wait for their reactions to Jesus to show, for these often have particular relevance to me. Normally, some particular person or attitude presents itself and I can ask the Spirit to show me what this means for me. It may be blindingly obvious in the first instant, so then I have to decide whether to accept this prompting.

Praying the Scripture, or *lectio divina*, has been especially helpful for me, and I invite you to consider doing this too. I start by consciously directing my attention inward, away from affairs of the world, and then I pray for God to be with me. I read slowly, taking care to notice any word or phrase that stands out prominently as I read. As soon as this happens I let the Bible rest, close my eyes, and allow that word or phrase to rest in my consciousness, savouring it with my heart. When I realise my mind has wandered, I return

PREFACE

gently to those words. Gradually the Spirit may reveal something, or I may be asked to carry those words with me for a day or so till the lesson becomes clear. In each of these actions, I am making the choice to return to the words given to me by God. I am giving up my own control to allow the Spirit to direct me. I am practising how to lead a new life. Please consider joining me in this style of reading.

It is tempting to keep reading and to squeeze as much meaning as possible from the text. In our other work, the more we read, the more informed we become and the more we understand the complexities of a topic. Reading with the mind is an important stimulus for the spiritual journey. What is more important with Scripture, though, is to allow the writings themselves to speak to us, to allow the Spirit to speak through them. As soon as a word or phrase jumps out, I stay with that and pray to be shown what it means for me.

After all, God is Spirit, and in spirit must God be worshipped. We cannot truly understand God's purpose for us with the mind, not even with a mystical setting of the mind. We can use our minds to prepare the ground and later to carry out the work. But the primary relationship with God is spiritual, without the interference of the mind. We enter into a mystery.

Analysing text is useful only as preparation for the inward movement from the head to the heart. We need to be ready for the Spirit's prompting to move from intellectual appreciation and enter the mysterious unknowing of the heart. Clinging to the intellect is a mistake for it prevents us from being receptive to the openings and purifyings of God's working within us.

Some of John's text is factual storytelling. This storytelling contains layers of meaning, perhaps a spiritual allegory that can reveal deeper insights or words that may be used for meditation through which the Spirit can speak to our souls or purify our hearts. Other texts are immune to rational thought, and it is a mistake to try to analyse them. These have to be meditated and prayed upon till, with great mercy, God illuminates their meaning in ways beyond words.

So, dear reader, these are my own reflections. I encourage you to allow your own to flow. Perhaps some of my thoughts will help. For the deeper meanings, it is up to the Spirit and you. I have not utilised every verse in John; maybe there are others waiting to speak to you. In sitting with these verses, may you find the Spirit has messages to enlighten your own path, illuminate difficulties, and suggest the next steps for you to take in your spiritual journey.

David Johnson
Wondecla, Australia
12th month 2016

PREFACE

Jesus said:

I can of mine own self do nothing.[1]

Whoever follows me won't walk in darkness, but will have the light of life.[2]

Love one another.[3]

I am the way, the truth, and the life.[4]

If ye love me, keep my commandments. And I will pray the Father, and he shall give you another Comforter, that he may abide with you forever; even the Spirit of truth.[5]

Those who love me will be true to my word, and Abba God will love them; and we will come to them, and make our dwelling place with them.[6]

I won't speak much more with you, because the ruler of this world, who has no hold on me, is at hand; but I do this so that the world may know that I love Abba God and do as my Abba has commanded.[7]

Abba, into your hands I commit my spirit.[8]

---

[1] John 5:30 KJV.
[2] John 8:12 TIB.
[3] John 13:34 KJV.
[4] John 14:6 KJV.
[5] John 14:15-17 KJV.
[6] John 14:23 TIB.
[7] John 14:30-31 TIB.
[8] Luke 23:46 TIB.

CHAPTER 1
JESUS

Jesus as a Human Being

Jesus was born a Jew into a world of fierce conflict between powerful elites and oppressed peoples.[8] The Jews of Palestine were surrounded by and had been invaded by successive colonisers and cultures—Syrian, Chaldean (modern Iraq), Persian (modern Iran), Greek, and Roman—for over seven hundred years (see appendix 1). Jesus was born perhaps 6 or 5 BCE, towards the end of the reign of Herod the Great (Matthew 2:1, Luke 1:5), who was an ambitious ruler of the Jews operating under the control of the Roman Empire.

Since childhood, Jesus would have known the history of these invasions, experienced the tensions between the Jewish people and the Roman colonisers, seen brutal massacres by the Romans, and experienced their intrusions into the sacred life of Judaism. He grew up in a country where violence, corruption, greed, and repression were commonplace.

Against this background history of invasion and war, with contests for power, territory, and wealth, comes Jesus, saying, "My kingdom is not of this world". Jesus asserts the coming of another kingdom, of following another ruler, of living under the guidance and justice and peace of another lord. He calls the people to change their ways. In this new kingdom, the present rulers have no place. In a world and culture where politics and intrigue and betrayal and murder are the norm, he still says, "Trust in the providence of creation, give your all to God; stop relying on earthly wealth; love one another; love your enemies; do good to them that hate you".[9]

Although hundreds who had been taught and healed by Jesus became his followers, many of those in power resented him. Eventually, Jesus was crucified with the connivance of Jewish priests and the Roman procurator Pontius Pilate[10] after a public ministry of about three years, probably in 33 CE.

Earlier prophets had spoken of the need for compassion for the poor and vulnerable yet led their people into killing. It was Jesus who drew the line against all violence and who in his life showed the need for total surrender to God while forgoing all worldly violence, power, status, and wealth.

Jesus spoke from his own experience, using parables and sermons to describe his own relationship with God, how it felt, and where his gifts in teaching and healing came from. We might like to devise complex theologies, but that was not Jesus' intent. Jesus spoke simply and directly both to unlearned and to well-educated people about a religious life accessible to all.

Jesus Does Nothing without the Life and Power and Instructions and Authority of God

Many times in John's gospel Jesus confirms he is there to do the will of *him who sent me* (John 4:34 NIV), and he says that *it is Abba God, living in me, who is accomplishing the works* (John 14:10 TIB). Often people have skipped over this fact that Jesus is clear he is not just a child of God but was also sent as a servant of God.[11] If Jesus can do nothing without God's creative energy, love, and guidance, then we cannot expect it to be otherwise for ourselves. Jesus makes it clear that we too are capable of becoming children ('sons') of God. We have the beginnings of that already within us, and it is up to each of us, in a shared relationship with God, to determine how far and how deeply and how closely we develop this potential.[12]

Luke records that after his baptism, Jesus, *full of the Holy Spirit, left the Jordan and was led by the Spirit into the wilderness* (4:1 NIV), then later returned to Galilee *in the power of the Spirit* (4:14 NIV). In the curing of the paralytic lowered down through the roof of a house, Luke makes it clear that *the power of the Lord was with Jesus to heal the sick* (5:17 NIV). In the exorcising of the mute demon, Luke records Jesus' words: *But if I with the finger of God cast out devils . . .* (11:20 NIV). Thus, Jesus was a man guided and empowered by the Holy Spirit of God. He did not act out of his own Self and his own capabilities. Other gospels certainly testify that Jesus was sent by and derived his power from God, but it is the Gospel According to John that makes this point a central theme.[13]

One example of this relationship is Jesus' statement, *I am the true vine, and my Father is the husbandman. Every branch in me that beareth not fruit he taketh away* (John 15:1-2). One interpretation is that the branches taken away are those of us who do not measure up. However, Jesus' words show he is recognising that any tendency *in me*, in himself as a human being, to ever stray from God's purpose is also pruned. He is totally subject to God's directions.

The early Christians accepted versions told to them by the disciples who had been with Jesus (Hebrews 2:3), versions which admitted this dependence on God. Thus the author of the Letter to the Hebrews could write: *Wherefore, holy brethren, . . . consider the Apostle and High Priest of our profession, Christ Jesus; Who was faithful to him that appointed him* (3:1), a description that implies that Jesus undertook what God asked of him. Other verses in Hebrews substantiate this view: *Though he were a Son, yet learned he obedience, by the things which he suffered* (Hebrews 5:8; see also 10:7).[14]

The author of Hebrews noted that this obedience was tested through suffering, which for us too seems to be the most effective way we overcome our egos and self-centredness, surrendering our lives to God. The suffering we speak of here as beneficial is not passive acceptance of evil but the suffering we consciously accept in actively undertaking God's work.

In the gospel of John, too, Jesus is very clear that his healing power and the words he speaks come from God or, in his words, his *Abba*.[15] Greek manuscripts used the word *pater*, meaning father, and this has led to the unfortunate use of 'Father' in English translations. The Jerusalem Bible does write *Abba* (Father) in Mark 14:36. Jesus spoke Aramaic and most likely used the Aramaic word *A'bba*, a term of intimacy, of trust, a word formed easily by the lips of infants. In Hindi a similar word is *Ba'pu*, and in English the softly spoken Pa'ppa is close. Jesus on earth, albeit a 'heavenly man', affirmed essentially, "I do not speak to you of my own accord, but God who sent me commanded me what to say. I know that God's command leads to eternal life. Whatever I say is just what Abba God told me to say" (see John 12:49-50).

Christian doctrines have emphasised Jesus' divinity. I want also to emphasise Jesus' humanity, that he was a person who felt both the joys and troubles of life, friendship, antagonism, hospitality, and homelessness. Through all these experiences he maintained a most extraordinary faith in the universal divine presence and love and goodness of *Abba*, God, 'Father', within him. John's gospel makes this point time and again.

Near the end of his life, Jesus witnessed twice to his surrender to God. In Gethsemane on the night before he was crucified, Jesus prayed, *My Father, if it is possible, may this cup be taken from me. Yet not as I will, but as you will* (Matthew 26:39 NIV; see also Mark 14:36; Luke 22:42), and he commented to Peter, *Put up thy sword into the sheath: the cup which my Father hath given me, shall I not drink it?* (John 18:11).

Jesus' final words, spoken as he was dying, are recorded by Luke: *Father, into your hands I commit my spirit* (Luke 23:46 NIV). This is not just a statement for the moment but a declaration of how he had lived his life.[16]

Jesus Embodies the Eternal Indwelling Christ, the Truth, the Word, the Light, and the Life

In the prologue (John 1:1–14), John identifies God with the Word, the creative force without which nothing was made that was made. Secondly, God is identified with the Light, the universal, divine Light within that is given to every person born. This Light is at first noticed as our conscience that indicates what is right and what is wrong. Thirdly, this Word is the source of Life that gives us power and ability. The Word is the source of Light so we can know and of Life so we can have energy.[17] The Word has many layers of meaning, for it incorporates both the creative power of God and also is one way the divine communicates with us. The Word of God then is the source of Life and the ground of our being.

John's gospel also identifies the experience people had of Jesus as the Christ, the one anointed fully with the Word, the Light and Life and Love of God.[18] Jesus is a person so truthful that his words and actions are faultless guidance towards God and a life of peace and holiness. John makes the timeless spiritual role of Christ very clear in his poetic prologue, though the utter Truth of it may not become completely and mysteriously apparent to us till much later.

This inward presence can only be approached through prayer, not through rational thinking. Jesus' advice in Luke 17:20 is precise on this point: *The kingdom of God cometh not with observation: . . . the kingdom of God is within you.* The analogy of leaven within a loaf of bread carries the same message—the life is within. We can each feel elements of this within ourselves and are invited into the inner journey to encounter it.

Using the metaphor of digging for treasure hidden in the field, Gerard Hughes expresses the same attitude: "the field within which the treasure is hidden is our own life, and the treasure is our own self, our Christ self. . . . As the treasure is within our inner self, to which we alone have access, neither the Church nor anyone in the Church can open the treasure for us".[19]

The Light manifests itself in many ways and to many peoples. The Hindu tradition also attests the experience of knowing this divine Light. For example, a stanza of the Bhagavad Gita (10:41) says:

> Whatever is beautiful and good, whatever has glory
> and power is only a portion of my own radiance.[20]

Although many spiritual traditions testify to the mystery of divine presence and spiritual light, John experienced that Jesus, as the Eternal Christ, is the source of this Light. If we too focus on Jesus and his teachings and presence, we can find a universal spirituality and a Christianity that predates and may carry our souls way beyond rehearsed prayers and doctrines. Jesus is a perfect Guide.

John's gospel is an extraordinary communication of religious thought that surpasses the primitive beliefs in specific gods or in a god who behaves like human beings. The gospel names a divine presence that, if we let it, may anoint and control the whole of our being and life. This Presence is named as the Christ, the universal source of all ages, the power of Light and Life and Love, of which each of us has a measure and to which each of us has potentially complete access. That is the point of John 1:9 and 1:16.

Jesus as Both Servant and Christ

These two themes, Jesus as servant and Jesus as Christ, are in no way contradictory or incompatible. They are perfectly conjoined. Jesus' example, his life and witness, his ministry and teaching, all show us that the inward life and power to live a life in the Truth come from humility and complete faithfulness, obedient always to the inward promptings and leadings of God.

What then is the will of God for us, a term that has been much abused? It is to recognise when we are out of step with God's intent. We are to be creatures of love and truthfulness, walking justly and mercifully and humbly attentive to God's instructions.[21] Suffering may be part of this journey.

Nicholas Peter Harvey, a Roman Catholic lay theologian, describes holy obedience as follows:

> Deeply present . . . and explicit in the story of Jesus, is a strong notion of obedience, not in the corrupted and diminished modern sense of just doing what you are told, but as a key function of the relationship indivisibly with the living God and all that is. True obedience has connotations of listening, of receptivity, of honouring the other in his or her sheer otherness. . . .
>
> It is revealing to note that Jesus is said to have learned obedience by suffering, that is to say by passionately taking the consequences of his own decision to pursue his destiny in the way that he did. If we think of suffering simply as something imposed on him by his enemies we miss the point . . . : there is in play here a chosen and offered suffering, a suffering therefore in a category quite other than that which is sheerly imposed and endured. It is not at all a case of 'what can't be cured must be endured', but of a willing plunge into this particular suffering which once accomplished turns out to be healing.
>
> The way of faith and hope and love is hinted at in Jesus' references to the Father's will [and manifests] an awesome faithfulness in pursuit of a

call which is also a gift, and which points towards death . . . [not] understood by those around [him], . . . [for] no utilitarian calculus could conceivably suggest a fruitful outcome of the chosen course.[22]

Each of us is invited to follow the inward Light in trust, seeking the possibility of a life of real holiness admitted by Jesus for himself (e.g., John 10:34-38). Such a Christ-like life was confirmed as an experience of the early Christians (John 1:12; 1 John 2:5-6, 3:7) and the Letter to the Ephesians: . . . *until we all attain unity in our faith and in our knowledge of the Only Begotten of God, until we become mature, attaining to the whole measure of the fullness of Christ* (4:13 TIB).

It was also articulated by George Fox, the founding Quaker, and by the early Quaker evangelist William Dewsbury. In 1673, Fox wrote:

So as man and woman come again to God, and are renewed up into his image, righteousness and holiness by Christ, thereby they come up into the Paradise of God, the state which man was in before he fell, and into a higher state than that, to sit down in Christ that never fell.[23]

Dewsbury, in 1655, knowing in himself the sense of judgment (condemnation) when he had done wrong, urged readers:

Return within everyone in particular; examine your hearts, and mind the light in your consciences, and it will always let you see where your hearts are, and what they delight in, for it is the heart the Lord requires; . . . there is your teacher within you, the light of your consciences; loving it, and obeying it, is your life; hating it and disobeying it, is your condemnation.[24]

The common pattern is a long period of inward inspiration, yearning, searching, cleansing, and transformation as we are led closer to God, to the point where our own will is replaced by the willingness to do lovingly and happily as God asks. This inward change is followed by gifts of courage and hope and joy to witness that of God in our actions in the world.

CHAPTER 2
THE ETERNAL MYSTICAL VISION REACHING OUT TO US—THE CALL

Praying the Word

> *John 1:1 In the beginning was the Word, and the Word was with God, and the Word was God. 1:2 The same was in the beginning with God.*
>
> *1:3 Through the Word all things came into being, and apart from the Word nothing came into being that has come into being.* (TIB)
>
> *1:5 And the light shineth in darkness; and the darkness comprehended it not.*

The prologue of the gospel of John starts with the same historic declaration as Genesis and the gospel of Mark: *In the beginning.* John is linking Jesus and all he is about to say with the creation and sustaining of a spiritual life on earth. This prologue lays out a main message of the Gospel—Jesus is part of the energy of creation, the Word, and the source of Light and Life, a Light that is in every person.[25] This surely is a tremendous claim to make, yet it is made with certainty. Many people baulk at the assertion that Jesus is divine, preferring to hold that he is just an extraordinary human being. John's purpose in writing the gospel is to convince us otherwise, not by philosophical argument but by drawing us into a spiritual experience.

This poetic prologue is in two parts. The first part (1:1–5) is both a mystical statement and a prayer. It is a prayer of acknowledgement of God as the source of all and ground of our being, a prayer of both humility and praise. The Word is identified as being present at the beginning of creation, in parallel to the statement, *And God said, Let there be light: and there was light* (Genesis 1:3).[26] This Word is divine and has been since creation, it was there before creation for without it was nothing made, and it will remain afterwards. God's Word (the *him* of KJV 1:3, 4) is the creator, the source of everything that was made, the creator of all creation. This Word is also the source of Life and of Light. The ancients understood the mystical reality: *By your word, YHWH, the heavens were made, by the breath of your mouth all the stars* (Psalm 33:6 TIB).

Unfortunately for our human minds, there is no logical answer to the question, What is the Word? We cannot be given the answer by someone else. We start by meditation and prayer, entering our inner darkness, for the responses can only come from God.

The human experience is that our inner darkness may start as just emptiness or a confusion of thoughts. It can become a place of loneliness and abandonment, part of the inner stripping in preparation for spiritual growth. Yet the inner darkness can also become a safe emptiness, a refuge, as we become aware that somewhere inside us, hidden, is the Presence of God. It is the place to wait patiently for first glimmerings of the Light, and this darkness can be very calm, safe, soft, and receptive.

The Word and the Light are divine gifts that we experience in small measure and that increase as we faithfully follow what the Light asks of each of us moment to moment. There is no way to understand these poetic statements with a logical mind; they are the outpouring of a Middle Eastern spiritual message from two thousand years ago, yet it can have surprising relevance if it is prayed rather than analysed.

> *Then came one named John, sent as an envoy from God, who came as a witness to testify about the Light, so that through his testimony everyone might believe. He himself wasn't the Light; he only came to testify about the Light—the true Light that enlightens all humankind.* (John 1:6-8 TIB)

The prologue (1:6-9) brings this mystical statement to an earthly setting, as John the Baptist testifies to the marvel of the Light born as Jesus on earth. This is the true Light, the Truth, born into every person.[27] As Thomas Merton describes it,

At the center of our being is a point of nothingness which is untouched by sin and by illusion, a point of pure truth, a point or spark which belongs entirely to God, which is never at our disposal, from which God disposes of our lives, which is inaccessible to the fantasies of our own mind or the brutalities of our own will. This little point of nothingness and of *absolute poverty* is the pure glory of God in us. . . . like a pure diamond, blazing with the invisible light of heaven. It is in everybody.[28]

He was in the world, and the world was made by him, and the world knew him not. He came unto his own, and his own received him not. But as many as received him, to them gave he power to become the sons of God, even to them that believe on his name: Which were born, not of blood, nor of the will of the flesh, nor of the will of man, but of God. And the Word was made flesh, and dwelt among us, (and we beheld his glory, the glory as of the only begotten of the Father,) full of grace and truth. (John 1:10-14)

The equivalence of Word and Light and Truth, all in Jesus, is found throughout John's gospel. First, the Word, the breath of God, is the creator of all. Second, there is the divine Light that sustains life,[29] and this Light is in all. Third, Jesus was the Word and the Light as a physical reality while he was alive on earth. Western minds have trouble grasping the interrelationship of these three, that they are one—and more, that everything is simply a function of this divine creative energy that we can experience as the Light within or as the divinely spoken Word.

This mysterious quality of the Light, that it is both inwardly seen and heard, is a human experience, expressed, for example, by George Fox in 1653:

. . . so that everyone might come to know who their teacher was, Christ Jesus and the Lord God, as the prophets and the apostles and the true Church did, and so to know both God and Christ's voice by which they might see all; the false shepherds and teachers they had been under and see the true shepherd, priest, bishop and prophet, Christ Jesus.[30]

In 2016, Quaker Margery Post Abbott described "everyday prophets" as "people who listen for the Voice of Light, who might walk humbly even as they come to speak boldly the path of compassion and justice".[31]

Our darkness cannot at first even begin to understand the Light and these mysteries. It was clear in Jesus' presence, and the spiritual presence of the Light may still make it clear to anyone. John's unique mystical vision is astounding in its breadth and depth and subtlety. Jesus gives this Light and Life. *For God, who commanded the light to shine out of darkness, hath shined in our hearts, to give the light of the knowledge of the glory of God in the face of Jesus Christ* (2 Corinthians 4:6). The lived experience of being with Jesus is clear in the First Letter of John:

> *That which was from the beginning, which we have heard, which we have seen with our eyes, which we have looked upon, and our hands have handled, of the Word of life; (For the life was manifested, and we have seen it, and bear witness, and shew unto you that eternal life, which was with the Father, and was manifested unto us;).* (1 John 1:1-2)

This Light of Christ within is not the light of our reasoned thoughts or a light made by nature; it is a mystical light, the Light of the Word.

In the late 1640s, George Fox described his experience of the Light as follows:

> But as all believe in the light and walk in the light, which Christ hath enlightened every man that cometh into the world withal, and so become children of the light, and of the day of Christ; in his day all things are seen, visible and invisible, by the divine light of Christ, the spiritual, heavenly man, by whom all things were made and created.[32]

> ... and in this I saw the infinite love of God. I saw also that there was an ocean of darkness and death, but an infinite ocean of light and love, which flowed over the ocean of darkness. And in that also I saw the infinite love of God; and I had great openings.[33]

This Light is a light that lighteth *every* person in the world, no exceptions (John 1:9). Early Friends seized upon verse 1:9 and submitted to all its ramifications. Everyone has that goodness, no matter how latent it may seem. Early Friends took this not just as a fact of intellectual understanding but as a fact of faith and of behaviour. Since there is that of God in all, we cannot injure or cheat or deceive or kill anyone, for each of these would be acts against God. We really have to do unto others as we would they do to us.

The experience of those first followers of Jesus is stated by John: *as many as received him, to them gave he power to become the sons of God* (John 1:12). What an extraordinary claim—that individuals might become members of the immediate family of God.[34] We are being offered the possibility of being merged into this new consciousness. Jesus is also a present teacher and priest. This is a different concept of God from the remote, powerful, authoritarian God of the Old Testament.[35]

John is making a statement of what many saw and he witnessed for himself, something that can seem far away to many of us now, especially those of us who are used to having factual proof put in front of us. So we start this journey into John's gospel either holding on to this demand for factual proof and in effect requiring Jesus' role be proved to our satisfaction or allowing ourselves to suspend such worldly judgment and enter more humbly into this journey. The implication of the phrase *as many as received him* is that this decision is a free choice.

Many of us start our spiritual journeys requiring that the book or faith we are drawn to prove good enough for our committed attention. We tend to overlook our own deficiencies while also being aware there is something much more to life than we are presently experiencing. Yet our spiritual growth lies in facing our deficiencies. What some of us might have as a dreadful inkling is in fact true: it is not Jesus and God who have to prove themselves worthy to us; each of us has to become worthy of the gift of divine presence. We have the seed for that change within us.

John the Baptist as the Messenger—First Sounds of the Call

> And this is the record of John, when the Jews sent priests and Levites from Jerusalem to ask him, Who art thou? And he confessed, and denied not; but confessed, I am not the Christ. And they asked him, What then? Art thou Elias? And he saith, I am not. Art thou that prophet? And he answered, No. Then said they unto him, Who art thou? that we may give an answer to them that sent us. What sayest thou of thyself? He said, I am the voice of one crying in the wilderness, Make straight the way of the Lord, as said the prophet Esaias. And they which were sent were of the Pharisees. And they asked him, and said unto him, Why baptizest thou then, if thou be not that Christ, nor Elias, neither that prophet? John answered them, saying, I baptize with water: but there standeth one among you, whom ye know not; He it is, who coming after me is preferred before me, whose shoe's latchet I am not worthy to unloose. (John 1:19–27)

> The next day John seeth Jesus coming unto him, and saith, Behold the Lamb of God, which taketh away the sin of the world. This is he of whom I said, After me cometh a man which is preferred before me: for he was before me. And I knew him not: but that he should be made manifest to Israel, therefore am I come baptizing with water. And John bare record, saying, I saw the Spirit descending from heaven like a dove, and it abode upon him. And I knew him not: but he that sent me to baptize with water, the same said unto me, Upon whom thou shalt see the Spirit descending, and remaining on him, the same is he which baptizeth with the Holy Ghost. And I saw, and bare record that this is the Son of God. (John 1:29–34)

John the Baptist has been preaching the need for people to examine their lives and to return to worshipping God alone. As a sign of cleansing, he is baptising them with water. The religious authorities question him.[36] He identifies the one who is to come, Jesus, the Light, and he witnesses that it is Jesus, not himself, who is the divine Messiah.[37]

I am the voice of one crying in the wilderness (John 1:23) are the words of John the Baptist, the timeless voice of the prophet who has set himself apart in the wilderness, away from all contemporary behaviour, away from the false gods and wasteful comfort.[38] He is speaking the words given him in God's presence. And where is this wilderness? This wilderness is both within us and without us, for the 'voice' is the Spirit calling within each of us to move from present behaviours that are damaging to our spiritual growth to a life that embraces spiritual values in all its being.

After his baptism in the Jordan River by John the Baptist, a mystical vision is recorded of the Spirit descending like a dove onto Jesus, accompanied by the voice of God.[39] This must have been a pivotal moment in Jesus' life. He had been baptized in water and immediately afterwards was baptized by the Holy Spirit. Luke 3:23 noted Jesus was about thirty years old at the time. According to both Mark and Luke, this baptismal vision marks the transformation and empowerment of Jesus to start his public ministry.[40]

John draws our attention to whoever or whatever has been our guide, just as John the Baptist alerted people to the need to reinvigorate the spirituality of their lives in advance of the work to be done by Jesus. For the disciples who sought John in Ephesus in the first century after Jesus' death, as it is for us now, John is saying that these previous guides, or any other 'gods' or philosophies we may have followed, will not bring us closer to God in the way Jesus can. John's view is that these were the forerunners; these guides helped refocus our lives, but they were not the ones who could bring fullness of the Spirit.

John the Baptist behaved as the first calling often does for each of us, as a voice of uneasiness within us that prompts us to realise and to admit we are not as close to God and to a fulfilled life as we might have imagined. We are not as happy as we would like to be; we may not have abundant natural joy. We become aware of an emptiness, of our own shallowness, that we need to change, and yet we are not clear how to do it. Such awareness commonly comes from someone else around us whose words or deeds enter our being as a witness in our heart and show us that not all is well with our present stance.

John the Baptist is also asserting that a whole new inner cleansing and change must occur, a spiritual baptism, a change that cannot be achieved with external washing. Yet there is one who stands among us, indeed within us, awaiting the opportunity to begin the inner work required.

The Calling—What Do You Seek?

> *Again the next day after John stood, and two of his disciples; And looking upon Jesus as he walked, he saith, Behold the Lamb of God! And the two disciples heard him speak, and they followed Jesus. Then Jesus turned, and saw them following, and saith unto them, What seek ye? They said unto him, Rabbi, (which is to say, being interpreted, Master,) where dwellest thou? He saith unto them, Come and see. They came and saw where he dwelt, and abode with him that day: for it was about the tenth hour. One of the two which heard John speak, and followed him, was Andrew, Simon Peter's brother. He first findeth his own brother Simon, and saith unto him, We have found the Messias, which is, being interpreted, the Christ. (John 1:35–41)*

When Jesus arrives, two of John's disciples follow him. Later, Andrew and his companion are asked the timeless question: *What seek ye*, that is, "What do you want in life?"

Imagine those two young fishermen, probably in their early twenties, living in the familiar community of the same fishing village that had been home to their forebears. Since they sought out John the Baptist, they must have been spiritual seekers who had thought about the course and meaning of their lives. Then this most unusual man arrives who they have heard has extraordinary insight and powers. And he turns, looking into their eyes, and asks them directly, "What do you want?"

The formal calling of the first four disciples, Andrew, Peter, James, and John, is explained in Mark (1:16–18). The context is that the fishing industry on the Sea of Galilee was regulated by Roman colonial forces, and only those who had purchased licences were permitted to fish, with the produce sold through approved buyers. The potential for corruption by local authorities is obvious; they paid off Roman soldiers while profiting from and burdening their own people. Public antipathy to the Romans was widespread. Some people became violent in their opposition (zealots), and some acquiesced and became collaborators (tax gatherers and high priests). As Jesus' life and ministry showed, he chose a third way, the path of nonviolent resistance, neither armed revolt nor self-centred collaboration. So the calling of these early disciples had both spiritual and practical elements—such is the way of a life committed to Truth.[41]

We should remember that their Hebrew culture had been permeated for hundreds of years by the prophecy: Keep your eyes open for the Messiah.[42] Philip is similarly excited and clear: *we have found him, of whom Moses in the law, and the prophets did write, [it is] Jesus of Nazareth, the son of Joseph* (John 1:45).

I, too, had such a yearning in me, the hope that one day I might find a source of truthful spiritual guidance, a place where my restless soul could find answers. Many long to find continuing contact with that of God. Young people are often as desperate in their desire for God as were those two young seekers, already on their journey spending time as disciples of John the Baptist. This desire is emplaced within us by God, just as Jesus inflamed this desire within the hearts of those young fishermen when he appeared among them.

For each of these young men, time stood still. Perhaps they were aware of the wind or a distant noise of the water or some nearby chatter. But for this moment, their hearts and minds stand still. They are on the brink. Do they stay with all that is well known, living a familiar life of fishing and village work, or do they walk into the unknown, at the beckoning of the Spirit?

I notice that neither brother clearly answers Jesus' question, What do you seek? It was the same for me at the start of my spiritual journey. Neither could I have answered that question clearly and precisely. In the beginning we are drawn into the journey, and we consent to follow without knowing where we are going.

Each of them is drawn to learn more, so they ask where Jesus dwells. The invitation is immediate and positive: *Come and see.* This episode has two levels—one is the factual level, in that Andrew and Peter are intrigued by this prophet and they ask where he is staying so they can find him again and spend time with him. However, they know they are not going out of curiosity to see what sort of house it is, how big it is, what type of furniture it contains, how many animals are there, or what is in the garden. They are going for a much deeper reason. The deeper level is not where Jesus lives physically, for they sense this man dwells in a life of spiritual certainty for which they yearn. They perceive Jesus has spiritual gifts beyond anything they have known. Maybe he dwells in the Light and not in the darkness.

Where does each of us dwell? In a house, yes. But what about spiritually—do we dwell in the place described in Psalm 23:6 (*Surely goodness and love shall follow me all the days of my life: and I will dwell in the house of the LORD for ever*) and in Psalm 90:1 (*Lord, thou hast been our dwelling place in all generations*)? This word 'dwell' has a multilayered meaning in the Scriptures. When Andrew asks, *Master where do you dwell?*, he could be asking, "Where are you staying tonight?" or "Master, in what spiritual space do you reside that gives you these special qualities?"

We can choose a physical home that draws us and arouses our spiritual being. But 'dwell' implies more than that; it implies our willingness to enter a spiritual space where, in time, that of God comes to dwell in us.[43] Whether we acknowledge it or not, in fact we do dwell in sacred space. Do we dwell in the light or in the dark? So, is *Come and see* an invitation or a promise?

There is a reaching out by the Light of Christ within each of us that arouses our yearning for a deeper spiritual life, our yearning for God. How often has that happened to each of us? Have we allowed it to happen?

Is it possible for us to respond to Jesus' call, *Follow me*, like those young fishermen, or like Levi the tax collector, who immediately got up and followed Jesus (Mark 2:14)? It sounds so succinct and clear, and yet we have such trouble imagining ourselves in that position. All our worldly insecurities and rational objections rise up protesting within us. Yet, as John asserts (1:12-13) and many have found, in doing so we are given the life and the power to undertake lives and even public witness in ways we had not previously thought ourselves capable of.

The Bible stories make it clear that Jesus changed the lives of those around him. People left their occupations and homes to be itinerant disciples; hundreds afflicted by disease, blindness, or infirmity were healed; many burdened by doctrine or dogma were liberated into a life of inner peace guided by the Holy Spirit. For Thomas Ellwood, it was a decision to cease the superficial flattery of doffing hats and bowing at the knee, bringing social disapproval and ostracism. For George Fox, it meant leaving home and family, and for William Penn, it meant declining the status, prestige, and comfort of an aristocratic life and career. For Margaret Fell, it was opening her home, thus risking abuse, property loss, and imprisonment to support the persecuted early Quakers.

Each of us will experience a prompting to change our behaviour. It may be to no longer drink alcohol, to avoid slipping curses into our language, to never again buy raffle tickets, to scale back ambitions, to take up a daily practice, to stop wearing jewellery, to increase charitable giving, to seek reconciliation with another, to stand publicly in solidarity with oppressed people. These are to be sensed inwardly rather than be imposed by external regulation. Obedience to the call begins with even the smallest prompting.

John identifies this as the first issue for us to encounter in the spiritual journey; he has placed it in the first of the twenty-one chapters of his gospel. He knows that any inward journey actually starts with an outward step—beginning a new path, taking a step away from parts of our past. This always involves a decision to do things differently, and each step will require us to bear a cost.

John's stance in the gospel, and presumably the one he articulated to those who came to see him in Ephesus, was that Jesus is the most perfect teacher of the way to God. I can imagine him saying, "Much you will need to leave behind, and if you want to learn more, stay, and I will tell you the stories of Jesus".

John is really asking, "Are you ready to change and take a new path?" The question is not "Do you believe in Jesus Christ" but "Are you ready to leave much behind and embark very seriously on the spiritual journey?"

CHAPTER 3
HOW MUCH CHANGE MIGHT WE EXPERIENCE?

Jesus Introduced to the World as an Extraordinary Being: The Wedding at Cana

> And when they wanted wine, the mother of Jesus saith unto him, They have no wine. Jesus saith unto her, Woman, what have I to do with thee? mine hour is not yet come. His mother saith unto the servants, Whatsoever he saith unto you, do it. And there were set there six waterpots of stone, after the manner of the purifying of the Jews, containing two or three firkins apiece. Jesus saith unto them, Fill the waterpots with water. And they filled them up to the brim. And he saith unto them, Draw out now, and bear unto the governor of the feast. And they bare it. When the ruler of the feast had tasted the water that was made wine, and knew not whence it was: (but the servants which drew the water knew;) the governor of the feast called the bridegroom, And saith unto him, Every man at the beginning doth set forth good wine; and when men have well drunk, then that which is worse: but thou hast kept the good wine until now. (John 2:3-10)

The first event in Jesus' ministry related by John is the story of the water made wine at the wedding feast in Cana.[44] This miracle of Jesus in Galilee is the first sign that Jesus is indeed an exceptional individual. For many of those who would later be told of his deeds, or hear Jesus themselves, this story from an obscure northern town, far away from Jerusalem, that a man had turned water into wine was a sign of a major prophet. No one had done anything like that before in living memory. As we know, there was more to come.

Initially, Jesus refuses to be involved. God's work is not to be done just at the behest of human desires. For me, this human element makes Jesus real. He, like me, is at first hesitant to accept the prompting. Then, perhaps recognising the difficult position of the host who has run out of wine for the wedding reception, Jesus is led to help out. In this first miracle, Jesus is merely helping alleviate the situation; he has not yet started on his healing and life-saving ministry. Do we not find this ourselves as we enter the spiritual quest seriously, that our life starts to become easier even before we experience major changes within ourselves?

Jesus is introduced by his mother Mary. Why his mother? In particular, why the mother rather than the typical authority figure of the father? It is his mother as the ultimate giver of life, the bearer, the nurturing figure. His mother introduces and brings forth Jesus into his first miraculous act of ministry.

Moreover, in the ancient texts, Wisdom is always female, the voice of Sophia.[45] Jesus is the son of Wisdom. In this episode, as John relates the story, it is the female voice of Wisdom, Jesus' mother, who says, "When Jesus asks something of you, do it". Learning to listen to and obey the voice of wisdom is important in the spiritual life. That is, the spiritual journey has a strong element of faithfulness or obedience, right from the start. *Whatsoever he saith unto you, do it* was a necessary instruction at that time, yet it is also on a deeper level a timeless instruction.

The wisdom spoken here is not worldly wisdom gained by practical experience handling matters of business and human affairs. Such wisdom is commonly oriented to resolving situations with the aim of worldly gain. The spiritual voice of wisdom comes from God: *For the LORD giveth wisdom: out of his mouth cometh knowledge and understanding* (Proverbs 2:6). It derives from a deep spiritual understanding in our hearts of what God is asking to be done that leads to peace and righteousness and preserves us from following paths of darkness and 'evil'.[46]

In a telling statement (John 2:9), John notes that the ruler did not know from whom this miraculous drink emanated, though the servants did. The poor perceive what those with wealth and possessions cannot.

John is making it clear that Jesus has the power to turn ordinary water into excellent wine, or the mundane mind into spiritual intoxication. As the governor of the feast observes, in this case the best wine is served later. Such is the experience of the spiritual journey. The best and sweetest times may not be served up by God early but instead come well into the journey. The amount of wine in this story is considerable. Each stone jar held at least fifteen gallons (sixty to seventy litres), and six jars would have held over 360 litres of wine. In modern terms, some 480 bottles would be a stupendous amount for a small village wedding. This amount of wine signifies the boundless blessings of life in the Spirit.

For those steeped in the Hebrew faith, this episode recalled the stories of Elijah and Elisha. Elijah had encountered the impoverished widow at drought-stricken Zarephath and prophesied that her barrel of meal and cruse of oil would not fail till the rains fell again (1 Kings 17:10–16). Similarly, Elisha had compassion for a woman whose husband had died. She was now at the mercy of his creditors, who planned to sell her two boys as slaves (2 Kings 4:1–7). Elisha told her to collect empty jars and to shut herself indoors. Through her obedience to these instructions, her jars were miraculously filled with oil that she could sell to repay the debts and support her family. This ancient prophet had been able to rescue a poor and marginalised woman from distress, showing compassion and in the process providing a wondrous spiritual sign.[47] The unbelievable, sustaining flow of oil is paralleled by the vast amount of wine delivered for the wedding feast and later by Jesus feeding the thousands of people by the lake. So John has introduced Jesus as an extraordinary person, a worker of miracles, and placed him in the line of the old prophets. In John 1:38, Jesus is linked back to Moses as a man who dwelt with God, and in John 2:6–9 to the prophets Elijah and Elisha.

The physical changing of water into wine contains a daunting implication, for it suggests that to enter the Presence of God, a correspondingly large change is required inwardly of each of us. Further, it implies that this inward miracle can be accomplished with Jesus' assistance. The guiding rule for this journey is made clear by Jesus' mother as the voice of spiritual wisdom —*whatsoever he saith unto you, do it*. Obedience is required, and the promise is spiritual life. That applies to the leadings and promptings within each of us. In this journey it no longer matters what we each think should be done; instead, we must be prepared to do whatever the Light (or Jesus) shows us is the way.

I can imagine John making the point strongly to new disciples that this is a new way of living; many of their old rules and habits will need to be left behind if they are to follow the Light and Jesus. William Penn wrote about the first Quakers:

> They were changed men [and women] themselves before they went about to change others. Their hearts were rent as well as their garments, and they knew the power and work of God upon them. . . . And as they freely received what they had to say from the Lord, so they freely administered it to others. The bent and stress of their ministry was conversion to God, regeneration and holiness, not schemes of doctrines and verbal creeds or new forms of worship, but a leaving off in religion the superfluous and reducing the ceremonious and formal part, and pressing urgently the substantial, the necessary and profitable part, as all on serious reflection must and do acknowledge.[48]

Clearing Out in Preparation for the Journey

> *And the Jews' passover was at hand, and Jesus went up to Jerusalem And found in the temple those that sold oxen and sheep and doves, and the changers of money sitting: And when he had made a scourge of small cords, he drove them all out of the temple, and the sheep, and the oxen; and poured out the changers' money, and overthrew the tables; And said unto them that sold doves, Take these things hence; make not my Father's house an house of merchandise.* (John 2:13–16)

The Passover and Feast of Unleavened Bread is a Hebrew religious and holiday period, a harvest festival that falls in March–April (see table 1). In John's gospel, Jesus went three times to Jerusalem for the Passover (John 2:13, 6:4, 12:1). The events in chapter 2 are placed at 28 or 29 CE.[49] It is also possible this event happened more than once.

The Passover remembers the preparation for and the start of the Israelites' journey from Egypt, the great forty-year physical and spiritual journey through the wilderness that is an allegory for our own journey. It commemorates the exodus from Egypt after four hundred years of slavery, after the night when the angel of death passed over the houses of the Hebrews whose doors were marked with sacrificial blood, while in the houses unmarked by blood all the first-born males of the Egyptians died (Exodus 12:1–42).

This ritual killing, visited upon Egyptian babies and their parents, appals me, and although I can see the allegories, the redemptive violence is more than I can understand. However, the Jews of Jesus' time would have understood the significance of the flight from Egypt as the start of the great journey, as emphasised in Exodus 12:2: *This month shall be unto you the beginning of months.*

Table 1. Major Jewish Festivals

(sources: *NIV Study Bible* (2011); Exodus 23:14–17; Leviticus 23:1–44; Deuteronomy 16:16)

Festival	Reference	Time	Description	Purpose
Passover and Feast of Unleavened Bread	Exodus 12:1–14 Leviticus 23:5–7	March–April	Eating lamb with bitter herbs, and bread without yeast	Remember deliverance from slavery in Egypt
First Fruits	Leviticus 23:9–14	March–April	Presenting sheaf of first barley	Joy and thankfulness for God's bounty
Weeks (Harvest)/ Pentecost	Leviticus 23:15–22 Deuteronomy 16:9–12	May–June	Joyous festival with offerings, including first wheat harvest	Joy and gratitude for blessings of the harvest
Ingathering (Tabernacles)	Exodus 23:14–17 Leviticus 23:33–36 Deuteronomy 16:13–15	Sept.–Oct.	Celebration of the harvest, living in booths, libations of water	Remember journey from Egypt, honour the productivity of Canaan

What does Jesus do in his first public act recorded by John? He walks in, secure in his own authority to do so, and, taking a corded whip, drives the animals from the temple, sets free the doves, and overturns the money changers' tables. There must have been shock and pandemonium in the temple courtyard, with merchants outraged and customers scattering. Were people affronted at this interruption to their duties or even ashamed that they too were about to be sucked into the falseness of the monetary charade? Priests and temple guards came running. "Who is doing this?" For many, such an act would invite severe punishment. But Jesus stands with the courage to confront them all, sure in his authority, saying, "Get this stuff out of here, it has no place in the temple". And no one was able to argue honestly that he was wrong.

This episode of Jesus clearing the temple forecourt is placed in the Synoptic Gospels on the day after Jesus arrives in Jerusalem, after Palm Sunday and just a week before his death. John places it earlier, as the first of Jesus' many acts to confront the falseness of the religious teachings and practices of his time. By this act, he challenged the profit motives of the temple community.[50] The selling of animals for ritual slaughter, the potential dishonesty and the money-grubbing of the money changers, all happened with the knowledge of the priests and Jewish hierarchy, and the profits were shared.[51] Jesus challenges this. Let us ponder the courage and impact of this episode.

First, Jesus has driven the means of ritual slaughter from the temple. He is placing an end to a practice that had been a hallmark of ancient Hebrew culture and was exemplified by sacrifices of young animals and horrifying examples such as Abraham's willingness to kill his own son, the slaughter of the Egyptian children at the first Passover, and the slaughter of the priests of Baal at the behest of Elijah. Although ritual slaughter did not finally stop till the destruction of Jerusalem in 70 CE, my sense is that Jesus knew that all such rituals were unnecessary and that this ritual slaughter was certainly unwarranted. Jesus also confirmed with a Jewish teacher that the fundamental commandments to love God and love each other were far more important than all the burnt offerings and sacrifices (Mark 12:32-34).

The early Christians noted that the endless practice of such animal sacrifices was ineffective in bringing people to perfection (Hebrews 10:1-11). Rabbinic Jews might have continued the practice, but the followers of Jesus did not.

The Letter to the Hebrews (chapters 7–9) enunciates a primary teaching of these early Christians—that Jesus is a priest in the line of Melchizedek, not in the line of Levi. Melchizedek was the high priest of the Most High God who brought forth bread and wine for Abraham and predated the appointment by Moses of the tribe of Levitical priests.[52] The old covenant based on Mosaic laws and regulations is to be replaced by a new covenant. Further, Jesus, by his own sacrifice, forever ended the external Mosaic rituals of handwashing and animal sacrifice and replaced them with a discipline of obedience to the inward Light.[53]

Second, Jesus is placing an end to financial gain and corruption through the temple system. The temple, scribes, and priests were central to Jewish life. The religious leaders and Sanhedrin were hereditary positions that were drawn from the wealthy landowners of the Sanhedrin class, entrenched in a fruitful relationship with the Romans. The temple was the place to demonstrate adherence to social and religious customs. This priestly leadership was the arbiter of the law, one that could on the one hand confer social status and on the other ensure a person was stoned to death.

The Passover, one of the great festivals, was a time for committed Jews to travel to the great temple in Jerusalem and to immerse themselves together in their faith. There would have been crowds of people. This would also have been a time of great profitability, with much money changing hands and much effort to demonstrate status and to attain religious approval. The parallel is obvious to our own consumer-dominated Christmas period, most of which revolves around retail trade profitability and gimmickry that distorts our Christian spiritual heritage.

The Passover also celebrates the deliverance of the people by God from Egypt, from bondage into spiritual freedom. Jesus is making it very clear that the temple is not a place for gathering material wealth. Is that not the case with all of us, that our spiritual journey starts seriously when we confront our own material desires? In fact, there is little progress till we do. We may not be ready to sell all we have and give to the poor. Yet, are we earning honestly and spending wisely or are we greedy or buying unnecessary possessions?

Jesus answered those who sought a sign confirming his authority to drive the traders from the temple. Both Jesus' reply and John's commentary are recorded in the gospel:

> *Jesus answered and said unto them, Destroy this temple, and in three days I will raise it up. Then said the Jews, Forty and six years was this temple in building, and wilt thou rear it up in three days? But he spake of the temple of his body. When therefore he was risen from the dead, his disciples remembered that he had said this unto them; and they believed the scripture, and the word which Jesus had said.* (John 2:19–22)

By including these words early in the gospel, John is drawing attention to the traditionally sacred period of three days (e.g., Exodus 3:18, 5:3, 8:27). This time frame recalls examples from Hebrew history, such as the days of darkness imposed on Egypt when the Pharaoh refused to release the Hebrews from bondage (Exodus 10:22), a significant fast (Esther 4:16), and the time Jonah was in the whale's belly (Jonah 1:17).

John is extending the meaning of Jesus' clearing of the built temple to recognising that God dwells within an inner temple, one that is inside each of us. Jesus asserts the built temple is not the important place to interact with God. The important place, the most sacred place, the most ready place, is within our own hearts. We need to be in contact with God everywhere our body goes, not just in the church or temple. It is easy to gloss over this teaching of Jesus, which became fundamental in the religious life in the early church.

This early Christian teaching is evident in the final sermon of Stephen before his stoning to death: *Howbeit the most High dwelleth not in temples made with hands; as saith the prophet* (Acts 7:48).[54] Paul must have heard these words, as he was a witness to Stephen's death, though the mystery was not finally instilled in him until after his conversion, for it was later that Paul wrote *Know ye not that ye are the temple of God, and that the Spirit of God dwelleth in you?* (1 Corinthians 3:16) and *for ye are the temple of the living God; as God hath said, I will dwell in them, and walk in them; and I will be their God, and they shall be my people* (2 Corinthians 6:16). Paul is recalling the words of Jeremiah (31:33) that God would develop a new covenant with the people, a covenant written in their hearts and not just on the tablets of stone handed down by Moses. Paul reiterates the message in a letter to his spiritual son Timothy: *That good thing which was committed unto thee keep by the Holy Ghost which dwelleth in us* (2 Timothy 1:14).

The real temple is not the building of stone, for each of us is the temple of God, and it is from within ourselves that we need to overcome worldly desires for wealth and status, and it is from within each of us that these materialistic profiteers are to be banished. As George Fox wrote in 1652:

> There I declared the everlasting Truth of the Lord and the word of life for several hours, and that the Lord Christ Jesus was come to teach his people himself and bring them off all the world's ways and teachers to Christ, their way to God; and I laid open all their teachers and set up the true teacher, Christ Jesus; and how they were judged by the prophets, Christ, and the apostles; and to bring them off the temples made with hands, that they themselves might know they were the temples of God.[55]

The challenge of a new way of living is clear to anyone familiar with the Hebrew Scriptures. John is linking Jesus to the ancient Hebrew succession of divinely inspired, prophetic work. To drive that point home, John comments in the last verse of this second chapter that Jesus *needed not that any should testify of man: for he knew what was in man* (2:25). These are both the words of someone who had seen Jesus in action and also a clear statement that Jesus had the inward authority of divine understanding to know the inmost parts of those around him.

Jesus calls us to let go of possessions and habits no longer useful. The social norm of going to church, although important in building community, is no longer the benchmark of performance in the faith. Jesus calls us to personal transformation into the living Christ. We are not required to measure up to how others in the church rate us but to face God inwardly, where there is no hiding from rigorous examination by the Light within.

As Thomas Merton puts it:

> The real building of the Church is a union of hearts in love, sacrifice, and self-transcendence. The strength of this building depends on the extent to which the Holy Spirit gains possession of each person's heart, not on the extent to which our exterior conduct is organised and disciplined by an expedient system.[56]

CHAPTER 4
REBIRTH—A VERITABLE LEAVING BEHIND OF THE OLD

Jesus Confirms Rebirth by the Spirit to Nicodemus

> *There was a man of the Pharisees, named Nicodemus, a ruler of the Jews: The same came to Jesus by night, and said unto him, Rabbi, we know that thou art a teacher come from God: for no man can do these miracles that thou doest, except God be with him. Jesus answered and said unto him, Verily, verily, I say unto thee, Except a man be born again, he cannot see the kingdom of God. Nicodemus saith unto him, How can a man be born when he is old? can he enter the second time into his mother's womb, and be born? Jesus answered, Verily, verily, I say unto thee, Except a man be born of water and of the Spirit, he cannot enter into the kingdom of God. That which is born of the flesh is flesh; and that which is born of the Spirit is spirit. Marvel not that I said unto thee, Ye must be born again. The wind bloweth where it listeth, and thou hearest the sound thereof, but canst not tell whence it cometh, and whither it goeth: so is every one that is born of the Spirit.* (John 3:1–8)

Why, of all people, did John choose Nicodemus to profile at this stage of his teaching? Nicodemus was a Jewish leader, one who had clearly recognised the true spiritual nature of Jesus, in contrast to many of his colleagues. Nicodemus is one of the Jewish leaders who were so well schooled in their own laws that they could not really grasp Jesus' teaching. Yet, as we discover, throughout his ministry Jesus is revealing the essence of ancient teachings, the essence obscured by the multitudinous laws and rituals of the established Hebrew culture. In his words, he had come to fulfill the law. Later,

Nicodemus cautions the Sanhedrin elders who wish to kill Jesus without allowing him the natural justice of presenting his own defense (John 7:50-51), and three years later he accompanies Joseph of Arimathea, another Jewish elder, to collect and prepare the body of Jesus for burial (John 19:38-40). So, Nicodemus is an example of a common, gradual transition in the spiritual life: the initial awakening to new possibilities, the need for space to voice his uncertainties, the intellectual and spiritual rebalancing, and later the entering into a deep and committed relationship.

In this first interaction, Nicodemus came to Jesus by night, in secret. It is worthwhile spending a few minutes imagining his state of mind. Nicodemus found himself not in agreement with many of his fellow Pharisees and then finally decided to visit this Jesus by himself. What was he thinking as he was drawn to approach Jesus? Was that not my way also? When at first I began to read the gospels and to open myself to the possibilities, did I go openly to the Church and proclaim my new direction? No, I sat quietly by myself to start reading and see what happened. I came secretly, without telling others.

Nicodemus responded to Jesus' miracles because they bore the witness of God's work. The story of Nicodemus also reminds us that it is the Spirit, who reaches out to each of us from the examples of others, to which our heart responds, and it is the Spirit that leads us to start and continue on our spiritual path to God. Few of us perform major miracles, yet as we each allow ourselves to be witnesses for God's work, we too engage and enliven others.

When the Light first comes to us, it begins in our darkness—in our internal night. We sense its presence and are drawn to learn more. This point in our lives is one of the most important we have, and it is good to remember this time and be thankful. It is the point at which we are first reached. What we do from then on is up to us. So it was for Nicodemus; this was the night he was first reached. He could have stayed in the comfortable circle of his legal Pharisaic colleagues, but he chose to step out and investigate. At that point he had started to leave some of his old self behind.

I am reminded of Thomas Ellwood who in 1659 listened to Edward Burrough and James Nayler at meeting and admitted, "I drank in his [Burrough's] words with desire, for they not only answered my understanding but warmed my heart with a certain heat, which I had not till then felt from the ministry of any man".[57] At the Penington home after supper that night, Ellwood listened to their discussion of the universal grace of God to all mankind. Next morning, after Ellwood, his father, and his sister had departed, Burrough remarked to the Peningtons: "As for the old man, he is settled on his lees, and the young woman is light and airy, but the young man is reached and may do well if he don't lose it ".[58]

The second special point in our spiritual journey is when we realise seriously that the spiritual path demands real change—the need for us to be reborn. That is, the Light shows us we are not yet fully acceptable to God, and we accept that we need to change. How very grateful can we be that the Light has reached out to us and that again we have the choice to proceed or stay where we are? This story of Nicodemus parallels some of my own steps in the spiritual journey. Perhaps many of us have also traveled the path that Nicodemus did that night.

Nicodemus's opening words are those of a diplomat and trained teacher. He has heard or seen the miracles of Jesus and knows from his religious training that such miracles are signs of the Presence of God and that this man must be a prophet, an important teacher. The older prophets, such as Elijah and Elisha, were known to have performed miracles, and so he goes to see Jesus, presumably asking to learn from this teacher the secrets of the ways of God. The older prophets had plenty to say about the erroneous ways of the Jewish people and what they needed to do in order to repent and to regain God's favour. In contrast, Jesus does not reply in the standard prophet mode. He does not specify a return to living in the laws handed down by Moses; his teaching is radically different. Jesus teaches that everyone must be born of the Spirit to enter the Presence of God.

At first Nicodemus is uncomprehending, yet in a way that is inwardly sincere and honest. He cannot understand a person being born twice—emerging from the womb a second time as a baby from his mother! The interchange has an air of banter. Jesus' response, *Art thou a master of Israel, and knowest not these things?* (3:10), could be taken as sarcastic criticism, but maybe it is just humorous chiding. John typically uses a misunderstanding to draw out the real meaning. Yet our minds, too, when we hear the word 'reborn', think, "Not likely". We have to shift into the spiritual, nonrational mode to come close to understanding what is required and what must happen. The change required is more serious than many at first grasp—no wonder Jesus says it means to be reborn—and the metaphor of changing water into wine springs to mind.

Verses 3:3–5 are the only ones in this gospel in which Jesus specifically says the phrase 'Kingdom of God'. *Except a man be born again, . . . Except a man be born of water and of the Spirit, he cannot enter into the Kingdom of God*—not just enter, but enter into. This saying recalls the great promise made by Ezekiel: *A new heart also will I give you, and a new spirit will I put within you: and I will take away the stony heart out of your flesh, and I will give you an heart of flesh. And I will put my spirit within you, and cause you to walk in my statutes, and ye shall keep my judgments, and do them* (Ezekiel 36:26–27). Jesus' own human experience was the same, for following his immersion baptism, the Holy Spirit descended upon him and he was never the same again.

Jesus is not a great proponent of kings and kingdoms, and he does not travel the land announcing he is a great leader. Although many are waiting for a great spiritual and perhaps military leader to rid the country of the imperial Romans with their idolatrous gods, Jesus is not this type of king. His 'kingdom' is not of this world. Yet he seems almost reluctant to say so, and he only admits his divine role as the Messiah, the Christ, when he is in a one-on-one conversation and is building a personal relationship with someone—with the Samaritan woman, with Peter, with the blind man he has cured (John 4:26, 6:69, 9:35–38). In the trial scenes he refuses to announce it even when questioned by Pilate (18:25–38). John uses others, Andrew and John the Baptist and the Samaritan woman, to proclaim Jesus (John 1:41, 1:29–36, 4:28–30).

The tenor of this approach is that Jesus comes to each of us individually, in a deeply personal relationship. It is not something heralded by megaphone statements. When Jesus admits to the cured man *it is he* [the Son of God] *that talketh with thee* (John 9:37), it is a quiet and simple voice, intimating, "Yes, you have found me, I am right here, close to you, and you and I have formed a bond that need never be broken".

Jesus reiterates the difference between flesh and spirit. They are not mixed, and whereas the ways of the body and the world can be understood by the bodily mind, the ways of the Spirit can only be apprehended by the Spirit. To try to understand and catch the Spirit with the mind is impossible, a hopeless task. Yet that is a difficult lesson to learn, for how often do I strain my mind to grasp the Spirit's movement? I should learn to cease straining.

> *The wind bloweth where it listeth, and thou hearest the sound thereof, but canst not tell whence it cometh, and whither it goeth: so is every one that is born of the Spirit.* (John 3:8)

Jesus draws us away from wanting to run our inner life according to logical regulations by using the above analogy with the wind. As in many languages, the word for 'wind' or 'breath' is the same as for 'spirit' (in Hebrew *ruach*, in Sanskrit *prana*, in Greek *pneuma*, and in Chinese *chi* or *qi*). In Hebrew, *ruach Elohim* is the Spirit of God, or we might say the breath of God, the breath that was breathed into our nostrils to make us each a living soul (see Genesis 2:7).

In Norman Marrow's rendering, *The breath of wind stirs and breathes at its pleasure; you can hear it, but you don't know where it comes from or where it goes to. So it is with everyone who has undergone a birth of the Spirit, the very breath of life* (TFG). The Spirit breathes in us as it wills, and we hear the Word and then it is gone. We believe in the wind without knowing either its source or its end, without knowing precisely how it works its way through the air around us, and in the same way we must believe in the Spirit. This Spirit may not follow a logical path, as our minds may expect and desire and even demand, for the path of the Spirit can be a wandering path, at times moving very strongly and then at times unexpectedly still with no clear direction. Such is the experience of God.

Many people who are infused with and follow the Spirit have a similar effect on those around them. Their contemporaries cannot quite understand where the impulses come from that move their friend and are never sure what might happen next. The Spirit moves in ways not easily fathomable by mortals. Isaac Penington wrote:

> There is a faith which is born of man's self, and a faith which is the gift of God. . . . As there are two births, the first and the second, so they each have their faith.[59]

> O! how doth the soul that is begotten of the divine breath, that is born of the living power and virtue, depend upon God for his continual breathings! There is nothing that hath so much from God, and yet nothing is so little able to live without him.[60]

At this point, Nicodemus fades from the story. There is no neatly wrapped conclusion for him or for us. The encounter he willingly sought with Jesus has left him in silence as he ponders what to do and comes to terms with the spiritual demands of Jesus' ministry to him. So is it for us, as we often take time in our own silence to spiritually digest the implications of a message from the Spirit. Only much later do we learn at the end of the gospel that it was Nicodemus, along with Joseph of Arimathea, who came to collect Jesus' body after the crucifixion (John 19:38-40). What a changed man! There is hope for all of us.

Rebirth Is a Universal Gift

The requirement to be reborn spiritually to enter the Presence of God has an important corollary. It does not matter who you were born as physically—it does not matter what nation, or tribe, or race, or people, or colour, or status. There are no chosen people. Every person has the potential to be reborn spiritually; everyone has, as John noted earlier, the Light within.

> *For God sent not his Son into the world to condemn the world; but that the world through him might be saved. He that believeth on him is not condemned: but he that believeth not is condemned already,*

> because he hath not believed in the name of the only begotten Son of God. And this is the condemnation, that light is come into the world, and men loved darkness rather than light, because their deeds were evil. For every one that doeth evil hateth the light, neither cometh to the light, lest his deeds should be reproved. But he that doeth truth cometh to the light, that his deeds may be made manifest, that they are wrought in God. (John 3:17–21)

John returns to this theme as Jesus explains his role on earth. His role is not to condemn but to save. To the Jewish society, so focused by the Pharisees on adherence to the smallest laws and judgments of wrongdoing, Jesus presents a diametrically opposite view. We are similar to the Pharisees, for we are often quick to judge what others have not done quite correctly.

As Jesus did repeatedly during his earthly ministry, the Light within us not only reveals our wrongdoings but also shows us the way to healing, where we may have Life more abundantly (John 10:10).

Old Testament passages record the frustration and anger felt by the sovereign Lord, God, Yahweh, at the wrongdoings of the Hebrews. Yet Jesus is also recalling the teachings of Ezekiel, who spoke the words given to him and emphasised that God would much prefer that people be saved than die:

> As surely as I live, declares the Sovereign LORD, I take no pleasure in the death of the wicked, but rather that they turn from their evil ways and live. (Ezekiel 33:11 NIV)

Jesus, or it may be John inserting his own commentary, reconfirms the message of the prologue—that Jesus is the Light come into the world (3:17–21). The light and the dark are mutually exclusive. Those who persist in refusing to acknowledge the presence of this Light are thereby condemning themselves to darkness and thus to ignorance and spiritual death. Those who do evil are unwilling to bring their inner selves into the Light; they hold back lest they be shown their errors. They prefer to remain complacent in their wrongdoings rather than feel reproved. It takes courage and trust to expose ourselves inwardly. In contrast, the good deeds of all those who follow Truth and are willing to come into the Light are clear for all to see, and more, their good deeds are done through them by God. All that is good is wrought by God.

Most importantly, the start of this passage states that when Jesus came into the world the purpose of his whole life was that people might be saved. The name Jesus, given before he was born (Matthew 1:21; Luke 1:31), is a Greek form of the Hebrew name Joshua, which means 'the Lord saves'. Jesus did not come to condemn with a scale of appropriate punishments; he came to forgive and to save. Parallel texts later in John (7:38, 8:12, 10:10) state that Jesus came to give life. That is the message of his work among people, his healing and curing of the body, his spiritual teachings, and the examples of his way of life.

Fox and the early Friends were similarly clear on the pivotal role of the Light within—each of us has a choice, either to follow the Light or to stay in the dark.

> 'The path of the just is a shining path,' the path of the unjust is darkness. So there are but two paths. Now the unjust cannot abide to hear talk of the light, but call it natural, and created and made, or conscience, they do not know what to call it, whose darkness cannot comprehend the light, though it shines in the darkness.[61]

As the lyrics of Australian songwriter Peter Kearney put it,

> Even though there is a light in the world
> We can still choose to let the night unfold,
> And walk in the dark,
> The dark might suit us very well.
> We can talk about peace, and get ready for war
> while our standard of living is killing the poor.
> Our hearts are so numb, just what does it mean
> to come into the light . . . into the light.[62]

John the Baptist Reminds Us That Humility Is an Essential Gift to Practise

> *Then there arose a question between some of John's disciples and the Jews about purifying. And they*

> *came unto John, and said unto him, Rabbi, he that was with thee beyond Jordan, to whom thou barest witness, behold, the same baptizeth, and all men come to him. John answered and said, A man can receive nothing, except it be given him from heaven. Yet yourselves bear me witness, that I said, I am not the Christ, but that I am sent before him. He that hath the bride is the bridegroom: but the friend of the bridegroom, which standeth and heareth him, rejoiceth greatly because of the bridegroom's voice: this my joy therefore is fulfilled. He must increase, but I must decrease.* (John 3:25-30)

The narrative returns to the relationship between Jesus and John the Baptist. John had been preaching repentance and baptising the people who flocked to hear him, though the Baptist acknowledges he is but the messenger.[63] The messenger, preacher, or prophet can only point the way. The inner change, the redeeming and saving, can only be done by God's power.

Repentance is a term widely used in the Old Testament, in the Synoptic Gospels, and in early Christian writings, though not once does it occur in the Gospel According to John. In Hebrew, repentance is represented by two verbs: *shuv* ('to return') and *nicham* ('to feel sorrow'). The New Testament usage of repentance is a translation of the word *metanoia* from the Greek texts, a word that has the connotation of change, the change of mind with a sense of regret.

Does John not use 'repentance' because he considers it to be a concept well taught elsewhere, or does he want to emphasise something different? Many people are affronted and reject the call to repentance. We often want to justify ourselves and to resist change.

Perhaps it is helpful to know the underlying meaning of *metanoia* as a call to accept inwardly any wrongdoings that become manifest in the Light and, with a sense of regret but not guilt, begin the changes required in life. A feeling for the meaning is given in Psalm 119:59-60: *I thought on my ways, and turned my feet unto thy testimonies. I made haste, and delayed not to keep thy commandments.*

Jesus rarely condemns, with the exception of the hypocrisy of the Pharisees and the Sadducees. Jesus emphasises the new path, the new way of life. He often tells people to go and sin no more. *Metanoia* involves accepting that previous ways may be revealed as mistaken and untenable and turning to a new way where we can be reconciled with God.

When his disciples became concerned at the number of people flocking to Jesus, John the Baptist answers with humility—he is not carried away by feelings of hurt pride nor a longing for earthly status and power: *John answered and said, A man can receive nothing, except it be given him from heaven* and *He must increase but I must decrease.*

This telling piece of ministry can be a hard admission for most of us. It takes humility to accept what the Light shows us. Further, we may all tend to think we have some control over what we are and can take credit for our good work. John the Baptist is saying, "No, all your abilities are a gift from God", and yet we commonly take them for granted. Then he notes a natural extension of this humility in that we are to allow our own sense of self and ego to diminish so that the Light and Jesus' presence within us may grow.

The extent of John's humility is a model for us. Quaker Elias Hicks wrote in 1820,

> For if thou willingly surrenders thyself as an offering to God—to do his will, as by the Light in thy own heart and conscience he is pleased to manifest it to thee—thy understanding will be more and more opened into those things that concern thy present and everlasting peace.[64]

Complete Rebirth

The change needed within us is more than we imagined. Here is the truth of the matter, which is shocking and hard to accept; this rebirth is nothing short of the dying of the 'old man', the former self, with its reliance on one's own strength and knowledge and qualifications.

How hard it is to stop justifying myself because some parts of me are good. This will be difficult language for many, but the truth of it cannot be denied for it is the experience of the holiest people in history as well as the calling within us. If you are hearing this you are probably also hearing your own resistance, as I was. Consider the possibilities of complete humility and powerlessness in this matter, of letting go of that resistance, of praying for help in cutting it loose. For only in facing the inner death can we be brought to spiritual rebirth and the start of that regeneration, during which we must daily and resolutely maintain our fervent attentiveness to the Light within. As William Dewsbury preached in 1688:

> You have line upon line, precept upon precept, here a little and there a little, to direct your minds to the Light of Christ Jesus. As the first Adam was made a living soul, so the second Adam is a quickening Spirit. This know for certain: no man or woman can be quickened and raised up into the life of the second Adam until the life of the first Adam be taken away from them.
>
> . . . Now except we become born again, we cannot enter into the kingdom of God. There is no becoming the new creatures, until we be slain to the old man. Thou must be slain in thy pride, haughtiness and the corruption of thy own will, and all selfishness, Thou must have God to burn it up in thee.[65]

CHAPTER 5
JESUS INSTITUTES THE NEW WORSHIP IN SPIRIT AND TRUTH, IRRESPECTIVE OF GENDER, CLASS, OR RACE

Samaritan Woman at the Well

Chapter 4 of the Gospel According to John starts with a clear statement of what is happening and why. Jesus is to leave Judea and travel north towards Galilee, and between the regions of Judea and Galilee lies Samaria.

The Samaritans were religious enemies of the Jews of Judea, with a long history of conflict between the two groups (Ezra 4:1-6; Sirach 50:25-26). Samaria had been populated by Assyrian colonists who had then intermarried with the Hebrews. When Nehemiah enforced the Mosaic law against mixed marriages, the Jewish priest Manasseh, who had intermarried, was expelled from Judea, and he led a secession, taught Mosaic law, and erected a temple for the worship of God at Mount Gerizim. This mixed community accepted only the first five books of the Old Testament and the book of Joshua, ignoring the prophets and hence the prophetic validation of the temple at Jerusalem. Animosity continued, with Samaritans refusing passage to Jews travelling from Galilee up to Jerusalem for the feasts. In ca. 120 BCE the Jewish leader John Hyrcanus marched his army north to destroy the Samaritan temple on Mount Gerizim.

The Samaritans were regarded as the lowest of the low, despised and perhaps even untouchable. Later, the temple authorities tried to insult Jesus by saying, *Aren't we right to say that you are a Samaritan—a heretic—and that you're possessed by a devil?* (John 8:48 TIB). There is some evidence that Jews would even cross the Jordan and travel through the desert on the eastern side of the river and then back across the Jordan to avoid breathing air that Samaritans had breathed.

That is why the parable of the Good Samaritan (Luke 10:29-37) has such biting effect.[66] In that story, first the Jewish priest, who should have been prepared to minister to a person in need, passed by on the other side of the road without rendering any assistance to the man who had been robbed. Then came the Levite, a custodian of the temple, who should have known the requirements of the law to do justice and mercy, and he too passed by on the other side of the road. Jesus thus portrays these two essential leaders of the Jewish faith as having failed in their obligations. Then finally the Samaritan, a despised Gentile, does what compassion and mercy demand after the two Jewish leaders had failed miserably. Jesus could not have made a more caustic statement about the Jewish leadership. He could not have made a more startling requirement that the followers of Judaism extend the spirituality of compassion to all.

The term 'Jews' is used in the Bible to refer to the whole nation of Jewish people in respect to their birth, place of origin, and religion (e.g., 2 Kings 16:6, 18:26; Esther 9:1-30; Jeremiah 40:12; John 18:39; Acts 10:23, 39) or generally to a crowd of Jewish people (e.g., John 8:52, 12:11). Jesus and his disciples were also Jewish people. In the Gospel According to John, the term 'Jews' can refer to the local crowd, to the Jewish culture, or to Jewish people generally, and especially to the Jewish leaders—temple authorities, Sadducees, Pharisees, scribes, and priests.

As the gospel narrative develops, it becomes clear that the Jewish leaders became increasingly antagonistic towards Jesus (John 5:18; 8:37; 11:8). In the decades after Jesus' death, the Jewish leadership and Roman authorities together ensured the continued persecution of the early followers of Jesus (see appendix 2).

The Gospel According to John has been used to justify anti-semitism.[67] It is not righteous for the wrong acts of some Jewish priests in the first century to be visited upon others, including those who have been born centuries later. Let us recognise also that the gospel references to 'Jews' do not mean Jews alone. The stories refer to all those who hide behind legalities, traditions, and prejudices that are oppressive and deny compassion. These tendencies, these behaviours exhibited by first-century Jewish leaders, these

'Jews', are inside each of us as well. Margaret Fell wrote the following about George Fox speaking at a church in 1652:

> And the first words he [Fox] spoke were as followeth: 'He is not a Jew that is one outward, neither is that circumcision which is outward, but he is a Jew that is one inward, and that is circumcision which is of the heart'.[68]

So with this background, let us explore the fourth major episode in Jesus' ministry—after the making of wine from water, the upending of the tables in the temple, and the instructions to Nicodemus. The first three all take place in the context of Jewish communities, but in the fourth Jesus brings his ministry into contact with the heathen Samaritans. Certainly Jesus was not about to evade them. He needed to travel beyond Samaria, so through Samaria he went. This is symbolic; Jesus is ready to bring the Light into every person, no matter what their race or spiritual state.

Within each of us too are hidden parts that need to be illuminated and cleansed by the Light within. The story of the Samaritan woman is an example of how to respond to that Light.

> *He left Judaea, and departed again into Galilee. And he must needs go through Samaria. Then cometh he to a city of Samaria, which is called Sychar, near to the parcel of ground that Jacob gave to his son Joseph. Now Jacob's well was there. Jesus therefore, being wearied with his journey, sat thus on the well: and it was about the sixth hour. There cometh a woman of Samaria to draw water: Jesus saith unto her, Give me to drink. (For his disciples were gone away unto the city to buy meat.) Then saith the woman of Samaria unto him, How is it that thou, being a Jew, askest drink of me, which am a woman of Samaria? for the Jews have no dealings with the Samaritans. Jesus answered and said unto her, If thou knewest the gift of God, and who it is that saith to thee, Give me to drink; thou wouldest have asked of him, and he would have given thee living water. The woman saith unto him, Sir, thou hast nothing to draw with, and the well is deep: from whence then hast thou that living water? Art thou greater than*

> *our father Jacob, which gave us the well, and drank thereof himself, and his children, and his cattle? Jesus answered and said unto her, Whosoever drinketh of this water shall thirst again: But whosoever drinketh of the water that I shall give him shall never thirst; but the water that I shall give him shall be in him a well of water springing up into everlasting life.* (John 4:3-14)

Jesus has been travelling in the hot sun, and about midday (the sixth hour) he arrives at a famous location—the place where the Hebrew patriarch Jacob had found a good well to provide water for his people and animals.[69] Sychar (or Shechem, near the present city of Nablus) is some fifty-five kilometers north of Jerusalem, not that Jesus would have walked it in one morning. The disciples had gone to buy food.

While Jesus is resting, a woman approaches the well, probably as she does every day. Yet women normally went together in the evening, when it was cooler, to draw water for their families (Genesis 24:11). Why was she alone in the heat of the day? Who knows her thoughts on this hot day, when she would normally have been alone, and saw a strange man by the well who then asked her for a drink? She cannot understand why a Jew, a religious enemy, would ask her, a Samaritan woman, for a drink, particularly since she, who was considered unclean, had handled the drinking vessel.

Jesus replies that if she had known who he was, it would have been she asking him for water—living water. John now uses this interaction and the woman's misunderstanding to develop his theme. The woman cannot understand how Jesus can get any water because he has no bucket to lower into the well. Jesus replies that he speaks not about water to drink but of spiritual life and an eternal well to be found within each of us.

> *The woman saith unto him, Sir, give me this water, that I thirst not, neither come hither to draw. Jesus saith unto her, Go, call thy husband, and come hither. The woman answered and said, I have no husband. Jesus said unto her, Thou hast well said, I have no husband: For thou hast had five husbands;*

> *and he whom thou now hast is not thy husband: in that saidst thou truly.* (John 4:15-18)

When the woman asks for water again, Jesus tells her to get her husband. The woman honestly admits she has no husband; perhaps she is a loose woman in her culture. Jesus acknowledges her truthful statement, noting she has had five husbands, which she cannot deny. Isn't this common in the spiritual journey, that when we encounter God, the Spirit immediately raises some misdeed or deficiency within us? It is easy to be disappointed and give up. As errors are shown by the Light, we know Truth has been revealed. So it was with the woman at the well. As soon as she really engaged with Jesus, her misdeeds were exposed to her. Yet she acknowledged the truth immediately; she did not deny them or flee. She stood in Jesus' presence, in the Light. Yet there was no sense of condemnation.

There may well have been quite the opposite: a sense of deep connectivity, a latent intimacy. Hebrew traditions contain examples of marriage invitations being spoken near the water well, by Abraham's servant seeking a wife for Isaac (Genesis 24), by Jacob on seeing Rebekah (Genesis 29), and by Moses on seeing Zipporah (Exodus 2). A walk by the sea, along a creek, or near a lake has been the setting for many in love, though most are unaware of the blessings of life in the water by which they are walking. A spiritual marriage between Jesus and the Samaritan woman is being broached beside the well at Sychar.

> *The woman saith unto him, Sir, I perceive that thou art a prophet. Our fathers worshipped in this mountain; and ye say, that in Jerusalem is the place where men ought to worship. Jesus saith unto her, Woman, believe me, the hour cometh, when ye shall neither in this mountain, nor yet at Jerusalem, worship the Father. Ye worship ye know not what: we know what we worship: for salvation is of the Jews. But the hour cometh, and now is, when the true worshippers shall worship the Father in spirit and in truth: for the Father seeketh such to worship him. God is a Spirit: and they that worship him must worship him in spirit and in truth. The woman saith unto him, I know that Messias cometh, which is*

called Christ: when he is come, he will tell us all things. Jesus saith unto her, I that speak unto thee am he. (John 4:19–26)

And immediately, she recognised she was in the presence of a prophet. The woman is spiritually ripe. We do not have the rest of her life story, but it seems to me her life would never have been the same from that moment on. So it is for us; once we are brought face-to-face with spiritual reality, our life is forever changed.

At this point, the woman moves from discussion about worldly water to the manner of worship, for she is very aware that her Samaritan religion believes Mount Gerizim is the place to worship, whereas Jews assert the temple in Jerusalem is the place to worship God.

Jesus comments in essence that she and those like her do not understand how to truly worship God. In the future, worship shall be neither in the temple on Mount Gerizim nor at the temple in Jerusalem. This is an extraordinary statement. From then on, worship is not to be defined in terms of this or that temple; worship is to be internal, in spirit and in truth. No falsity is allowed. God is to be worshipped in spirit. Words and liturgies are not mandatory.

For Fox and others, this was a critical statement that meant the established churches had completely missed the point of Jesus' advice and also the ways of the apostles. Jesus had established a new worship, a new covenant, as was clearly understood by the early Christians.[70]

Further, Jesus uses the wonderful future present, *the hour cometh and now is*. This is a statement of the continuing revelation of the Spirit, meaning that from now on the Spirit is available every moment and we can live expecting this. This experience of the early apostles is mentioned elsewhere, for example, the promise at the end of Matthew, *and, lo, I am with you always, even unto the end of the world* (28:20).

This statement is the basis for the early Quaker practice of worshipping in silence, with internal listening and seeking, leaving aside thoughts, and the turning away from temples and churches and doctrines. Jesus has emphasised the spiritual lesson related to the clearing of the inner temple, the sacred space within each of us. In the words of

Paul: *Know ye not that ye are the temple of God, and that the spirit of God dwelleth in you?* (1 Corinthians 3:16).

William Penn emphasised that such worship is not in our own power. It is the result of God's working within us:

> Christ drew off his disciples from the glory and worship of the outward temple, and instituted a more inward and spiritual worship, in which he instructed his followers. "Ye shall neither in this mountain, nor yet at Jerusalem," says Christ to the Samaritan woman, "worship the father. God is a spirit, and they that worship him, must worship him, in spirit and in truth."[71]

> True worship can only come from a heart prepared by the Lord. . . . And whatever prayer be made, or doctrine be uttered, and not from the preparation of the Holy Spirit, it is not acceptable with God; nor can it be the true evangelical worship, which is in spirit and truth; that is, by the preparation and aid of the Holy Spirit. For what is a heap of the most pathetical words to God Almighty; or the dedication of any place or time to him?[72]

Jesus is saying the true worship of God is by the Spirit, not perfunctory recitations and our endless requests to make the world as we would like it. The true prayers are those instilled in the heart by the Spirit, not those generated by our minds. The true worship takes place by listening in silent stillness, 'waiting on the Lord' to hear and then doing what each of us is asked, and so fulfilling God's purpose in creating us.

> *And upon this came his disciples, and marvelled that he talked with the woman: yet no man said, What seekest thou? or, Why talkest thou with her? The woman then left her waterpot, and went her way into the city, and saith to the men, Come, see a man, which told me all things that ever I did: is not this the Christ? Then they went out of the city, and came unto him.* (John 4:27-30)

The disciples return and are amazed to find Jesus talking with this Samaritan woman. It was not normal for a Jewish man to address a strange woman, especially for a teacher to speak with a woman in public. Yet that is the way of the Spirit—it does not distinguish gender or race or class. The woman leaves her waterpot, the baggage she has been carrying for many years, and rushes to the city.

She is the perfect preacher of the Word, for having heard it she returns to tell others. Note it is a woman who does this, not a man. This simple woman, a Gentile, not a learned Jewish priest, is the most effective and perfect preacher of the Word. The men of the city respond immediately to this message from Jesus and come to learn more. In 1674, George Keith wrote about the meaning of this passage:

> So first of all, she was taught . . . by Christ himself; she was taught immediately, and being thus taught, she believed on him, and then she went and Preached him. This is an excellent Pattern, and an Example unto all true Ministers, and Preachers of Christ. First to be taught by himself, before they go Preach him unto others . . . she was called immediately by the Spirit of Christ in her heart; she ran not unsent, it appears the Lord sent her, and was with her by his Spirit, by the good effect her Testimony had; for, as it is said, *many of the Samaritans of that City believed on him,* &c. And this was through her Preaching. They did not despise her because she was a Woman, they did not say unto her (as many now say) thou art a Woman, thou should not Preach; . . . The manner how she preached Christ, is observable, she preached him from her own experience, as what she found done by him to her own condition.[73]

This was the clear justification for the early Quaker admission of women into ministering for worship and actively participating in the lives of Friends. Jesus made no distinction between men and women, and neither would the first Friends. The key issue was then and is still—has this person been endowed with the gift of ministry, of being taught inwardly by the Spirit, and of being sufficiently disciplined to wait until the words of God are presented before giving utterance? Many established churches are still struggling with the issue of female ministers. The Quaker position has always been that God gives the Holy Spirit to all, without exception.

The Samaritan woman's preaching is simple—no long discursive and analytical sermons and no long-winded justifications based on old texts or traditions. She simply says, *Come and see what I have seen.* This is a statement of what she knew from experience. Simple statements and ministry instilled unto the heart by the Spirit are best.

> *In the mean while his disciples prayed him, saying, Master, eat. But he said unto them, I have meat to eat that ye know not of. Therefore said the disciples one to another, Hath any man brought him ought to eat? Jesus saith unto them, My meat is to do the will of him that sent me, and to finish his work. Say not ye, There are yet four months, and then cometh harvest? behold, I say unto you, Lift up your eyes, and look on the fields; for they are white already to harvest. And he that reapeth receiveth wages, and gathereth fruit unto life eternal: that both he that soweth and he that reapeth may rejoice together. And herein is that saying true, One soweth, and another reapeth. I sent you to reap that whereon ye bestowed no labour: other men laboured, and ye are entered into their labours.* (John 4:31-38)

Jesus now converses with his disciples, emphasizing that his job is to do the work that God has put him on earth to do and drawing attention to the work they also must do. This is the first time in the gospel that John makes explicit Jesus' role as a servant of God. We can imagine the reactions of those who had heard and meditated with John on these stories of Jesus—they might feel this man is God. But no, Jesus and John are very clear: This is God working through Jesus.

Jesus' statement that *My meat is to do the will of him that sent me, and to finish his work* reveals the source of sustenance of the spiritual life. Jesus acknowledges there is a spiritual analogy of food for the worldly body. If we ask ourselves what is the food of spiritual growth, the answer is that it is doing the will of 'him' who sent Jesus, of finishing the divine plan. The spiritual food is given for doing, not for personal enjoyment. If this was true for Jesus, no doubt it is true for us. Early Friends and those who allow themselves to be changed in response to the Light within them, allow themselves to forgo their own plans and to follow what the Light is showing them within. As a result, they find themselves changed and empowered people.

Jesus emphasises the urgency of the work. How long do we have? How long can we delay the spiritual work while we muck around with other things?

The period of four months reflects the farming cycle from sowing of seed to reaping the harvest. In that time, the green fields of wheat have turned pale brown and the seed heads look white in the sunlight. Yet in the spiritual realm we do not have to wait four months, nor any time, for the spiritual fields are white; they are ready to harvest now. Jesus has sown the seeds, and those who bring their soul towards God can work now. The sower and the reaper in the spiritual realm can rejoice together. No four-month waiting period is required! The task is now!

The spiritual journey is to be done in the here and now. It is not a matter of waiting for later forgiveness and redemption—the work is now. That applies both to our work in the world and also to ourselves.

> *And many of the Samaritans of that city believed on him for the saying of the woman, which testified, He told me all that ever I did. So when the Samaritans were come unto him, they besought him that he would tarry with them: and he abode there two days. And many more believed because of his own word; And said unto the woman, Now we believe, not because of thy saying: for we have heard him ourselves, and know that this is indeed the Christ, the Saviour of the world.* (John 4:39–42)

Finally, Jesus spends time with the people, and they come to hear his voice themselves. The words of these eyewitnesses are very instructive. They do not see Jesus as just a man; the key thing they perceive is the presence of the mystical Christ, the Presence and 'offspring' of God. The words of the woman and the Samaritan people are clear: "Is this not the Christ?"

Is that not so with us, too, that we may first be drawn to the spiritual life by the experiences and evidence in the lives of others and then we begin to hear the voice ourselves, which confirms us on the path?

John has established Jesus as the guide to worshipping God and to finding the Christ within each of us and working among us.

George Fox asked,

> Now where is this spirit, and where is this truth? Is it not within people? . . . and so, every man and woman must be brought to truth in their own hearts, and brought to the spirit of God in their own hearts. This is the standing and perfect worship, and it will stand when all the worships of old Adam are gone.[74]

Healing the Nobleman's Servant

Jesus resumes his travel northwards to Galilee, where he encounters a nobleman seeking a cure for his stricken son.

> *So Jesus came again into Cana of Galilee, where he made the water wine. And there was a certain nobleman, whose son was sick at Capernaum. When he heard that Jesus was come out of Judaea into Galilee, he went unto him, and besought him that he would come down, and heal his son: for he was at the point of death. Then said Jesus unto him, Except ye see signs and wonders, ye will not believe. The nobleman saith unto him, Sir, come down ere my child die. Jesus saith unto him, Go thy way; thy son liveth. And the man believed the word that Jesus had spoken unto him, and he went his way. And as he was now going down, his servants met him, and told him, saying, Thy son liveth. Then enquired he of them the hour when he began to amend. And they said unto him, Yesterday at the seventh hour the fever left him. So the father knew that it was at the same hour, in the which Jesus said unto him, Thy son liveth: and himself believed, and his whole house.* (John 4:46-53)

The healing of the nobleman's son is similar to the healing of the centurion's servant in Matthew 8:5-13. Whether there were multiple healings from a distance or whether these two passages record slightly different versions of the same event is not so important. Cana is a hill town in southern Galilee, just north of Nazareth, and Capernaum is forty-five kilometres to the north, on the shore of the Sea of Galilee. Jesus is continuing his journey north from Judea through Samaria and is met along the road by the nobleman pleading for his sick son to be made well. People in Cana would remember the miracle at the wedding feast, and perhaps many have heard of the events in Jerusalem during the Passover. Jesus' response is to recognise that people need signs and wonders to encourage them in the spiritual life.

I notice also that the nobleman has come well along the road to meet Jesus. He has had to make the effort, going forward in faith, with commitment of time and energy to travel the path. I wonder what the nobleman was thinking as he set out and travelled the road. Maybe he was at first half believing but not totally committed until Jesus, or the Light, worked some change within him that could not have happened any other way. At that point, he would believe fully in the Spirit. This was my experience.

Except ye see signs and wonders, ye will not believe reminds me of the many times I, and perhaps others, have sought some reward in our prayers. We may even attempt a little internal contract that we will stay in meditation and prayer if God will let us feel this presence. We too are asking for signs before we are ready to believe. Eventually, we have to outgrow this need and seek God unconditionally. Then we have some chance of unconditional love and healing.

After the initial joy and consolations that draw us into the spiritual journey, there is much work to be done, and John is effectively saying here, early in the process, that we all need to learn to seek God without requiring regular signs and little rewards.

When the nobleman does make the effort, Jesus is ready for him. He accepts Jesus' word that his son will recover, and he starts towards home. Such is faith. Then he discovers the miracle is true, for his servants confirm the healing, and the hour it happened matches exactly when Jesus spoke to him. This is my experience—when I pray for healing, I can sense the prayer has been heard, and yet the healing may not become apparent till later. It all depends on my being willing to travel the road myself and have faith.

Perhaps the man set off hopeful, partly believing in what he had heard about the miraculous powers of Jesus. Then the final verses confirm that when the healing occurs, the whole house believes. When a miraculous change is effected within us, our faith is increased and we become completely trusting in Jesus. This is the common experience—trusting in the Light and following the Light leads to more Light.

Equality

The stories of the Samaritan woman and the healing of the nobleman's son show how Jesus brings spiritual life, living water, and then healing. The Samaritan woman accepts what the Light reveals within her and becomes a minister. Jesus institutes the new covenant for worship with continuing revelation of God.

Jesus ministered equally to Jews and Gentiles, to men and women, to commoners, scholars, and nobility. There were no barriers. The Light is available to all. Spiritual equality regardless of ethnic origin, gender, age, rank and class was confirmed for early Christians by both Peter and Paul:

> *. . . I will pour out of my Spirit upon all flesh: and your sons and your daughters shall prophesy, and your young men shall see visions, and your old men shall dream dreams: And on my servants and my handmaidens I will pour out in those days of my Spirit; and they shall prophesy.* (Acts 2:17-18; Joel 2:28-32)

> *What you have done is put aside your old self with its past deeds and put on a new self, one that grows in knowledge as it is formed anew in the image of its Creator. And in that image there is no Greek or Hebrew, no Jew or Gentile, no barbarian or Scythian, no slave or citizen. There is only Christ, who is all in all.* (Colossians 3:9-11 TIB)

CHAPTER 6
THE DAY OF VISITATION AND HEALING

The Day of Visitation

After this there was a feast of the Jews; and Jesus went up to Jerusalem. Now there is at Jerusalem by the sheep market a pool, which is called in the Hebrew tongue Bethesda, having five porches. In these lay a great multitude of impotent folk, of blind, halt, withered, waiting for the moving of the water. For an angel went down at a certain season into the pool, and troubled the water: whosoever then first after the troubling of the water stepped in was made whole of whatsoever disease he had. And a certain man was there, which had an infirmity thirty and eight years. When Jesus saw him lie, and knew that he had been now a long time in that case, he saith unto him, Wilt thou be made whole? The impotent man answered him, Sir, I have no man, when the water is troubled, to put me into the pool: but while I am coming, another steppeth down before me. Jesus saith unto him, Rise, take up thy bed, and walk. And immediately the man was made whole, and took up his bed, and walked: and on the same day was the sabbath.

The Jews therefore said unto him that was cured, It is the sabbath day: it is not lawful for thee to carry thy bed. He answered them, He that made me whole, the same said unto me, Take up thy bed, and walk. Then asked they him, What man is that which said unto thee, Take up thy bed, and walk? And he that was healed wist not who it was: for Jesus had conveyed himself away, a multitude being in that place. Afterward Jesus findeth him in the temple, and said unto him, Behold, thou art made whole: sin no more, lest a worse thing come unto thee. The

> *man departed, and told the Jews that it was Jesus, which had made him whole. (John 5:1–15)*

This story is the miraculous healing of a man crippled for thirty-eight years. There is no investigation of what led to the problem, whether the man was a sinner, or what might be any legal ramifications or costs. No commitment in faith was identified, as is often done in other healing miracles. The man who was crippled did not ask for healing as the nobleman had for his son; Jesus simply accepted the person at that moment and healed him. Jesus arrived, saw what was needed, and asked the man if he was ready, and the man confessed his weakness and inability. Jesus then issued a specific instruction to do something. This is a common pattern in my own spiritual life. *Wilt thou be made whole?* We all have to give our consent to be cured, either by going to a doctor and accepting the medical advice and treatment or, on the spiritual plane, by consenting to follow the Light and the instructions of the Spirit. We are free to choose. Later, the man was given the courage to witness to the healing by Jesus rather than deny it due to fear of the authorities.

Jesus comes to a distressed person, visits him for a short time, and makes him whole. This was a day of visitation for that man, a special day in his life when he was presented with the spiritual opportunity to choose between faithful witness to the Light or denial of the Light out of fear or desire for worldly gain.[75]

Later, Jesus finds again the man he has cured and reminds him to sin no more or a worse fate could befall him. Jesus has released the man from his past and commands him to live purely in the future. No backsliding—the command is to follow the Light.

What worse fate? If we miss our day of visitation, it may not return and we can be left to rue the day we did not turn onto the new path indicated by the Light. If we are inattentive to the Light when we have it, we may find our hearts hardened and darkened. Spiritual darkness may ensue, making it harder to follow the path, perhaps even leading to spiritual death due to our committing sins. Spiritual injury is worse than physical disability or death. As Gandhi once remarked about being nonviolent, it is better to suffer damage to your body, which will generally heal, than to suffer damage to your soul that is incurable.

God's Work Not Subject to Human Timetables

> *It was because Jesus did things like this on the Sabbath that the Temple authorities began to persecute him. Jesus said to them, "Abba God is working right now, and I am at work as well".* (John 5:16–17 TIB)

The healing of the lame is one of the signs predicted for the Messiah (Isaiah 35:5), and the gospels record many instances of such healing (e.g., Matthew 15:30; Luke 7:22). Yet the Jewish leaders take issue with work being done on the Sabbath.

Jesus does not explain or justify this Sabbath healing on compassionate grounds, as he did when he replied to the Pharisees that of course people work on the Sabbath for many of them have untied animals from a manger, and no one would leave a child sick or an animal to suffer without pulling it from a well (e.g., Luke 13:10–17, 14:1–6). So, why should he not heal on the Sabbath a person who is suffering? No—Jesus reminds us that God works continually, otherwise how would the world continue to receive life, and light, and love? Jesus is operating at a spiritual level, and there is no need for rational justification on the basis of worldly needs. God works, and Jesus works, every day.

Life is a response to the spirit no matter what day or what hour. When there is a need for healing, do it—do not withhold because of some worldly or contrived reason. There is no boundary between times to operate on a secular basis and times to operate on a spiritual basis. The day of visitation can come at any time.

We are made aware that God is always working. It is we who become tired, lazy, or unwilling, generally for reasons that suit ourselves. The need is to put Self aside and allow God to continue working through us. We are allowed rest when the work is done.

God Is the Source of Jesus' Life and Powers

> *Therefore the Jews sought the more to kill him, because he not only had broken the sabbath, but said also that God was his Father, making himself equal with God. Then answered Jesus and said unto them, Verily, verily, I say unto you, The Son can do nothing of himself, but what he seeth the Father do: for what things soever he doeth, these also doeth the Son likewise. For the Father loveth the Son, and sheweth him all things that himself doeth: and he will shew him greater works than these, that ye may marvel. For as the Father raiseth up the dead, and quickeneth them; even so the Son quickeneth whom he will.* (John 5:18–21)

Then comes the startling admission by Jesus: *The Son can do nothing of himself.* Previously, Jesus had told his disciples that he is spiritually sustained by doing *the will of him that sent me* (John 4:34). Now he makes the clear and extraordinary statement, "I can do *nothing* by my own power". Surely this is a dramatic moment in John's story of Jesus. For the first time in all the gospels, Jesus confirms he is not omnipotent and that he relies absolutely on God for his energy and wisdom and healing abilities.

This statement, *The Son can do nothing of himself,* is one of humility and reliance on God (John 5:19; see also John 5:26, 5:30, 8:28). Jesus does not say, "I can do most things, but really I need to rely on God to help with the more spectacular miracles", or, as we might say, "I can handle most of life and just call on God when I am in a tight spot!" No, Jesus says he can do nothing, absolutely nothing, by himself; everything he has and does is from God. Jesus makes this point three times in this section.

In 5:18–22, Jesus faces the accusation that he has said he is equal with God, a claim for which the Jewish leaders sought to kill him. They are imprisoned in their traditional legal framework and cannot understand the breadth of his spirituality. Jesus' statement (5:19–20) is not so much a doctrinal confirmation that Jesus is the complete revelation of God as it is an acknowledgement by Jesus as a human being that his entire life and abilities are gifts of God. He refutes their accusation by acknowledging that he can only work because God works through him. If that is the case for Jesus, then surely it is the case for us.

Without God, I am nothing. For me, in difficult times, when the Spirit goes, the paper bag just blows away.

The New Covenant

> *For Abba God judges no one, having entrusted all judgment to the Only Begotten.* (John 5:22 TIB)

Jesus has instituted a new covenant between God and people, a covenant predicted by Jeremiah (31:31-34) and Ezekiel (11:19-20). John 5:22 is a very different narrative from much of the Old Testament. It is my experience that God is not a judge and punisher in the Old Testament sense, for the God of Jesus is merciful and loving. The new covenant brings an end to the Old Testament model that God is a watchful, wrathful judge who delivers punishments like a worldly king or judge in the legal realm. The new covenant proclaims that love is the way, as is fully explained later in the gospel. In this new covenant, for which the time is coming and now is, God is to be worshipped in Spirit and in Truth. God is Spirit. God is merciful, loving, and the source of blessings.

Any reproving and judging is entrusted to the Light and to Jesus in person when he was on earth. Yet we know how little judging he did. Most of his ministry was healing, forgiving and inviting people into a new life, a life where individuals changed direction and sinned no more, a life of abundance. He only passed judgment on those who persistently refused to listen and modify their ways, especially those who were hypocritical in their behaviour. Jesus' Light did appear directly to Saul on the road to Damascus, reproved him, and made a way forward for him to be changed. The mystery of God calls me, and the Light of Christ shows me my errors and the narrow path to follow. This Guide is not a bewildering set of regulations; it is the Light within, available to all, at all times.

For all of us, there will be days when the Light visits us strongly to call us into new ways of being. These days of visitation are so vital that we must be alert and responsive. Do we watch and pray lest we become lost?

> *Verily, verily, I say unto you, He that heareth my word, and believeth on him that sent me, hath everlasting life, and shall not come into condemnation; but is passed from death unto life. Verily, verily, I say unto you, The hour is coming, and now is, when the dead shall hear the voice of the Son of God: and they that hear shall live. For as the Father hath life in himself; so hath he given to the Son to have life in himself; And hath given him authority to execute judgment also, because he is the Son of man. . . . I can of mine own self do nothing: as I hear, I judge: and my judgment is just; because I seek not mine own will, but the will of the Father which hath sent me.* (John 5:24-30)

The new covenant confirms a new way of worshipping in Spirit and in Truth, irrespective of the location of any temple or church. Then Jesus again speaks of the spiritual possibilities in the future present: *The hour is coming, and now is, when the dead shall hear the voice of the Son of God: and they that hear shall live.*

Jesus also confirms that, even as the Son of man, nothing he does can be done without the life given to him by his *Abba*, father, and that he is always faithfully obedient to *Abba*, the one who sent him.[76] Jesus acknowledges he is the servant of God. He is recognizing that it is that of God, the Christ, directing and living through him as a man. We are invited to also recognise that if we can allow ourselves to be given over to that possibility, letting go of all else, that life and that Christ may begin to shine in each of us.

May we take a moment to consider this wonderful possibility? Those who continue to hear and listen to the inner voice, the Word, who follow the Light within and accept their errors, can be moved from a state of spiritual deadness, aloneness, and uncertainty to a state of spiritual life and closeness to God.

This was the understanding of the early apostles. They found that by following Jesus' teachings closely they became purified, even felt they were God's children, not just as an intellectual concept but as a lived experience.[77] It did not matter whether they were Jew or Gentile, slave or free, male or female–the experience is independent of creed, status, and gender.

Repudiating the Lack of Love

> *And the Father himself, which hath sent me, hath borne witness of me. Ye have neither heard his voice at any time, nor seen his shape. And ye have not his word abiding in you: for whom he hath sent, him ye believe not. Search the scriptures; for in them ye think ye have eternal life: and they are they which testify of me. And ye will not come to me, that ye might have life. I receive not honour from men. But I know you, that ye have not the love of God in you.* (John 5:37–42)

When the heart is hardened by habit or self-interest, when the neck and jaw are stiff with self-justification, it is impossible to listen to what Jesus wants us to hear. Some have observed that if we do not listen to God, the pain rises to a level we cannot but notice. Suddenly we become aware that we are in error and need to change.

The same impassioned frustration and rebuke was felt by Jesus' own village leaders in Nazareth (Luke 4:24–30) and by the Pharisees, who covered their lack of compassion with ritual righteousness (Matthew 23:37–39; Luke 11:37–52) or questioned his non-compliance with ritual hand washing (Mark 7:5–23). This direct challenging is recorded many times in John's gospel. My own experience of Jesus' presence is the same. There is no hiding of sins in the Light.

In this first time in John, Jesus confronts and criticises the Jewish leaders. They refuse to accept him despite their belief in the Hebrew Scriptures as the path to salvation, and yet these same Scriptures refer to him. That the Scriptures testify of Jesus may refer to Moses's prophecy, *I will raise them up a Prophet from among their brethren, like unto thee, and I will put my words in his mouth; and he shall speak unto them all that I shall command him* (Deuteronomy 18:18). Jesus maintains that prophecies of the Messiah do in fact refer to himself. He cannot understand why they or we hold back from his teachings.

Then comes the frightening repudiation that the Jewish leaders lack love in their hearts. What a terrifying judgment. Thus, Jesus introduces what will become the overriding message of his ministry—love one another. Has this judgment ever happened to any of us? Have we ever done something without love in our hearts?

CHAPTER 7
BREAD OF LIFE

Sign of Feeding the Multitude

> *After these things Jesus went over the sea of Galilee, which is the sea of Tiberias. And a great multitude followed him, because they saw his miracles which he did on them that were diseased. And Jesus went up into a mountain, and there he sat with his disciples. And the passover, a feast of the Jews, was nigh.*
>
> *When Jesus then lifted up his eyes, and saw a great company come unto him, he saith unto Philip, Whence shall we buy bread, that these may eat? And this he said to prove him: for he himself knew what he would do. Philip answered him, Two hundred pennyworth of bread is not sufficient for them, that every one of them may take a little. One of his disciples, Andrew, Simon Peter's brother, saith unto him, There is a lad here, which hath five barley loaves, and two small fishes: but what are they among so many? And Jesus said, Make the men sit down. Now there was much grass in the place. So the men sat down, in number about five thousand. And Jesus took the loaves; and when he had given thanks, he distributed to the disciples, and the disciples to them that were set down; and likewise of the fishes as much as they would. When they were filled, he said unto his disciples, Gather up the fragments that remain, that nothing be lost. Therefore they gathered them together, and filled twelve baskets with the fragments of the five barley loaves, which remained over and above unto them that had eaten.* (John 6:1-13)

Writing long after the events, John explains that the Sea of Galilee, as it was known in Jesus' time, was now called the Sea of Tiberias. The Romans did as many colonisers do; they changed place names to honour themselves and diminish the indigenous culture. By now, Jesus' miracles drew a large crowd from rural areas of Galilee, even as he sought time apart. The story itself is plainly told.

John places the events close to the second Passover of Jesus' ministry, providing a sacramental setting for this episode. Jesus' first concern is that the people will go hungry, for these are the 'sheep' he came to recover from lostness and he wishes to sustain them. In the first instance this is physical food, and when there seems not enough he is able to produce more. The amount of food becomes a bountiful excess, matching the situation of the wine at Cana. People came in need and were given much more than they could have expected. They came with nothing and Jesus gave them food to eat, sufficient to fill each and every one of them, and yet there was more.

The miraculous feeding stirs the people's desire to make Jesus their king (John 6:15)—to hope he will come to rule their earthly lives. However, Jesus understands this desire to stay on the earthly plane but refuses to be present for them to do this.

How often have we wished that God would just come and fix things that are wrong, a heartfelt desire that is often frustrated in our work and ministry? Commonly, we think we know the solution and expect God to fix it in this way. To our great disappointment or even despair, the plans do not succeed. It seems God is absent. The lesson is that we have to wait until it becomes clear what God is asking us to do. Such is also our own inner experience, that if we try to grasp too closely any spiritual grace we are given, to hang onto it physically, to pretend we can maintain it in any earthly or physical sense, it disappears.

Later, Jesus remarks that people were seeking him not because of the miracle itself but because *ye did eat of the loaves, and were filled* (John 6:26). Such is the spiritual parallel; when we come to experience the presence and the power we are similarly satiated with peace and with unity, and there seem to be no gaps unfilled except perhaps a yearning for more.

It is not our seeing a miracle but our experience of being spiritually fulfilled that convinces us to continue on the path. Jesus' advice is, *Labour not for the meat which perisheth, but for that meat which endureth unto everlasting life* (John 6:27). The analogy emphasizes that spiritual food is also needed, just as physical food is needed by the body. Many find Jesus' life and the Bible an endless source of spiritual food.

> *Then those men, when they had seen the miracle that Jesus did, said, This is of a truth that prophet that should come into the world. When Jesus therefore perceived that they would come and take him by force, to make him a king, he departed again into a mountain himself alone.* (John 6:14-15)

Although two other gospels record this miracle, it is John who explains that Jesus withdraws to be alone because the people sought to *take him by force, to make him a king*.[78] For those around him, Jesus had not come to be an earthly king, which is what they earnestly desired. Moreover, as the rest of his life would show, physical force is not the tool to gain access to the Presence of God.

Miraculous Walking on Water

> *And when even was now come, his disciples went down unto the sea, And entered into a ship, and went over the sea toward Capernaum. And it was now dark, and Jesus was not come to them. And the sea arose by reason of a great wind that blew. So when they had rowed about five and twenty or thirty furlongs, they see Jesus walking on the sea, and drawing nigh unto the ship: and they were afraid. But he saith unto them, It is I; be not afraid. Then they willingly received him into the ship: and immediately the ship was at the land whither they went.* (John 6:16-21)

With night coming on, the disciples wanted to head for home across the Sea of Galilee, even though Jesus had not returned. When the wind rises, the sea becomes very rough. Now they had rowed twenty-five to thirty furlongs (a furlong is two hundred meters).⁷⁹ So, five to six kilometres is a goodly distance to row. They saw a man walking across the sea's surface, coming closer, and they were afraid. Such an apparition would have been a very disturbing sight. The situation changes when they realise it is Jesus. He identifies himself and is welcomed into the boat. It seems that in just a moment they are landed safely at their destination.

In times of distress, when life seems turbulent and difficult and I perhaps even feel overwhelmed or at risk of drowning in my troubles, it is important for me to remember the Spirit is still present if not always obvious. It may well be that I have done what the disciples did, simply left Jesus behind! Yet he catches up in his own way. I have to recognise the presence, put aside any fears, and welcome the presence of the Light again. At that point, I commonly feel my balance return and become firmly grounded once again.

The story is also an allegory for prayer when we are subject to distracting, confused, anxious, or angry thoughts. We too have to struggle against these distracting thoughts in committed prayer, as did those disciples rowing in the turbulent sea. They did not cease, and neither should we. When we look up from the unsteady boat to the Light, it has an unexpected way of calming us and moves us rapidly to become grounded again.

Jesus' presence as the Light and the promised peace in our prayers—how calming that is! It intrigues me that John describes the scene as something that happened in the past, *So when they had rowed about five and twenty or thirty furlongs*, yet when Jesus is mentioned it is in the present tense, *they see Jesus walking on the sea*. It is as if John is making the point that it is when the Light is present that we are living in the present, in the moment.

George Fox's 1658 advice when beset by dangerous or corrupting thoughts and impulses was to look *over* the confusions to the Light, to look *across* the troubled sea.

> Be still and cool in thy own mind and spirit from thy own thoughts, and then thou wilt feel the principle of God to turn thy mind to the Lord God, whereby thou wilt receive his strength and power from whence life comes, to allay all tempests, against blusterings and storms. . . .

Therefore be still a while from thy own thoughts, searching, seeking, desires and imaginations, and be stayed in the principle of God in thee, to stay thy mind upon God, up to God; . . .

What the light doth make manifest and discover, temptations, confusions, distractions, distempers; do not look at the temptations, confusions, corruptions, but at the light that discovers them, that makes them manifest; and with the same light you will feel over them, to receive power to stand against them . . . For looking down at sin, and corruption, and distraction, you are swallowed up in it; but looking at the light that discovers them, you will see over them. That will give victory; and you will find grace and strength: and there is the first step of peace.[80]

John's Version of the Eucharist

They said therefore unto him, What sign shewest thou then, that we may see, and believe thee? what dost thou work? Our fathers did eat manna in the desert; as it is written, He gave them bread from heaven to eat. Then Jesus said unto them, Verily, verily, I say unto you, Moses gave you not that bread from heaven; but my Father giveth you the true bread from heaven. For the bread of God is he which cometh down from heaven, and giveth life unto the world. Then said they unto him, Lord, evermore give us this bread And Jesus said unto them, I am the bread of life: he that cometh to me shall never hunger; and he that believeth on me shall never thirst. (John 6:30–35)

The sacramental significance of these passages is explained by Jesus after his return to the synagogue in Capernaum. His Jewish hearers were well aware of the manna that came from heaven, from the sky, when Moses was leading the Israelites through the wilderness (Exodus 16:14–35; Numbers 11:6–9). Jesus considered that manna, which lasted only a day and which Moses forbade people to hoard, is bread that is eaten and perishes. In contrast, he turns the discussion to the eternal, lasting bread of life.

Those listening had been taught that the spiritual bread of the Hebrews is the Torah, the revealed will of God, as recorded in the books of the Pentateuch (Genesis, Exodus, Leviticus, Numbers, and Deuteronomy). Traditionally, these books were written by the prophet Moses and handed down through generations as the laws to govern people's lives. That is, the Torah was the guide, the bread of wisdom, and the spiritual sustenance of the Hebrews. It was a serious challenge to the established order for Jesus to stand in the synagogue at Capernaum and assert that he was the bread of life.

Imagine this story being told in the oral tradition instead of being read silently to oneself, spoken out loud with emphasis to dramatise the teachings.

> *But I said unto you, That ye also have seen me, and believe not. All that the Father giveth me shall come to me; and him that cometh to me I will in no wise cast out. For I came down from heaven, not to do mine own will, but the will of him that sent me. And this is the Father's will which hath sent me, that of all which he hath given me I should lose nothing, but should raise it up again at the last day. (John 6:36-39)*

Jesus repeatedly states that he has come down from heaven (John 6:33, 38, 41, 42, 50, 51, 58). Surely John has written this for a good reason, for it is the only gospel to make the point. Some interpret this statement as doctrine for Jesus being sent down by God to die on the cross. My own feeling is that Jesus knew his life had a special purpose, especially after his mystical transformation during his baptismal immersion by John the Baptist. Jesus knew he had been sent to do God's work in an extraordinary way. He knew he was not sent that he might pick and choose but to do as he was instructed and empowered by God. Middle Eastern and Indian traditions hold that a special spiritual messenger is sent when needed. Jesus was aware of his mission.

'Down from heaven' is the common term describing something sent by and from God. Examples include heaven being described as the holy habitation and source of blessings (Deuteronomy 26:15); the fire called down by Elijah upon the captain and his fifty soldiers of the king of Samaria (2 Kings 1:10-12); God looking down upon his creation (Psalms 14:2, 53:2, 80:14); and the great sheet that was let down in the vision that convinced Peter that there was no person profane or unclean, which was a staggering rebuttal of Jewish traditions (Acts 11:5-10). The phrase may have recalled, for people at that time, the dream of Nebuchadnezzar interpreted by Daniel that *the king saw a watcher and an holy one come down from heaven, and saying, Hew the tree down, and destroy it; yet leave the stump of the roots thereof in the earth . . .* (Daniel 4:23).

Jesus cut away the previous rituals of outward prayer and worship and instituted a new way, leaving only the roots connected to the ground of God from which new worship would grow. When Jesus says whoever *believeth on me shall never thirst* and whoever *believeth on me hath everlasting life* (John 6:35, 47), he is saying we should cease worrying about those rituals, for if we concentrate on being like him, the everlasting spiritual life will follow.

The early Christians were known as the people of the Way, as when Saul asked for letters to the synagogues in Damascus *so that, if he found any there who belonged to the Way, whether men or women, he might take them as prisoners to Jerusalem* (Acts 9:2 NIV).[81] Their lives were focused on the teachings of Jesus and on the wonder of his life and reappearances after his physical death; they believed in him. Their worship, as described later by Paul (1 Corinthians 14:26-33), was different to the synagogue liturgies. God for them was to be worshipped inwardly, in Spirit and in Truth.

> *The Jews then murmured at him, because he said, I am the bread which came down from heaven. And they said, Is not this Jesus, the son of Joseph, whose father and mother we know? how is it then that he saith, I came down from heaven? Jesus therefore answered and said unto them, Murmur not among yourselves. No man can come to me, except the Father which hath sent me draw him: and I will raise him up at the last day. . . . Verily, verily, I say unto you, He that believeth on me hath everlasting life. I*

> *am that bread of life. Your fathers did eat manna in the wilderness, and are dead. This is the bread which cometh down from heaven, that a man may eat thereof, and not die. I am the living bread which came down from heaven: if any man eat of this bread, he shall live for ever: and the bread that I will give is my flesh, which I will give for the life of the world.* (John 6:41–51)

Jesus' listeners were incredulous and were troubled by this discussion because this was Jesus, the son of Joseph and Mary—how could he say he had come down from heaven? They knew he was from Nazareth! Jesus made a huge leap by passing off this reference to the manna as past history, noting that all their fathers who ate manna in the wilderness were now dead.

Jesus asserts he is the bread of life, yet not him but that which is passed down to him from God. He receives this food because he does the will of God. As the bread of life, Jesus is grounded in the will of God and his own faithfulness to it.[82]

For early Christians, the reference to bread recalled the role of Melchizedek, the priest of the 'most high God', recognised as a legitimate priest of the true one and only God by Abraham (Genesis 14:18). That blessing of bread and wine had sacramental qualities, and the followers of Jesus considered him to be in the line of Melchizedek, the priest forever, not of the Mosaic priests of the line of Levi.

> *The Jews therefore strove among themselves, saying, How can this man give us his flesh to eat? Then Jesus said unto them, Verily, verily, I say unto you, Except ye eat the flesh of the Son of man, and drink his blood, ye have no life in you. Whoso eateth my flesh, and drinketh my blood, hath eternal life; and I will raise him up at the last day. For my flesh is meat indeed, and my blood is drink indeed. He that eateth my flesh, and drinketh my blood, dwelleth in me, and I in him. As the living Father hath sent me, and I live by the Father: so he that eateth me, even he shall live by me. This is that bread which came down from heaven: not as your fathers did eat manna, and are dead: he that eateth of this bread shall live for ever. These things said he in the synagogue, as he taught*

> *in Capernaum. Many therefore of his disciples, when they had heard this, said, This is an hard saying; who can hear it?* (John 6:52–60)

John 6:52–60 would have been extremely challenging to those of his hearers rooted in the literal meaning of his words. His audience had been reared in a culture requiring the sacrifice and burning of innocent animals. Special morsels of meat or flesh were distributed to priests and given for eating. It may be the Jews were scoffing when they asked, *How can this man give us his flesh to eat?* For many, though, it must have been an uncomfortable and disgusting idea that Jesus, though a remarkable healer and teacher, was not only foretelling his own sacrifice but also possibly the cutting up and distributing of pieces of his own flesh. No wonder many could not grasp the spiritual meaning of his words and just walked away.

However, Jesus is not talking of physical cannibalism. He made a strong stand against the ritual slaughter of animals that was rife in the Jewish Temple of his day. Instead, he makes it clear he is speaking spiritually of the need to sustain spiritual growth.

John does not write of the Eucharist being instituted as a formal ritual at the Last Supper.[83] In fact, in John's gospel the Last Supper is a lesson in humility, equality, and service through the washing of the disciples' feet. Instead, John describes Jesus' teaching of the Eucharist as an awareness to be carried at all times, as an inward experience, not an outward ritual. More than this, Jesus is challenging the idea that we control our lives. We are spiritual beings, and the life energy we have is spiritual and needs spiritual food. The Presence of God, the Christ, is the source of that spiritual food. We do not live on bread alone but on every word that comes out of the mouth of God.[84] The implication of the flesh and blood is that we cannot choose little bits of this spiritual food; we need to accept all Jesus is offering to be fully alive. The journey is not travelled by choosing who we will treat with love and respect or when we will act for God and when not. The path is one of total commitment. Many are not ready to hear this.

> *It is the spirit that quickeneth; the flesh profiteth nothing: the words that I speak unto you, they are spirit, and they are life.* (John 6:63)

Jesus does make it clear that he is speaking of a spiritual experience, not an earthly eating, as was indicated earlier when he said that whoever *believeth on me shall never thirst*. The 'quickening' is Life, as is clear in the translation of John 6:63 by The Jerusalem Bible:

> *It is the Spirit that gives life,*
> *the flesh has nothing to offer.*
> *The words I have spoken to you are spirit*
> *and they are life.*

Jesus takes the opportunity to ask his followers, "Who will also go away?"

> *Then said Jesus unto the twelve, Will ye also go away? Then Simon Peter answered him, Lord, to whom shall we go? thou hast the words of eternal life. And we believe and are sure that thou art that Christ, the Son of the living God.* (John 6:67-69)

Jesus is asking for a verbal statement that leads to commitment. In response, Peter confesses Jesus as the Christ. The impetuous, wayward Peter is the one who, in that moment of dissension, was given the clarity and certainty that Jesus is the Christ, the Truth, the perfect Guide. Perhaps he even felt some grief over those who had rejected and abandoned Jesus.

Not uncommonly, it is in a moment of difficulty or grief that certainty in the spiritual journey is inwardly gifted. The continuing transformation of Peter is a wonderful and reassuring example of this.

Yet Jesus has also named for the first time in this gospel Judas Iscariot, son of Simon, the man who later betrayed him (John 6:70-71). Having to handle such contrary presences is an integral part of our life's work. George Fox describes the importance of focusing on Christ and what is holy to discern that which is of God and that which is of human or earthly desires. Although some of the metaphors may seem strange, the need for constant inward attentiveness is clear.

Dear Friends,—Mind the steadfast Guide to the Lord, where we do all meet in the eternal spirit, in oneness, all being baptized into one body, having one food, the eternal bread of life, which the immortal feed upon, and all are made to drink into one spirit, which is the cup of the communion of the blood of our Lord Jesus Christ, which makes perfect and redeems from all that is earthly, up to God, who is holy, pure, spiritual and eternal. And let not any of you in your desires wander from that which is pure in you; then your conditions will be kept clear and pure to see all things as they are, and a clear separation will be made from that which is of man and of your own, and that which is of God; and there will be a growing up in that which is pure.[85]

Chapter 8
MEETING OUR RESISTANCES

Jesus in Jerusalem

> After these things Jesus walked in Galilee: for he would not walk in Jewry, because the Jews sought to kill him. Now the Jews' feast of tabernacles was at hand. His brethren therefore said unto him, Depart hence, and go into Judaea, that thy disciples also may see the works that thou doest. . . . Then Jesus said unto them, My time is not yet come: but your time is alway ready. . . . But when his brethren were gone up, then went he also up unto the feast, not openly, but as it were in secret. Then the Jews sought him at the feast, and said, Where is he? And there was much murmuring among the people concerning him: for some said, He is a good man: others said, Nay; but he deceiveth the people. Howbeit no man spake openly of him for fear of the Jews. (John 7:1-13)

The gospel story shifts from the distant rural villages of Galilee to Jerusalem, the spiritual centre of Judaism.

Six months have passed since the feeding of the multitude near Passover time (John 6:4). Jesus waited for the time of God's appointing to travel to Jerusalem to attend the Feast because he knew the leading 'Jewry' sought to destroy him. The gospel mentions many times that the Jewish leadership opposed Jesus and even threatened him with death. The first response by established authorities to any challenge is to ridicule, then oppose strongly, and then threaten serious physical violence and finally death.[86] Jesus lived and worked in the face of this 'fear' much of his ministry, as have many other holy people, such as Mohandas Gandhi, Dietrich Bonhoeffer, Oscar Romero, Ignacio Ellacuría, and Dorothy Stang. Yet Mark also notes that Jesus was in danger of remaining too long in Galilee because the ruler Herod Antipas had heard from the priests and probably his spies that the people intended to proclaim Jesus as king after the miracle of the feeding of bread and fishes (Mark 3:6; 6:14). It appears Jesus spent those months wandering within Galilee and keeping a lower profile, preparing for his last year of ministry in Judea. It would be another six months till his crucifixion.

Waters of Life

The Feast of the Tabernacles is an eight-day period during the autumn harvest (September–October) when the Jewish faithful prayed for winter rains (see table 1). In Jesus' time, during this feast people lived in small huts or bowers to recall God's protection during their ancestors' sojourn in the desert. Included in the celebrations were daily processions carrying libations of water to the temple.[87] This feast also carried a traditional hope for the coming of the Day of the Lord, who would sweep away all of the enemies of Jerusalem and make the waters of life gush forth (Isaiah 12:3; Ezekiel 47:1; Zechariah 14:8).

> *Then shall the LORD go forth, and fight against those nations, . . . And it shall be in that day, that living waters shall go out from Jerusalem; . . . And the LORD shall be king over all the earth: in that day shall there be one LORD, and his name one. . . . And it shall come to pass, that every one that is left of all the nations which came up against Jerusalem shall even go up from year to year to worship the King, the LORD of hosts, and to keep the feast of tabernacles.* (Zechariah 14:3–16)

This prophetic message would have had added significance when the Gospel According to John was written, in the years of despair after the destruction of the temple by the Romans (70 CE). John is making a strong case for Jesus' role as the real source of these living waters of salvation. By this time in his ministry, the Jewish hierarchy was openly antagonistic towards Jesus and sought to kill him, yet he came to the temple to teach. His presence stimulated open debate. Some people, who believed he was a prophet and even the Christ, spoke up for him (John 7:26, 31, 40–43). Others thought him a deceiver and were strongly against him. He had brought the Jewish community face-to-face with their own behaviour, as he questioned and criticised much of their religious and daily practice. Yet his profound teachings, good works, and miracles endeared him to many, at all levels in the community.

How closely did Jesus fit the traditional Jewish messianic expectations?[88] Certainly Jesus rejected the worldly kingship role anticipated and hoped for by many at the time. Yet many of the common people may well have still hoped he might become a king. This would indeed be a threat to both the status of the established authorities and also to those who were spiritually committed and dependent on traditional Judaism. On the other hand, Jesus delivered many signs of being a man of God: his miraculous healings, his inspired knowledge of the Hebrew Scriptures, and the wisdom of his teachings.

The Jewish community is in the same state we too find ourselves, once we are into the spiritual journey in earnest. Much has happened of great spiritual benefit, but we realise that only a part of us is conforming to the Spirit's guidance and that much more within us needs to be changed. It is not uncommon for each of us to feel the debate internally, between parts of us that are set on the new path and parts that wish to hang on determinedly to old habits.

For me, there have been many times when the work yet to be done seems too much to contemplate, even quite depressing. In the words of the father of the epileptic child Jesus was to cure, *Lord I believe; help thou mine unbelief* (Mark 9:24).

> *On the last and greatest day of the festival, Jesus stood up and shouted, "Any who are thirsty, let them come to me and drink! Those who believe in me, as the scripture says, 'From their innermost being will flow rivers of living water' ".* (John 7:37-38 TIB)

Jesus had watched the daily ritual of people taking water from the pool to the temple, seeking inner cleansing and spiritual growth. Yet he knows his own teachings hold the key to coming into the Presence of God. In the presence of Jesus, in the Light, the superficial nature of these rituals is apparent.

No wonder Jesus finally cried out in frustration that those who thirst in their spirit should come to him, for those who believe in his way will have access to spiritual waters flowing to ensure the life of their souls. Outward rituals cannot do it. Jesus had proclaimed himself the bread of life, and now he says that he is the source of the living water that will assuage the great spiritual thirst in people. The allegory of life-giving water was well known from Psalm 42:1: *As the hart panteth after the water brooks, so panteth my soul after thee O God.* We recall his conversation with the woman at the well in Samaria (John 4:7-15).

Early Quaker William Dewsbury appreciated the refreshment offered by Christ. He felt led

> to declare to souls where their teacher is, the light in their consciences, which the Lord hath given unto everyone a measure to profit, for the exercise of the conscience towards God and men, and waiting in the light for the power of Christ. He would lead them up to the living fountain of water, where their souls would find refreshment in the presence of the Lord, and their bread would be sure, and their water never fail, (as the Lord hath made manifest to my [Dewsbury's] soul) and to worship him in truth at New Jerusalem.[89]

Our Own Resistances

> *Many of the people therefore, when they heard this saying, said, Of a truth this is the Prophet. Others said, This is the Christ. But some said, Shall Christ come out of Galilee? Hath not the scripture said, That Christ cometh of the seed of David, and out of the town of Bethlehem, where David was? So there was a division among the people because of him. And some of them would have taken him; but no man laid hands on him. Then came the officers to the chief priests and Pharisees; and they said unto them, Why have ye not brought him? The officers answered, Never man spake like this man.* (John 7:40-46)

The narrative in the gospel has changed, for till this point the narrative has been cast as if we are part of the crowd watching the events. To be sure, we can also enter into their effect upon ourselves. However, the rest of the gospel is directed towards individuals, and we are each invited into a deeper relationship with Jesus. Many are wary and prefer to hang back. Jesus confronts those who, despite his wonderful ministry, continue in Jerusalem to resist his message. Jesus knew the potential of life and was frustrated by the formalism and unbelief. *Why go ye about to kill me?* Jesus had asked (John 7:19), making it clear how very strong was the resistance of many Jews against him.

How many of us have yearned for spiritual refreshment yet have resisted full acceptance and have held back because of some entrenched knowledge about 'what suits me', or some previously learned attitudes to the Scriptures, or long-held habits, or some prejudice about other supposed Christians? Jesus has made it clear we need to be reborn, to let these old habits and self-justifications die. We are commonly asked to change direction. That part of ourselves is no different to those in the ancient Jewish community who had Jesus' miracles and ministry before their eyes and yet resisted his spiritual advices.

Gerard Hughes observed:

> When people begin to use their imagination on Gospel scenes they are often surprised at the Christ they meet. To some he appears much more ordinary than they would have expected, . . . *Whenever and whatever we read of Christ in the Gospel, we are also reading our own self-portrait, for Christ is what we are called to become.* . . . Christ is not simply, nor primarily, a model of good behaviour whom we must imitate. [Christ] is the source of our life and the sense of it, for to be another Christ is the meaning of our existence.[90]

The image of Christ revealed in Jesus is a mirror to our own selves, just as he was to those around him two thousand years ago. In this mirror we see both our potential and our resistance to change. Jesus brought the reality of their own lives to the people around him, just as he does in each of us today. Is what held them back what is holding us back now?

What is the source of our resistance? When we look at what Jesus did, it does not seem possible, it defies rationality, and it does not fit worldly experience. That is the point! We can walk in Galilee observing the wonders of Jesus at work, affected by his teaching, struck by the miracles, but we cannot unite with the Christ, we cannot enter our new Jerusalem without letting go our unbelief.

Am I stuck in old ways? Do I lack courage, fearing what others may think? Does it offend my common sense? Am I afraid of what change will bring? What is this resistance to the Light within us, what the Quaker Norman Marrow called "that spirit of rebelliousness we call Satan" (Mark 1:9-13 TFG)[91]

Nicholas Peter Harvey addresses this question head-on:

> Hard questions arise here. What is my defendedness? Or against what am I defending myself? What is the painful place not yet known and recognised, not yet anointed? This deep defence, unconscious of its aim, produces compulsive behaviour, that sustained guardedness which is so skilful, so habitual, so determined to reveal nothing. But this is to stress the negative. May it not rather be that I am in flight from the promise made manifest to me from the beginning? The promise without which life has no meaning and the future is a blank?
>
> The meaning to be found is a meaning of God. That is to say not just another meaning but the truth of who I am. To come to this meaning involves the abandonment or breakdown of many other meanings. . . . We need to find out, or be shown, what meaning we cling to. There also has to be a clean break, and no break can be clean without being acknowledged.[92]

Not always is our resistance due to an unresolved deep hurt. Commonly, it is just laziness. Commonly, we find that something of which we are very fond, or a particular gift, comes between us and God. It may be we have come to rely upon an accepted knowledge or a taught behaviour, or something that has proved very useful in the past. It might well be something we feel, even now, that we could not do without. Or, it may be just the fear of venturing into the unknown. We begin to recognise whatever is no longer useful or tenable if it reappears in some guise or other, often in our prayers and interrupting our silence before God. We do not let go of our known territory easily.

> *Nicodemus saith unto them, (he that came to Jesus by night, being one of them,) Doth our law judge any man, before it hear him, and know what he doeth? They answered and said unto him, Art thou also of Galilee? Search, and look: for out of Galilee ariseth no prophet.* (John 7:50-52)

Those habits we depend upon, like the Pharisees' and Sadducees' dependence on their traditions, continue to persecute our own souls and the Christ within us. We might remember that Nicodemus expressed honestly his own reservations, and we may similarly resist encountering a new life in the Spirit. Yet Nicodemus was a committed seeker and spoke to his colleagues in the Sanhedrin, and is this not the same voice now asking us to listen to Christ before we judge, that we may judge rightly?

Fox wrote the following about temptation:

> Friends,—Whatever ye are addicted to, the tempter will come in that thing; and when he can trouble you, then he gets advantage over you, and then ye are gone. Stand still in that which is pure, after ye see yourselves; and then mercy comes in. After thou seest thy thoughts, and the temptations, do not think, but submit; and then power comes. Stand still in that which shows and discovers; and then doth strength immediately come. And stand still in the light, and submit to it, and the other will be hushed and gone; and then content comes. And when temptations and troubles appear, sink down in that which is pure, and all will be hushed, and fly away. Your strength is to stand still. . . . And earthly reason will tell you, what ye shall lose; hearken not to that, but stand still in the light, that shows them to you, and then strength comes from the Lord, and help contrary to your expectation.[93]

CHAPTER 9
THE BALANCED LIFE OF PRAYER AND MINISTRY

Mercy and Forgiveness

> *Jesus went unto the mount of Olives. And early in the morning he came again into the temple, and all the people came unto him; and he sat down, and taught them. And the scribes and Pharisees brought unto him a woman taken in adultery; and when they had set her in the midst, They say unto him, Master, this woman was taken in adultery, in the very act. Now Moses in the law commanded us, that such should be stoned: but what sayest thou? This they said, tempting him, that they might have to accuse him. But Jesus stooped down, and with his finger wrote on the ground, as though he heard them not. So when they continued asking him, he lifted up himself, and said unto them, He that is without sin among you, let him first cast a stone at her. And again he stooped down, and wrote on the ground. And they which heard it, being convicted by their own conscience, went out one by one, beginning at the eldest, even unto the last: and Jesus was left alone, and the woman standing in the midst. When Jesus had lifted up himself, and saw none but the woman, he said unto her, Woman, where are those thine accusers? hath no man condemned thee? She said, No man, Lord. And Jesus said unto her, Neither do I condemn thee: go, and sin no more. (John 8:1–11)*

I love this passage because it speaks so clearly about the balance between the contemplative and the active life. Jesus spends his nights in contemplative prayer and his days in ministering to people.[94] For those of us wondering how to balance our lives and feeling stressed or lacking in love and wisdom during our busy active lives, Jesus models the answer for us. The results that are possible in such a balanced life of prayer and action are manifest in the events described.

Jesus very commonly spent time apart, alone, in the mountains,[95] and in this case upon the Mount of Olives. At night he was apart from humanity and somewhere elevated, a physical parallel to the state of contemplative prayer. There is no statement that he regularly spent large amounts of time involved in the Jewish worship systems. We learn that he went regularly to the Temple or the synagogue to teach, but his main prayer time appears to have been alone at night. It is clear he needed such time alone. He is doing exactly what he recommended during his discussion with the Samaritan woman at the well. He forwent the established liturgies to worship, in Spirit, directly with God. Jesus taught by his words, by his example, and by his miracles, and he continues to teach us each inwardly. Fox encouraged others to follow Jesus' example:

> Nevertheless, I declared Truth unto them and turned them from the darkness to the light of Christ, whether they would hear or forbear, and how that God and Christ was come to teach his people himself.[96]

When Jesus arrived the next morning, the Jewish elders had captured a woman taken in the act of adultery. They posed to him two alternatives—follow the law and stone her to death or release her without following the law and then they could accuse him in a religious court. Which alternative? Jesus does what he so often has done before; he ignores the options they present and finds a third way. He refuses to be constrained by their legal, yes-or-no arguments.

For a few moments he ignores his questioners until they have repeated their comments, and by this time they have placed themselves in an irretrievable position. By asking the person who is without sin to cast the first stone, Jesus has forced each of those people to act in relation to God and not to human habit or law. What a fundamental change this is! The external law is no longer the benchmark—the individual relationship with God and the individual answering to God is the standard. If our actions cannot be clear and answerable to God, we had better wait.

When the crowd dwindles away till none are left, Jesus shows he is not here to condemn the world but to save it. His response is mercy and forgiveness. As with the Samaritan woman, Jesus does not judge or issue recriminations and punishments. When the sin is brought out into the Light and acknowledged in Jesus' presence, it can be wiped away. There is no judgment. The soul has been redeemed. Jesus starts from this moment and says only, go and sin no more. A new life is underway. Thank heavens for that.

How will I handle the sins or slights of others against me from now on?

The Light of Christ Within

> *The next time Jesus spoke to them, he said, "I am the light of the world. Whoever follows me won't walk in darkness, but will have the light of life.* (John 8:12 TIB)

The theme of light appealed to many in the ancient world who had been influenced by Greek thought, and this probably assisted the spread of Jesus' teachings into the non-Jewish world.[97] Greek thought also distinguished the state of darkness, the lack of wisdom, from the enlightened state of wise people with awakened souls. John 8:12 is saying that Jesus' teachings are that path from darkness to light.

Of the Light Within, the inward Light, the Light of Christ, I know only a little. Yet I can say that this Light arises not from my own abilities or understandings, nor in images of my fears, anxieties, or worldly desires. We cannot initiate, manufacture, tame, or control this Light. The Light is worked by God within us and is a gift given in the love of God for us. It is universal, available in every person, irrespective of age, gender, class, or ethnicity, and if we can become open and receptive it may be experienced at any time and in any place. In the words of Howard Brinton:

> This Light . . . comes into the world enlightening every person. . . . It is not to be confused with human reason and human conscience. Being above both, it is that whereby reason becomes more enlightened and conscience more sensitized. It is the Absolute Value that is the source of all relative

values, however imperfectly it may be comprehended by the human understanding. It is that Creative Power that first dawned on chaos and that draws all things upward into nobler states of being. It is also warm, living, and personal, forever pleading with us to give up our selfish doing and desiring, and to follow its Divine Leading.[98]

George Fox knew both the way the Light of Christ inspires a heavenly sense of the great love of God yet also that the Light shows those parts of us that are in error and out of the Light:

> And one day, when I had been walking solitarily abroad, and was come home, I was taken up in the love of God, so that I could not but admire the greatness of his love. And while l was in that condition it was opened unto me by the eternal Light and power, and I therein clearly saw that all was done and to be done in and by Christ, . . . But oh, then did I see my troubles, trials, and temptations more clearly than ever I had done! As the Light appeared, all appeared that is out of the Light, darkness, death, temptations, the unrighteous, the ungodly; all was manifest and seen in the Light.[99]

The Light manifests itself in many ways, commonly as a sudden inner awareness, as if one has been told or seen something new. Some may experience it as 'my intuition'. If we move our focus away from Self and start accepting the Light as a gift from God, more of the divine stream of Life may reveal itself operating within us. The Light

- shows us the possibilities of a holy life—living in love and serenity with compassion, mercy, gentleness, and self-control. Often another's words or deeds are witnesses of the Light in them and this reaches our own hearts.
- suffuses us with unaccountable warmth, gratitude, joy, or love for another person or the natural world. We may have sudden awareness of the great blessings bestowed upon us without any doing or deserving on our part.

- engenders awareness of God's Presence, with feelings of inspiration and deep gratitude or awe and a yearning to be drawn more towards God, hoping that Jesus or God will become more real and visible in our lives.
- provides unexpected moments of deep new understandings, or openings, of how things really are, the deep truth about ourselves.
- shows us our errors, what many call sins, commonly in stark relief. At first we may wish to deny or rationalise these; however, the way of humility is to accept these truths as God's love and desire for us to become purer in heart.
- reveals what is in accord with God's desires for us to do or say and the next steps on our spiritual journey in life.
- shows our heart what to pray, often giving forth words and emotions in place of our own inabilities.
- gives comfort, forgiveness and healing, leading us to inner peace. We may be asked to pray for the healing of others.

In saying "I am the light", Jesus is referring to himself as Christ, the long-awaited embodiment of divine perfection in all its fullness. That is why he is not Jesus Smith or Jesus bar Joseph—he is Jesus Christ. We have the Light of Christ, in small measure, gifted to each of us at birth. However, Christ refers to the fullness of that gift from God, and the only time we have seen it well recorded is in Jesus. The same overwhelming Presence of God is believed by many to have been manifested, for example, in Moses, Krishna, Mohammed (peace be upon him), the Buddha, and (by the Baha'is) Bahá'u'lláh.

This is a very different "I am" to the usual way we talk about our own individuality, for it has nothing to do with Jesus as a self-centred person. Jesus is referring to the Presence of God present within him. Hereafter in this book, I indicate this meaning by using the term "I Am".[100]

Jesus' statement *I am the light of the world: he that followeth me shall not walk in darkness, but shall have the light of life* (John 8:12) is a very special promise. It is not one to be fully understood by the rational mind. Thomas à

Kempis was sure of its meaning, for he used this verse at the start of *The Imitation of Christ* (Book I.1), noting: "These are the words of Christ by which we are taught to follow his life and way of life if we would be truly enlightened and delivered from all blindness of heart".[101]

The thought was implanted in me—what if Jesus is absolutely correct? Could this continuing state of darkness, uncertainty, and lostness in me be replaced by a life in the Light if I was simply willing to give up all else, believe in Jesus, and trust in Jesus? What if I started doing that? So I did.

My practice became daily meditation, quietening my mind, practising surrender, appealing to Jesus, waiting patiently, 'waiting on the Lord'. I consciously asked Jesus: What do you want me to do here?

Easier said than done. Our mind wanders so easily from God; we get tied up in our own little knots, unhelpful knots; and when we suddenly become aware of this, the common reaction is distress at having lost the focus on the Spirit. Some can also, unhelpfully, feel guilty. The seventeenth-century lay Carmelite Brother Lawrence made the following his practice in order to give himself wholly to God

> I worshipped Him the oftenest that I could, keeping my mind in His holy Presence, and recalling it as often as I found it wandered from Him. I found no small pain in this exercise, and yet I continued it, not-withstanding all the difficulties that occurred, *without troubling or disquieting myself* [italics added] when my mind had wandered involuntarily. I made this my business, as much all the day long as at the appointed times of prayer; for at all times, every hour, every minute, even in the height of my business, I drove away from my mind everything that was capable of interrupting my thought of God.[102]

> *Jesus continued, "When you have lifted up the Chosen One, then you will know that I AM and that I can do nothing of myself; I say only what Abba God has taught me. The One who sent me is with me and has not deserted me because I always do God's will.*

> ... *If you live according to my teaching, you really are my disciples; then you'll know the truth, and the truth will set you free"*. (John 8:28-30, 32 TIB)

This is a significant change in heart for most of us in that we are not to follow faithfully, just hoping that everything will turn out for the best. The relationship between each of us and God develops into a loving relationship in which we wish to do, and only do, what pleases God. Thomas Merton's prayer is an eloquent example of a person who deeply desires to do so:

> My Lord God, I have no idea where I am going. I do not see the road ahead of me. I cannot know for certain where it will end. Nor do I really know myself, and the fact that I think I am following your will does not mean that I am actually doing so. But I believe that the desire to please you does in fact please you. And I hope I have that desire in all that I am doing. I hope that I will never do anything apart from that desire. And I know that if I do this you will lead me by the right road, though I may know nothing about it. Therefore I will trust you always though I may seem to be lost and in the shadow of death. I will not fear, for you are ever with me, and you will never leave me to face my perils alone.[103]

Jesus is clear that the journey is about doing what we have been shown is the way, not just receiving the warm gift of spiritual awareness and standing still. We must follow and persevere, for the promise is that *then you'll know the truth, and the truth will set you free* (John 8:32 TIB).

There are many dimensions to this promise, for there is something wonderfully freeing about living in the Spirit. Much of our anxiety and uncertainty is replaced with a trust in providence, in God. We are no longer enslaved by our self-centred desires. The worry over what to do, what is next, what if, is replaced with a reliance and acceptance on God. A huge burden of stress is removed. Living in the Light is freedom.

What is set free? George Fox talks about his soul being in chains, imprisoned within him, and that afterwards his soul was set free. How many of really understand what the soul is? Maybe that is because it is so well imprisoned and hidden within us we have never had any experience with it and so know nothing about it.

In the final part of the chapter (John 8:33–58), the Jewish leaders begin a more direct confrontation, not only questioning Jesus' authority but also insulting him and then picking up stones to cast at him. Jesus enters a long dispute with the Jewish leaders. There he was two thousand years ago, having performed public miracles and taught others how to approach God, and he has to justify his ministry in the face of recalcitrant Pharisees. As Mark also noted in his gospel: *Full well ye reject the commandment of God, that ye may keep your own tradition* (Mark 7:9). The complicated arguments, nit-picking, and debating go on and on, for the Light shineth in the darkness and the darkness comprehendeth it not. Jesus maintains his ministry, even though (John 7:1, 32) some Jews are intent on trapping and killing him.

We each also have a part that is uncomprehending, fond of established tradition, likes to dispute points of law, and cannot recognise fully the Truth. Like those Jewish leaders, we like to retain our own little control mechanisms over what is happening and to choose what we will admit to our inner attention, wanting to maintain this semblance of control and to keep things as they have been. It is as if we have our own little set of internal Pharisaic laws—this is how I have always done it, this is how I pray, this is how it should be done, this is why I cannot give up that part of myself, this is why I need to keep this belief and habit.

> *Jesus said unto them, If God were your Father, ye would love me: for I proceeded forth and came from God; neither came I of myself, but he sent me. Why do ye not understand my speech? even because ye cannot hear my word. Ye are of your father the devil, and the lusts of your father ye will do. He was a murderer from the beginning, and abode not in the truth, because there is no truth in him. When he speaketh a lie, he speaketh of his own: for he is a liar, and the father of it. And because I tell you the truth, ye believe me not.* (John 8:42–45)

Again, Jesus makes clear his total union with and dependence upon God: *for I proceeded forth and came from God; neither came I of myself but he sent me.* More importantly, on a deeper level he is speaking with each of us now. There is a part in each of us that comes directly from God, that part we could not possibly fashion from our own efforts, that part that is full of truth, that is unchangeable, that is never false and never tells lies. On the literal level, Jesus is talking to the Jewish leaders of his time. On a second level, his words are speaking within each of us now. As the early Quakers testified their dependence upon God and that Jesus was again come as the Light to teach them, so it can be for us, in the here and now. Am I willing daily to receive, to believe in, and to follow the Light of Christ within?

Jesus' response is direct and plainly spoken, saying that much of the behaviour of some Jewish people came from the wrong place, not from God but from another source, not from truth but from lies. Jesus is telling us also to stop focussing on things that are not related closely to God, otherwise we cannot even hear God: *Why don't you understand what I am saying to you? It's because you cannot bear to hear what I say* (John 8:43 TIB).

For me, if the ears of my heart do not hear God's word, then I have far to go. We can listen to sermons and read much literature, religious and otherwise, and never notice their spiritual import until the very moment when we are reached by God's spirit. Thus, on one occasion when many heard Paul, one woman, Lydia, understood the meaning behind his words: *the Lord opened her heart, that she attended to the things that were said by Paul* (Acts 16:13). Many can hear, though only those whose hearts are ripe hear the spiritual validity and call.

Coming to Convincement

> *Which of you convinceth me of sin? And if I say the truth, why do ye not believe me? He that is of God heareth God's words: ye therefore hear them not, because ye are not of God.* (John 8:46-47)

Jesus challenges the Pharisees to convince him of sin. The meaning of this word 'convince' differs now from the meaning in the 1600s. Back then, convince meant to convict. The Light had made past sins absolutely apparent and the real Truth so obvious it had to be admitted.[104] In modern language, this could have been written, "Which of you convicts me of sin?" The modern English of the NIV translation makes this meaning clear: *Can any of you prove me guilty of sin?* Jesus is asking the question in a direct debate with his opponents. He is in no mood to give an inch.

Early Quakers recognised this inward experience of 'convincement'; being inwardly judged and found wanting was a vital step in the spiritual journey. The Light within bursts forth inwardly and reveals past errors that the individual has to admit and for which great remorse is felt. In other words, the individual is inwardly convicted by the Light.

This is not a matter of ongoing guilt but an acceptance of inward judgment, with confession and admission before God. By admitting and welcoming this truth, people find great relief and peace, especially if they make any reparations required for such healing. There is reconciliation with God, a sense of being redeemed. Some convincements, what others might call conversions, were relatively gentle, but some who were convinced felt painfully rebuked of their former sins. Those who went through this cardinal experience and surrendered to the Light and then became members of the Society were known as 'convinced Friends'. Richard Claridge (1649–1723) described his own convincement as a Friend:

> This was the way that Friends used with me, when I was convinced of truth; they came oftentimes to visit me, and sat and waited upon the Lord in silence with me; and as the Lord opened our understandings and mouths, so we had very sweet and comfortable seasons together. They did not ask me questions about this or the other creed, or about this or the other controversy in religion; but they waited to feel that living Power to quicken me, which raised up Jesus from the dead. . . . Now this was Friends' way with me, a way far beyond all rules or methods established by the wisdom of this world, which is foolishness with God; and this is

their way with others that are convinced of the truth.[105]

Quaker John Banks wrote the following account of his experiences as a teenager in 1654:

> So that I may truly say, as a true and faithful witness for God, and the sufficiency of his power and quickening Spirit, (amongst many more) I did not only come to be convinced by the living appearance of the Lord Jesus of the evil and vanity, sin and wickedness that the world lies in (and that I was so much a partaker thereof); neither did I satisfy myself that I was reached unto by the power of God. But by taking true heed thereunto, through watchfulness and fear, I came by little one after another to be sensible of the work thereof in my heart and soul, in order to subdue and bring down, tame and subject the wild nature in me, and to wash, purge and cleanse me inwardly from sin and corruption; for that end, that I might be changed and converted. . . . so through faith in the power of God and shining of his glorious light in my heart, I overcame the wicked one (the enemy of my soul) through a diligent waiting in the light and keeping close to the power of God, in waiting upon him in silence among his people, in which exercise my soul delighted.[106]

I found John 8:47 (TIB), *Whoever belongs to God hears the word of God. And that's precisely why you don't hear them—because you are not of God,* a terrible opening, for the ears of my heart so commonly heard a voice that was not of God. I was certainly not of God, much as I might have wished I were or thought it so. Chastened, I had to redouble my efforts in prayer to reject the intrusions of my Self, become more silent, listen more carefully, and behave more obediently.

We can be very wary of taking these steps to let go. However, there is no certainty in the little legal games we have played to date. The Pharisees had the comfortable safety of knowing the religious laws and the consequences of misbehaviour. In times of uncertainty, they could retreat into the predictable safety of those laws, both inner and outer rituals. Jesus was saying that those laws are not the true basis of salvation. For us today, they include our inner laws and habits and rituals—they must also die and be gradually replaced by a reborn and resurrected being that is deeply dependent on God's guidance. We can feel the hope for a life in the Eternal Christ, a life in which judgment is no longer an overriding feature of thinking and behaviour. It is replaced by humility, faith, hope, courage, love, and compassion—what Buddhists call *metta* or loving-kindness.

> *Then answered the Jews, and said unto him, Say we not well that thou art a Samaritan, and hast a devil? Jesus answered, I have not a devil; but I honour my Father, and ye do dishonour me. And I seek not mine own glory: there is one that seeketh and judgeth. Verily, verily, I say unto you, If a man keep my saying, he shall never see death. Then said the Jews unto him, Now we know that thou hast a devil. Abraham is dead, and the prophets; and thou sayest, If a man keep my saying, he shall never taste of death. Art thou greater than our father Abraham, which is dead? and the prophets are dead: whom makest thou thyself? Jesus answered, If I honour myself, my honour is nothing: it is my Father that honoureth me; of whom ye say, that he is your God: Yet ye have not known him; but I know him: and if I should say, I know him not, I shall be a liar like unto you: but I know him, and keep his saying. Your father Abraham rejoiced to see my day: and he saw it, and was glad. Then said the Jews unto him, Thou art not yet fifty years old, and hast thou seen Abraham? Jesus said unto them, Verily, verily, I say unto you, Before Abraham was, I am. Then took they up stones to cast at him: but Jesus hid himself, and went out of the temple, going through the midst of them, and so passed by.* (John 8:48–59)

Jesus models for me many of the attitudes we have to learn. His patience is exemplary, even when he is insulted and told he is just a Samaritan and is possessed by a devil. As many knew then and many more know now, he was quite the opposite. Yet he does not respond with anger or trade a bigger insult. He replies that he is not in this work for himself but for the glory of God. Do we each undertake our work for the glory of God?

Jesus then continues to preach to them that his teachings are the way to spiritual life and, indeed, to eternal life. Every time Jesus points the conversation to the spiritual plane, the people return to questioning whether he has seen Abraham who died centuries before.

Do not the same tussles occur within ourselves? Each time we receive a spiritual opening, we are commonly recalled to earth by some limitation of our understanding or a worldly desire. It takes much patience and concentration to hold onto the divine imperative, whether in worship or action.

Jesus reverts a third time to the spiritual plane, using the "I Am", a statement of divine presence that the Pharisees cannot understand or accept: *Jesus said unto them, Verily, verily, I say unto you, Before Abraham was, I am* (John 8:58). This can only be fully apprehended in a mystical state—it defies rational explanation. It does remind us that 'that of God' has always been in us and our ancestors, and it still lives in us.

The statement "I Am" represents the Presence of God, the same statement of universal existence given to the ancient Hebrews through Moses and then restated in the book of Revelation.[107] It is framed in the present tense, for it is when we are in the present, not when we are imagining the past or future, that we find God.

The Pharisees cannot understand or accept what seems blasphemous to them. They cannot hear the Word of God because their internal ears are closed.

The Jewish crowd can no longer resist their violent impulses, and they pick up stones. Jesus does not organize his companions to fight—he slips away and hides. He is not yet ready to deal with the crowd, though he does not lack courage and conviction, as will become apparent later. We too may need to be patient until we are made ready to undertake direct action. In a deeper sense, the spiritual possibilities are hidden when violence takes hold within us.

Yet throughout his ministry, Jesus demonstrated there is no need to remain totally silent. Many times he showed his willingness to engage verbally with evil and to name it.

However, the way is one of nonviolence—to stand up for justice and righteousness without violence. When violence is perpetrated, we are called to withstand it by absorbing iniquities, naming them, and responding without transmitting or reflecting back the violence.[108]

Chapter 10
OUR BLINDNESS

Restoring Sight to the Blind

> And as Jesus passed by, he saw a man which was blind from his birth. And his disciples asked him, saying, Master, who did sin, this man, or his parents, that he was born blind? Jesus answered, Neither hath this man sinned, nor his parents: but that the works of God should be made manifest in him. I must work the works of him that sent me, while it is day: the night cometh, when no man can work. As long as I am in the world, I am the light of the world. When he had thus spoken, he spat on the ground, and made clay of the spittle, and he anointed the eyes of the blind man with the clay, And said unto him, Go, wash in the pool of Siloam, (which is by interpretation, Sent.) He went his way therefore, and washed, and came seeing. (John 9:1-7)

Jesus refuses to be drawn into a discussion of whether a man is blind because of sins, either his own or those of his parents. He is refuting the Old Testament theme that God punishes people because of their sins.[109] That belief is not consistent with my understanding of a God of love and life. That people who do bad things end up in situations that cause them pain seems more like a natural law to me. You cannot tell fibs and cheat without expecting you will end up in the company of others who do the same to you. Also, I cannot accept that those thousands of innocent village people who suffered the American bombings in Vietnam, Laos, Cambodia, and Iraq, or those who suffered the massacres in Rwanda, Croatia, Kurdistan, the United States, Australia, or anywhere else, had these terrible destructions visited upon them as punishment because they were bad.

The course of life has good and bad things in store for us. Jesus always accepts the reality in front of him and seeks God's guidance on how to handle it. Thus it was with the wine at the wedding, with the nobleman's dying son, with the cripple at Bethesda, with those who were hungry, with the woman taken in adultery, and now with a man blind from birth.

Moved by compassion, Jesus restores sight to the blind man. The Light within us shows us our inner reality every day. Is my response when meeting situations of conflict or pain to immediately seek healing? It is a big change to ignore our inner self-justifications and fears. Our inner blindness has to be cured so we can see clearly new paths, or those parts of ourselves that are spiritually false or useless, and in being willing to see them to allow the Light to heal them. In this sense we are starting to be reborn inside, though not in a spectacular public revival sense. In the silent depths of our inner being, a new heart is being created. Create in me a clean heart, O God.[110]

> *They brought to the Pharisees him that aforetime was blind. And it was the sabbath day when Jesus made the clay, and opened his eyes. Then again the Pharisees also asked him how he had received his sight. He said unto them, He put clay upon mine eyes, and I washed, and do see. Therefore said some of the Pharisees, This man is not of God, because he keepeth not the sabbath day. Others said, How can a man that is a sinner do such miracles? And there was a division among them. They say unto the blind man again, What sayest thou of him, that he hath opened thine eyes? He said, He is a prophet.* (John 9:13-17)

When the Pharisees hear of this miraculous healing on the Sabbath, they interrogate the man and his parents. The man is resolute and confesses Jesus as a prophet. This episode is a parallel to the healing of the lame man (John 5:1-16). The Pharisees must have been well aware that restoring sight to the blind was one of the Messianic signs predicted in the Old Testament, as was the curing of the lame man (Isaiah 29:18; 35:5-6, 42:7,16). Jesus is recorded as restoring sight to the blind in the other gospels, for example, Bartimaeus outside Jericho (Mark 10:46-52; Luke 18:35-43) as well as countless other instances (Matthew 21:14; Luke 7:21-22). Healing was happening again, and yet the Jewish leaders could not accept it.

Refute the Voice of the Pharisees That the Voice of the Spirit May Prevail

When the authorities again question a cured man about the right of Jesus to perform miracles, to work on the Sabbath, the man replies that he was once blind and now can see. Such is the effect of the Light of Jesus for us all. Given such a result, what meaning is there in artificial regulations such as Sabbath prohibitions? The letter killeth, but the Spirit giveth life.[111]

> *These words spake his parents, because they feared the Jews: for the Jews had agreed already, that if any man did confess that he was Christ, he should be put out of the synagogue. Therefore said his parents, He is of age; ask him. Then again called they the man that was blind, and said unto him, Give God the praise: we know that this man is a sinner. He answered and said, Whether he be a sinner or no, I know not: one thing I know, that, whereas I was blind, now I see.* (John 9:22-25)

The authorities then question the parents, who are afraid, knowing they might be thrown out of the synagogue. Since the synagogue was the centre of Jewish spiritual and social life, such excommunication was a thing to be feared. The Pharisees call on them to *Give God the praise* or, in the NIV translation, to *Give glory to God*, that is, to hold nothing back for yourself. It was a solemn charge to be completely truthful before God,[112] which ironically the man who had been blind has done, though not in the way expected or demanded by the temple rulers. He even asks if they wish to hear the story again (!) and asks, if he tells it, *will ye also be his disciples?* The interaction has taken on a humorous, slightly sarcastic tone: "How many times do I have to tell you, or are you just slow learners?" Such is the case for many, even at times within ourselves.

Note that this man, now with his sight fully restored, has become a true disciple who is able to stand up in witness to the world. He goes on to teach the temple elders this lesson of God's work, ending with the statement: *If this man were not of God, he could do nothing.* This is a surprising statement in that it is exactly what Jesus has previously said of himself

(John 5:30). This formerly blind man has seen so clearly, whereas the Pharisees, who believe they know and see everything, are blind to this reality. Jesus catches up with this man later and is told of these exchanges. This man whose sight is restored is the first recorded by John to offer the statement of complete faith: *And he said, Lord, I believe, and he worshipped Him* (John 9:38).

The Pharisees are left in a terrible position because they refuse to admit their own blindness, and hence Jesus cannot and will not heal them. It is those who accept the defects shown by the Light who can be healed and given spiritual sight.

Yet the final result is for those whose eyes are opened; they do believe (John 9:37–38). The assertion that Jesus is the Light (John 9:5) recalls the same words in John 8:12. John is bringing together once again his themes of Light and healing in this story of giving sight to the blind man. The blind man is healed physically and also receives deep spiritual insights. Spiritual healing works at both the physical and spiritual levels.

I notice how the voice of the Pharisees comes back repeatedly through the narrative of this gospel to challenge and try to divert the voice of the Spirit in Jesus, often with a note of fear or desire to control. In this episode of curing the blind man, Jesus has had to do it twice; first to discount the ideas that sin had led to the blindness and secondly to justify his working on the Sabbath. Each time in the gospel, Jesus confronts and rebuts this voice, which is a voice of schooled habits, a voice of legal regulations, and at times a voice of judgment, a voice of hypocrisy, a voice of self-justification, a voice of fear at the loss of influence and power. Jesus rejects this voice and returns to the voice of the Spirit. If he had to struggle with it, so do we.

Our spiritual journey and our active lives, both as individuals and in the community, contain this struggle between the demands of worldly expectations, desires, and self-justification on the one hand and the voice of the Spirit on the other. The voice of the Pharisees still lives on. We feel it in our prayers, we feel it in our conversations, and we feel it in our community relationships. That is our struggle to undertake, just as Jesus had to. His example reminds us to rebut or decline this voice every time we need to do so. That is how we do God's work in the world. The Spirit gives us the guidance of what to do and the strength to do it. Jesus shows us the Way.

> *And I will bring the blind by a way that they knew not: I will lead them in paths that they have not known: I will make darkness light before them, and crooked things straight. These things will I do unto them, and not forsake them.* (Isaiah 42:16)

CHAPTER 11
DO WE FOLLOW THE VOICE OF THE SHEPHERD?

The Good Shepherd

Verily, verily, I say unto you, He that entereth not by the door into the sheepfold, but climbeth up some other way, the same is a thief and a robber. But he that entereth in by the door is the shepherd of the sheep. To him the porter openeth; and the sheep hear his voice: and he calleth his own sheep by name, and leadeth them out. And when he putteth forth his own sheep, he goeth before them, and the sheep follow him: for they know his voice. And a stranger will they not follow, but will flee from him: for they know not the voice of strangers. This parable spake Jesus unto them: but they understood not what things they were which he spake unto them.

Then said Jesus unto them again, Verily, verily, I say unto you, I am the door of the sheep. All that ever came before me are thieves and robbers: but the sheep did not hear them. I am the door: by me if any man enter in, he shall be saved, and shall go in and out, and find pasture. The thief cometh not, but for to steal, and to kill, and to destroy: I am come that they might have life, and that they might have it more abundantly. I am the good shepherd: the good shepherd giveth his life for the sheep. But he that is an hireling, and not the shepherd, whose own the sheep are not, seeth the wolf coming, and leaveth the sheep, and fleeth: and the wolf catcheth them, and scattereth the sheep. The hireling fleeth, because he is an hireling, and careth not for the sheep. I am the good shepherd, and know my sheep, and am known of mine. As the Father knoweth me, even so know I the Father: and I lay down my life for the sheep. And other sheep I have, which are not of

> *this fold: them also I must bring, and they shall hear my voice; and there shall be one fold, and one shepherd.* (John 10:1–16)

John has been slowly working through his narrative of Jesus' ministry, starting with the timeless call to the first disciples (What do you seek?), then the changing of the wine and the telling Nicodemus of the need to be reborn. Both stories indicate the scale of change we go through if we wish to follow Jesus. There have been healings of those sick, lame, or blind, which certainly have implications for ourselves, and the instigation of a new worship in Spirit and in Truth, available to all regardless of race, colour, gender, or creed. Yet many have shown resistance, in Jesus' time and ever since. Do we, too?

The parable of the good shepherd invites us to take the step of following Jesus, given the evidence of his wondrous abilities in the previous chapters. The relationship between ourselves and Jesus becomes more personal. Do we accept and follow?

The shepherd knows each of his sheep and cares for them individually. In going out, he would be checking each was there by name and ensuring that none was missing. Then as he goes forth, he is leading, drawing them on to where there is suitable food and water. He will not lead them into danger. Yet the sheep may not always know where they are going, so they follow in trust. They hear his calling and follow. Similarly, can we be confident that wherever we are led we can go with trust, knowing that the way is being opened before us, even if the final destination is not immediately clear?

Given my now very clear idea of Jesus, why would I follow any other shepherd?

The good shepherd is described as one ready to give his life for the sheep, whatever is needed and much more, even what is most precious—his own life. There is no mention of what benefit the shepherd may derive from the relationship, nor is a relative value put on the sheep. In fact, there is no limit to what the shepherd will do for the sheep. In contrast, the hireling cares for the sheep only for material and temporal gain and does not have a deep love for the sheep.

In good times, the shepherd and the hireling are indistinguishable. But when the wolf appears the hireling commits two errors—first he leaves the sheep, and then, not even standing nearby and wondering if he can help, he flees the situation, abandoning his flock to the imminent ravaging by the wolf. In times of danger, the difference between the good shepherd and the hireling is immediately apparent.

In times of injustice, the hireling will not stand up to defend the sheep; he seeks to save himself. He deserts his flock and runs away. Can we identify the hireling within us, that part which always has our own self-interest at heart? Who is there to protect from that which seeks to destroy the soul? As a consequence, the sheep are scattered, dispersed far from the safety of their fold, which (in the allegory of sheep as the soul) exposes them to all sorts of temptations and vices—vanity, riches, pride, lust, and greed. This happens to us as communities only because we individually find ourselves prey to such tendencies.

The good shepherd has a close relation to the sheep. He knows his sheep, which implies that he knows each and every one. He knows which has a sickness and what to do for it, which sheep might be younger and tender and need more care, which might need to be kept close and not allowed to stray. In reverse, the shepherd is known ("of mine") by his own sheep. Note in all this that the sheep know the good shepherd by what he does, not by what he says. No matter what the hireling might have said to the owner of the sheep before he took them out to pasture, in the event it is what he does that distinguishes him from the shepherd. The implication is that although the hireling will only be there for the safe and good times, the shepherd is there always.

In the words of Psalm 23:1-3 (NIV), *The LORD is my shepherd, I lack nothing. He makes me lie down in green pastures, he leads me beside quiet waters, he refreshes my soul. He guides me along the right paths for his name's sake.* No need to struggle to find these things; just follow the Light, for it will lead us.

Finally, the shepherd recognises that there will be other lost sheep and it is his duty to go find them and bring them into the fold to safety. It is not sufficient to sit and wait; he will reach out to them. Our souls feel the reaching out that draws us into the safety of that divine love that protects from all misery and vice.

Jesus is drawing on ancient understandings from the Old Testament. The teaching of being led in trust using the analogy of a flock of sheep, also found in the writings of the prophets and the psalms, was an ancient tradition easily understood by the common people.[113] Jeremiah, Ezekiel, and Micah had all noted the scattering of the sheep and the need to regather them in the care of a trusted and good shepherd. For example, Ezekiel speaks of shepherds, referring to the religious authorities, who have failed miserably:

> *Woe be to the shepherds of Israel that do feed themselves! should not the shepherds feed the flocks?*
>
> *Ye eat the fat, and ye clothe you with the wool, ye kill them that are fed: but ye feed not the flock. The diseased have ye not strengthened, neither have ye healed that which was sick, neither have ye bound up that which was broken, neither have ye brought again that which was driven away, neither have ye sought that which was lost; but with force and with cruelty have ye ruled them. And they were scattered, because there is no shepherd: and they became meat to all the beasts of the field, when they were scattered....*
>
> *As I live, saith the LORD God, surely because my flock became a prey, and my flock became meat to every beast of the field, because there was no shepherd, neither did my shepherds search for my flock, but the shepherds fed themselves, and fed not my flock.* (Ezekiel 34:2-5, 8)

Ezekiel describes what has gone wrong for the flock. First, the shepherds selfishly regarded the sheep as being for their own benefit—for their own food and clothing. Second, they did not care for the sheep when they were sick or injured. Further, the shepherds allowed the sheep to be scattered and lost so they became victims to all the beasts—to all temptations and vices. Ezekiel does not call down wrath upon these shepherds but instead emphasises the role of the future shepherd who will regather the sheep and care for them properly. All those hearing Jesus would have been aware of these ancient teachings.

Jesus, being very aware that the sheep of his time have no shepherd (Matthew 9:36), fits himself into the role prophesied by Ezekiel: *And I will set up one shepherd over them, and he shall feed them* (Ezekiel 34:22-23). John summarises it clearly in John 10:27 *My sheep hear my voice, and I know them, and they follow me.* The role of the shepherd is to care for the flock, and Jesus promises to give his followers that care and to be the shepherd for their souls. The sheep follow their shepherd, George Fox preached, "so that they might all come to know Christ their teacher, their counsellor, their shepherd to feed them, and their bishop to oversee them and their prophet to open to them, and to know their bodies to be the temples of God and Christ for them to dwell in".[114]

Jesus Gives of His Own Free Will

> *No one takes my life from me; I lay it down freely. I have the power to lay it down, and I have the power to take it up again. This command I received from my Abba. (John 10:18 TIB)*

Jesus has entered this ministry of his own free will; he has given up whatever other inclinations or ambitions might have come to him. He has laid these down, preferring to follow the commandments of his *Abba* (Father), God. In due course, he will lay down his physical life. Yet he is free, both in the daily ministry and at the final day, either to lay his own will down or take it up.

So it is with us. We are being called into Life. It is not just a matter of rational decision-making to enter finally on the Way; it is a matter of giving up our focus on worldly ways and trusting that Way will open. We cannot make it a bargain (I will do this as long as Thee, O God, do that). As Edward Burrough wrote, we are to trust in Jesus, our shepherd.

> The Lord God everlasting, who is true and faithful, hath fulfilled his promise in us, and unto us, and we are gathered from the mouths of all dumb

shepherds, and out of the mouths of all hirelings, who have made a prey upon us, and fed themselves with the fat, and devoured souls for dishonest gain. And we are come to the fold of eternal rest, where Christ Jesus is the chief Shepherd, and he is the shepherd and bishop of our souls, that feedeth his flock with living bread that nourisheth us unto life eternal. He hath called us by his name, and put us forth, and he feedeth us in green pastures, and we are fed with hidden manna, and lie down at noon with his gathered flock.[115]

Continuing Resistance: The Worldly Voice That Disputes the Voice of the Spirit

> There was a division therefore again among the Jews for these sayings. And many of them said, He hath a devil, and is mad; why hear ye him? Others said, These are not the words of him that hath a devil. Can a devil open the eyes of the blind?

> And it was at Jerusalem the feast of the dedication, and it was winter. And Jesus walked in the temple in Solomon's porch. Then came the Jews round about him, and said unto him, How long dost thou make us to doubt? If thou be the Christ, tell us plainly. Jesus answered them, I told you, and ye believed not: the works that I do in my Father's name, they bear witness of me. But ye believe not, because ye are not of my sheep, as I said unto you.

> Then the Jews took up stones again to stone him. Jesus answered them, Many good works have I shewed you from my Father; for which of those works do ye stone me? The Jews answered him, saying, For a good work we stone thee not; but for blasphemy; and because that thou, being a man, makest thyself God. Jesus answered them, Is it not written in your law, I said, Ye are gods? If he called them gods, unto whom the word of God came, and the scripture cannot be broken; Say ye of him, whom the Father hath sanctified, and sent into the world,

> *Thou blasphemest; because I said, I am the Son of God? If I do not the works of my Father, believe me not. But if I do, though ye believe not me, believe the works: that ye may know, and believe, that the Father is in me, and I in him. Therefore they sought again to take him: but he escaped out of their hand.*
> (John 10:19-39)

This discussion takes place in winter (December) in Jerusalem at the Feast of Dedication that celebrates the dedication of the new altar built by the Maccabees.[116]

Some in the crowd contend that Jesus is mad or has a devil, while others reply that such a person could not perform miraculous healings. The religious leaders also contend that Jesus is a blasphemer. Jesus' presence and actions have brought matters into focus, into the Light. People have to make their own decision—do I believe in this man or not? When pressed for a direct answer to the question of whether he is the Christ, Jesus refuses to give a categorical yes or no. Instead, he tells his questioners to think about what he has done, and if they wish to know God, listen to what he has told them. Jesus says that just as sheep know the voice of their master and follow him, so do those who are drawn to God understand the words he has spoken.

As always, it is left to us to make our own decisions. That is free will. Our course is not to be decided by the traditional authority, as the Pharisees had always done and as many preachers have continued to do from the pulpit. We, each of us, enter into relationship with God inside ourselves, not relying on hearsay from another. The emphasis is on the question posed by George Fox in 1652: What canst thou say?[117]

Jesus argues that his good works bear witness of God working through him. This further enrages the Jewish leaders, who say it is not right to equate oneself with God. Yet Jesus confounds them by reminding them of the evidence from Samuel (1 Samuel 15:10) and Psalm 82:6 that each person who hears and acts on the Word is doing that of God. Each of us has that potential of God within us. I feel that maybe Jesus was saying to the religious authorities of his own time, "You all have that of God, if only you would cease being so blind and do what is just!"

> *How long will ye judge unjustly, and accept the persons of the wicked? Defend the poor and fatherless: do justice to the afflicted and needy. Deliver the poor and needy: rid them out of the hand of the wicked.*
>
> *They know not, neither will they understand; they walk on in darkness: all the foundations of the earth are out of course.*
>
> *I have said, Ye are gods; and all of you are children of the most High.* (Psalm 82:2–7)

When the Jews are left with no further argument, they try to take Jesus by force, and presumably they carry out their earlier threat to stone him. When both spiritual evidence and rational argument have failed, they resort to violence. The same response is practised today by the powers of darkness.

> *. . . but he escaped out of their hand, And went away again beyond Jordan into the place where John at first baptized; and there he abode. And many resorted unto him, and said, John did no miracle: but all things that John spake of this man were true. And many believed on him there.* (John 10:39–42)

However, Jesus retains control over these events and withdraws to the edge of the desert to spend his last three or four months with his disciples before returning at the next Passover to Jerusalem. Many come to the desert to learn from him, knowing nobody in living history has done the things Jesus has done.

CHAPTER 12
CHRIST IS NOT JUST A HEALER BUT THE SOURCE OF LIFE

Raising of Lazarus from Death

We know of Martha and Mary from another gospel (Luke 10:38-42) in which the two sisters are identified in a house Jesus has entered. John introduces their brother Lazarus, and it is clear this home is one in which Jesus was well received and safe.

The raising of Lazarus from the dead, with its extensive introduction, is the final sign, the ultimate miracle performed by Jesus before his arrest and death. It is the culmination of the increasing gifts bestowed by the Spirit through Jesus, first the changing of water into wine, then the healings and the restoration of sight to the blind. Along the way, many have come to a new faith and life. Now he restores the dead to life. I find this chapter a seemingly endless source of revealing meditations.

> *Now a certain man was sick, named Lazarus, of Bethany, the town of Mary and her sister Martha. (It was that Mary which anointed the Lord with ointment, and wiped his feet with her hair, whose brother Lazarus was sick.) Therefore his sisters sent unto him, saying, Lord, behold, he whom thou lovest is sick. When Jesus heard that, he said, This sickness is not unto death, but for the glory of God, that the Son of God might be glorified thereby. Now Jesus loved Martha, and her sister, and Lazarus.*
>
> *When he had heard therefore that he was sick, he abode two days still in the same place where he was. Then after that saith he to his disciples, Let us go into Judaea again. His disciples say unto him, Master, the Jews of late sought to stone thee; and goest thou thither again? Jesus answered, Are there not twelve hours in the day? If any man walk in the*

> day, he stumbleth not, because he seeth the light of this world. But if a man walk in the night, he stumbleth, because there is no light in him. These things said he: and after that he saith unto them, Our friend Lazarus sleepeth; but I go, that I may awake him out of sleep. Then said his disciples, Lord, if he sleep, he shall do well. Howbeit Jesus spake of his death: but they thought that he had spoken of taking of rest in sleep. Then said Jesus unto them plainly, Lazarus is dead. And I am glad for your sakes that I was not there, to the intent ye may believe; nevertheless let us go unto him. Then said Thomas, which is called Didymus, unto his fellow disciples, Let us also go, that we may die with him.
> (John 11:1–16)

The responses from the disciples cover common responses to danger. They are well aware of the repeated attempts by the Jewish authorities to take Jesus into custody and the threats to stone him.[118] When faced with the prospect of serious danger in doing God's work, the disciples, perhaps like ourselves, are looking for an excuse.

At first Jesus reminds them that it is important to keep doing God's work while he, the Light, is present, before also reminding them they have a responsibility to their friend. Perhaps looking for an easy out, the disciples argue that if Lazarus is just asleep, he will recover and wake up eventually, so why go all the way to Bethany? Jesus replies plainly that the message received was that Lazarus was seriously sick; they are being called to go. Thomas confirms that this is still a perilous journey but says let us go and share the work, whatever befalls us. Thomas is the voice of courage to do the work needed. At that point, the work begins.

> Then when Jesus came, he found that he had lain in the grave four days already. Now Bethany was nigh unto Jerusalem, about fifteen furlongs off: And many of the Jews came to Martha and Mary, to comfort them concerning their brother. Then Martha, as soon as she heard that Jesus was coming, went and met him: but Mary sat still in the house. Then said Martha unto Jesus, Lord, if thou hadst been here, my brother had not died. But I know, that even now,

> *whatsoever thou wilt ask of God, God will give it thee. Jesus saith unto her, Thy brother shall rise again. Martha saith unto him, I know that he shall rise again in the resurrection at the last day. Jesus said unto her, I am the resurrection, and the life: he that believeth in me, though he were dead, yet shall he live: And whosoever liveth and believeth in me shall never die. Believest thou this? She saith unto him, Yea, Lord: I believe that thou art the Christ, the Son of God, which should come into the world.* (John 11:17-27)

Traditionally, resurrection entails a promised future comfort to those suffering in the present world. It seems to be a common feature of religious thought, almost a way of coping with the difficulties of life. For example, the Romans had the idea of living in the blissful peace of the Elysian Fields after death, and the idea of 'heaven' has been a mainstay of both the Hebrew and the Christian traditions. Martha alludes to the Hebrew concept of those who have led a righteous life being called to life again in the future, when the perfect world is made. Jesus denies this concept and instead asserts a different resurrection, a spiritual rebirth in the present.

Jesus, using the "I Am", urges Martha not to wait for the future but to pay attention to the here and now. Jesus refers to himself as the embodiment of the source of real life, as reborn into a spiritual existence in this present life: *I am come that they might have life, and that they might have it more abundantly* (John 10:10).

Jesus knew there is life after death. He knew that he would go to a house where there are many mansions (John 14:2), or, as he said to Mary, I go to *my God and your God* (John 20:17 NIV). The gospel evidence is clear that Jesus knew he would die and that he had been preparing himself and his disciples for that event. He did not avoid or deny it.

The alternative attitude to dying, on both the momentary and life scales, is marked by denial, anger, depression, bargaining, and, hopefully, acceptance—the phases of grief so well documented by Elisabeth Kübler-Ross.[119] Such passionate and troubling emotions are displayed by many people facing loss or death and by many of their relatives and friends. Yet even Kübler-Ross with all her knowledge could not avoid these emotional upheavals. The answer lies not in knowledge but in spiritual practice.

Jesus knew of a resurrection in this life. We each regularly face moments of letting go of things to which we are attached; when those parts of our previous Self die, we experience rebirth as a slightly different individual. Our way of living and of accepting change and death is preparation for our dying.[120] If we seek peace and ensure it during life, then when death comes it can be faced in peace, with a life and spirit already committed to God.

Early Christians experienced being *risen with Christ* (Colossians 3:1 KJV) or *resurrected with Christ* (TIB). . . . They had experienced being completely changed; having died inwardly, they were reborn (resurrected) into a new being. Many have experienced what Paul wrote (Romans 6:5–11) as the dying of the 'old man', or, as the TIB puts it, *our former selves have been crucified*. Marcelle Martin explains this:

> With sometimes searing intensity, the inward Light revealed how thoroughly each person had been under the influence of spiritually oppressive forces. However much a person may have talked about God and engaged in religious practices, his or her actions had been primarily under the control of human will, in conformity to social norms. Even those who had avoided most sinful behavior found that they had been inwardly bound or chained in ways they barely suspected. They were shocked to see how they had colluded with hypocrisy and the spiritual oppression of themselves and others. This way of living to which they had previously conformed was now viewed as a form of death.
>
> Like the hard husk around a seed, the old self that was living in spiritual darkness needed to break open and disintegrate. A death of the old self was necessary in order for the seed—the Light of Christ Within—to take root and grow. The process of being turned from darkness to light is a process of being brought through death to rebirth. The disintegration of the old, willful self makes way for the birth of a new self that will reveal the divine image.[121]

Jesus places the accent on living his way right now, believing completely in him and what he is teaching us to do. Though our bodies deteriorate and die, the spiritual truth of what we have lived lasts forever. Is that not what we experience of the lives of the saints and other wonderful people? The spiritual impact of their lives and its ability to change us is still with us though they are long gone. It is now our turn. There is no place for spiritual procrastination, leaving it to the afterlife. The job is *now*. Jesus focuses our attention on living every moment in gospel order, opening ourselves to continuing inward changes and the dying of what is no longer useful or right, not deferring heaven till later.

Finally, Martha witnesses Jesus as the long-awaited Christ. She, the practical woman compared to her sister Mary (Luke 10:40–41), was also a person of deep spiritual faith and insight. She recognised, like Andrew, Philip, Nathanael, Peter, and the woman in Samaria, that she was in the presence of the Christ.[122]

The line between our work in the world and spiritual realization can be very thin. It can come at any time, and part of our religious life is to be attentive at all times and to take what the early Quakers called 'opportunities' to commune with the Light, whatever the time of day or week it opens for us.

John takes the time to set the scene. Mary comes to Jesus, deep in sorrow. Could not this man who had opened the eyes of the blind have also healed Lazarus?

> *And when she had so said, she went her way, and called Mary her sister secretly, saying, The Master is come, and calleth for thee. As soon as she heard that, she arose quickly, and came unto him. Now Jesus was not yet come into the town, but was in that place where Martha met him. The Jews then which were with her in the house, and comforted her, when they saw Mary, that she rose up hastily and went out, followed her, saying, She goeth unto the grave to weep there. Then when Mary was come where Jesus was, and saw him, she fell down at his feet, saying unto him, Lord, if thou hadst been here, my brother had not died. When Jesus therefore saw her weeping, and the Jews also weeping which came*

with her, he groaned in the spirit, and was troubled. And said, Where have ye laid him? They said unto him, Lord, come and see. Jesus wept. Then said the Jews, Behold how he loved him! And some of them said, Could not this man, which opened the eyes of the blind, have caused that even this man should not have died?

Jesus therefore again groaning in himself cometh to the grave. It was a cave, and a stone lay upon it. Jesus said, Take ye away the stone. Martha, the sister of him that was dead, saith unto him, Lord, by this time he stinketh: for he hath been dead four days. Jesus saith unto her, Said I not unto thee, that, if thou wouldest believe, thou shouldest see the glory of God? Then they took away the stone from the place where the dead was laid. And Jesus lifted up his eyes, and said, Father, I thank thee that thou hast heard me. And I knew that thou hearest me always: but because of the people which stand by I said it, that they may believe that thou hast sent me. And when he thus had spoken, he cried with a loud voice, Lazarus, come forth. And he that was dead came forth, bound hand and foot with graveclothes: and his face was bound about with a napkin. Jesus saith unto them, Loose him, and let him go. Then many of the Jews which came to Mary, and had seen the things which Jesus did, believed on him. (John 11:28-45)

What an extraordinary miracle. The body dead for four days is sealed in a cave, with the door blocked by a stone. The stone is blocking the transformation of that which is dead to that which is again alive.

I reflect on what is the stone in me that blocks spiritual life. The stonyhearted attitude that denies compassion and forgiveness is very often the answer. Yet I cannot remove it all myself, and it is the interaction with others that helps roll that stone away. Then, with the stone gone, can the dead come to life of their own accord? No, it takes the presence of the Spirit to do that, and so Jesus cries out, "Come forth", that is, move out of the darkness and into the Light. Venture forth.

Political Scapegoat

> *But some of them went their ways to the Pharisees, and told them what things Jesus had done. Then gathered the chief priests and the Pharisees a council, and said, What do we? for this man doeth many miracles. If we let him thus alone, all men will believe on him: and the Romans shall come and take away both our place and nation. And one of them, named Caiaphas, being the high priest that same year, said unto them, Ye know nothing at all, Nor consider that it is expedient for us, that one man should die for the people, and that the whole nation perish not. And this spake he not of himself: but being high priest that year, he prophesied that Jesus should die for that nation; And not for that nation only, but that also he should gather together in one the children of God that were scattered abroad. Then from that day forth they took counsel together for to put him to death.*
>
> *Jesus therefore walked no more openly among the Jews; but went thence unto a country near to the wilderness, into a city called Ephraim, and there continued with his disciples.* (John 11:46-54)

The chief priests were Sadducees, and together with the Pharisees they controlled the tenor of Jewish religious and social life in their society. Elsewhere, Jesus warned specifically against the 'leaven' of the Pharisees and the Sadducees (Matthew 16:6-12; Luke 12:1-3, 20:46-47). The leaven of the Pharisees was their pedantic insistence on minute regulations; of the Sadducees it was their theological rejection of resurrection and their acquisitiveness for worldly status and wealth. Both were hypocritical seekers of worldly approval, status, and influence, making a show of long prayers yet commonly blind to spiritual realities and the need for compassion and mercy in front of them. Yet that leaven is also within me, as a latent desire for recognition or as a blindness, and I ask for it to be replaced with the leaven from heaven.

The Sadducees and Pharisees together see that Jesus is drawing the multitude away from them, which is threatening their influence and relationships with the Roman colonisers. They have reached the limits of their tolerance for Jesus and make concerted plans to kill him. The raising of Lazarus is the last straw for them. With each miracle, Jesus has increased his stature as a prophet and broadened his influence among the people. Every time the Jewish religious authorities have challenged Jesus, he has answered them and has prevailed spiritually and intellectually. Their power base is disappearing before their eyes. As is so common to the powers of darkness, they move from instant thoughts of arrest to a concerted plan of violence.

It became expedient for these authorities that Jesus must die, becoming a scapegoat to preserve the worldly interests of the Jewish leaders. How often do we see that? Let us be wary, however, of casting judgment.

The scapegoat is not only utilised by the worldly powers. Too often have I also sacrificed an inner motion suggested by the Light in order to preserve my own sense of comfort and security. The change required by God is more than I had imagined.

Jesus now withdraws with his disciples for the last time to a place on the edge of the desert.

CHAPTER 13
CONFRONTING THE POWERS WITHOUT VIOLENCE

What Were the Disciples Thinking?

> *Then Jesus six days before the passover came to Bethany, where Lazarus was, which had been dead, whom he raised from the dead. There they made him a supper; and Martha served: but Lazarus was one of them that sat at the table with him. Then took Mary a pound of ointment of spikenard, very costly, and anointed the feet of Jesus, and wiped his feet with her hair: and the house was filled with the odour of the ointment. Then saith Judas Iscariot, Simon's son, which should betray him, Why was not this ointment sold for three hundred pence, and given to the poor?* (John 12:1-5)

Before the third Passover mentioned in this gospel, Jesus spent time in the remote community at Ephraim near the edge of the desert before travelling to Bethany. A special meal is prepared at the house of Simon the Leper *(*Matthew 26:6; Mark 14:3*)*, and Lazarus is present. Martha serves food. Mary anoints Jesus' feet. What a situation for Jesus, eating with close friends, including the Simon whose own son Judas Iscariot Jesus knew would later betray him.

Jesus then travels up to Jerusalem, knowing the religious leaders are out to get him. He has known for a long while that the final confrontation is coming. But what about the disciples? What was their frame of mind? Apparently they were quite unaware and could not understand even Jesus' own foretelling of his impending death (Luke 18:31). We readers have the benefit of hindsight and know what is about to happen, whereas the disciples at that time did not know the complete story.

As I recall the gospels, so often the disciples were struggling to understand what Jesus was saying and doing. Earlier in his ministry Jesus had to explain the meanings of his parables and teachings. In this sense, the gospels have

CONFRONTING THE POWERS WITHOUT VIOLENCE

faithfully preserved the teachings with necessary explanations so that they are still applicable and relevant to ourselves as disciples. Yet as Jesus enters Jerusalem, things are happening that the disciples only come to understand after Jesus' death and resurrection (John 12:16).

What did the disciples think as Jesus was greeted by enthusiastic crowds? Maybe they thought that people had finally come to accept Jesus as the Christ. Maybe Jesus would go and teach at Jerusalem, debate with the Pharisees, and slip away again, as he had done several times in the previous three years. Yet maybe they also thought that things would be different—after all, they had heard the angel speak to Jesus (John 12:28-29)—and perhaps this was the year something very wonderful would happen and Jesus would finally triumph and bring all to understand the Word.

The common thought was stated later by Cleopas and his friend on the road to Emmaus: *we trusted that it had been he which should have redeemed Israel* (Luke 24:21). Inevitably, they could remember that Jesus had changed water to wine, had healed the lame and cured the blind, and had even brought Lazarus back to life after he had been entombed dead. What spectacular miracle was about to be performed to finally refute or convert the Jewish authorities and restore peace and well-being to the Jewish communities?

What sort of glory might they have imagined? Despite Jesus' puzzling predictions, they had no idea of the shocking end in store, less than a week away.

As for ourselves, do we have ready-made expectations for our own journey? What sort of misplaced glory do we imagine along the way for ourselves?

> *On the next day much people that were come to the feast, when they heard that Jesus was coming to Jerusalem, took branches of palm trees, and went forth to meet him, and cried, Hosanna: Blessed is the King of Israel that cometh in the name of the Lord. And Jesus, when he had found a young ass, sat thereon; as it is written, Fear not, daughter of Sion: behold, thy King cometh, sitting on an ass's colt. These things understood not his disciples at the first: but when Jesus was glorified, then remembered they that these things were written of him, and that*

> *they had done these things unto him. The people therefore that was with him when he called Lazarus out of his grave, and raised him from the dead, bare record. For this cause the people also met him, for that they heard that he had done this miracle. The Pharisees therefore said among themselves, Perceive ye how ye prevail nothing? behold, the world is gone after him.* (John 12:12-19)

Jesus had given clear instructions to his disciples to go and get the colt of an ass (Mark 1:2-7; Matthew 21:2-7; Luke 19:33-35), fulfilling a prophecy by Zechariah (9:9). John is the only gospel writer to specify the use of palm branches being laid during Jesus' entry to Jerusalem, a traditional sign for the coming of a victor or king. Mark and Matthew simply record branches of trees. Many may also have come to see for themselves the man who had performed the miraculous raising of Lazarus from the dead. Might we sympathise with the people who expected this person to be their worldly saviour? After all, for most of us who are pursuing the spiritual journey, is there not also a barely hidden desire that this journey will also lead us and others to safety and comfort in a worldly sense?

Concerning the Pharisees who were determined to deal with the problem of Jesus by getting rid of him, John includes the ironic quote, *Perceive ye how ye prevail nothing? behold, the world is gone after him.* The Pharisees were aghast at the loss of their followers and power: "Look, everyone has left us to follow him", they deplored. Yet it was an unconscious prediction, for certainly many in the known world of that time would indeed leave the Jewish faith and follow Jesus.

> *Mark my words and make no mistake: if a grain of wheat doesn't fall into the ground and die, it survives, yes, but as one grain only. If it does die, it yields great increase. Those who cling to their lives have to give them up; those who set little store by their lives in the world of here and now shall keep them, timelessly unscathed.* (John 12:24-25 TFG)

When Jesus teaches the need for loss of life, we recall the advice to Nicodemus that we need to be reborn to enter the Presence of God. Jesus uses an analogy relevant to village people and common farming folk—that of the corn (or grain) of wheat. If the wheat does not fall into the ground, if it remains in a basket or silo, it remains just an isolated grain, with its potential and productive goodness unrealised. Yet if it falls to the ground and is itself destroyed—if the grain dies—then the new plant, the new growth, is given forth. In Jesus' words from the parable of the sower, it will yield a hundred-fold return (Luke 8:8). And in this idiom lies the expectation that this seed will be reproduced again and again, producing crop after crop, the good works of the Spirit spread out through the community.

It was Jesus' intention to give his whole life to God and in the end to give up his life into the hands of the princes of the world. For he knew that in doing so he would become unified with God. All the gifts of his life and ministry flowed from that decision to give up his own will, to let that die.

Verse 12:25 explains this clearly. If we are determined to have our own way in the world, to have our own pleasures and our own wealth control our worldly lives and actions, then we risk losing our spiritual lives. If we can forgo these, then we gain our spiritual lives.

This language occurs in many early Christian writings and also in works by mystics of other religions. Teresa of Avila talks of purging ourselves, which is the first of the three stages of approaching God—purgation, illumination, and union. We might call these stripping and emptying, then awareness and increase of the inward Light, and finally the full surrender of our life into God's hands. The Bhagavad Gita has the same message: "For the man who forsakes all desires and abandons all pride of possession and of self reaches the goal of peace supreme" (2:71).

Overemphasising Jesus' advice to deny oneself (Mark 8:34; Luke 9:23) has led to punishing penances, subjugation, and abuse. It undermines the natural, personal trust in the guidance of the inward Light, which is then overridden by external authority. This can lead to terrible inner discord and unhappiness.

The problem is not so much the advice itself as having the advice forced on people from an authoritarian mould of righteousness rather than being followed from an inner leading for change. Jesus was very clear that the latter is the way. The more helpful approach is to commit to a life following the leadings of the Spirit. We voluntarily give up many of our habits and possessions as it becomes our will to follow that of God. The way is lit inwardly, not externally. Perhaps the following quote from Thomas à Kempis will be helpful:

> Child, it behooves you to give all for all, and keep nothing of yourself from me. Know that self-love hurts you more than anything else in the world. Things cling to you and hold you to a greater or lesser degree, according to the love you have for them If your love is pure, simple and well-ordered, you will be free from bondage to any earthly thing.[123]

This all seems very negative and strange to those of us who have been fed a diet of the value of self-development and self-confidence and self-esteem as the basis for a healthy and rewarding life. Note that each of these common terms is centred on the Self. Yet the examples of our spiritual heroes and saints show that the Self in each has been put aside. The fact is that doing so leads to a wonderful and lively appreciation of the beauty of God's world and of the spiritual qualities in everyone around us.

This is very close to the Quaker maxim, "Answer that of God in everyone". We must be released from the focus on our own Self and our own well-being to be able to immediately and naturally be led by the Spirit to recognise and answer that of God, in those we meet. The psychological concept of 'projection' is that we tend to see in others what we want for ourselves and to be critical if it is not there. In contrast, the spiritual search is not for that which corresponds to our Self in others but for that of God. We may not recognise that of God in another as valuable in the first instance.

The episodes of Jesus' life recounted in the gospels reveal that this is exactly what he did and what he modelled for us. Whatever situation he was faced with, he recognised the spiritual quality and need in the moment or in the person. He answered that of God, that of love, that of compassion, that of truth.

> *[Jesus replied,] "Now my soul is troubled. What will I say: 'Abba, save me from this hour?' But it was for this very reason I came to this hour. Abba, glorify your name." A voice came from heaven: "I have both glorified it, and will glorify it again." The crowds that stood nearby heard this and said it was a clap of thunder; others said, "It was an angel speaking."*
> (John 12:27–29 TIB)

Jesus faces a point of decision: whether to follow God or, knowing the difficulty ahead, withdraw to safety. He asks for a way out. Then he realises that facing this difficulty is the way; this is the reason he has been brought this far.

So finally, we are all one day brought to a point of decision. It may be, Do I give up this quite minor habit, as the Spirit is asking of me? Or, Do I forgo my own plans to help someone else today? Do I refuse this tempting offer? Or it may be a more severe situation: Do I stay here and work in this place of conflict or do I move away for comfort and safety? Jesus gives us the words for such times: For this point of my life was I born. This is not to say we always are called to give up everything we want to do or to martyr ourselves. Many times, we are called to let others do the work or to move away from danger. However, if we are clearly asked to change or stay, then we know that is the reason we have been brought thus far on our journey.

What does 'glorify' mean, I ask myself when I read this passage. The dictionary definitions include 'make glorious' (that is, honourable, magnificent, splendid), 'exalt to the glory of heaven,' 'invest with radiance,' and 'transform into something more splendid'. I can have some idea of what it means though I have no real experience of such a thing.

What is clear to me is that Jesus is preparing to enter the next phase of his ministry on earth, and it will be something way beyond normal behaviour. And he is entering it in complete trust in the love of God.

Jesus' Final Public Summary of His Ministry

> *Then Jesus said unto them, Yet a little while is the light with you. Walk while ye have the light, lest darkness come upon you: for he that walketh in*

> *darkness knoweth not whither he goeth. While ye have light, believe in the light, that ye may be the children of light. These things spake Jesus, and departed, and did hide himself from them.* (John 12:35-36)

There is a continual movement by Jesus to be amongst people and then to withdraw where they cannot see him. He is present, the Light is present, and then he withdraws and darkness returns. This is a cycle in my own life. One aspect of faith is confidence that the Light will return. It is very important when the Light is present to believe and trust in that Light and to walk in it. That is how we become children of the Light, and that is how our measure of the Light is increased. Jesus spiritual advice is: Make use of the Light when you have it.

> *But though he had done so many miracles before them, yet they believed not on him: That the saying of Esaias the prophet might be fulfilled, which he spake, Lord, who hath believed our report? and to whom hath the arm of the Lord been revealed? Therefore they could not believe, because that Esaias said again, He hath blinded their eyes, and hardened their heart; that they should not see with their eyes, nor understand with their heart, and be converted, and I should heal them. These things said Esaias, when he saw his glory, and spake of him. Nevertheless among the chief rulers also many believed on him; but because of the Pharisees they did not confess him, lest they should be put out of the synagogue: For they loved the praise of men more than the praise of God.* (John 12:37-43)

The resistances and unbelief continue. Some have left Jesus and some have followed. If we do not open our hearts to the Light, then God leaves us in darkness. Each is free to choose. None is forced.

> *Jesus cried and said, He that believeth on me, believeth not on me, but on him that sent me. And he that seeth me seeth him that sent me. I am come a light into the world, that whosoever believeth on me should not abide in darkness. And if any man*

> *hear my words, and believe not, I judge him not: for I came not to judge the world, but to save the world. He that rejecteth me, and receiveth not my words, hath one that judgeth him: the word that I have spoken, the same shall judge him in the last day. For I have not spoken of myself; but the Father which sent me, he gave me a commandment, what I should say, and what I should speak. And I know that his commandment is life everlasting: whatsoever I speak therefore, even as the Father said unto me, so I speak.* (John 12:44–50)

For me, Jesus is not saying here that he is God; he is saying that those who believe in his teachings, believe in what he has said and done, and see clearly the spiritual source of all his work are also perceiving God. God can be understood and approached through Jesus. In all this he is not the judge but the saviour. His message is that we should look forward and work towards a way out of darkness and into light and life. Judgment is no use, neither the judging of others nor of ourselves. After all, the first only sets up barriers and the second can result in unproductive guilt.

Finally, Jesus reiterates a message he has given before: while on earth, he has faithfully said and done what God asked of him. Jesus is the instrument of God's work in the world, a servant of God. If that was good enough for him, surely it is good enough for us.

The choice to be a disciple is a free choice, even if Jesus puts it starkly: Follow me or go your own way.[124] Again, he makes the same point in different words in John 12:44–50, where he acknowledges that all he has done and does comes from God. Jesus has made a passionate plea to be heard. He knows he does not have much longer. This man knows his life is coming to an end, and he faces a terrible ordeal. He has spent three years teaching and healing, and it seems people are just not listening to what is so much needed. He does not cry out, "Obey all the laws of the temple rulers". He cries out, "Believe what I have been telling you, for it is the Word of God and it will lead to eternal life".

The spiritual life is first and foremost a *life*. Many may think of the spiritual life as imposing heavy constraints, that a life devoted to the Spirit would be somehow lacking in fulfillment, without enjoyment of common activities, restricting, dull, almost lifeless! But that is not true. The Light does encourage and help us to dispense with many previous habits and possessions. The spiritual life is a different life. Many things that previously seemed so attractive are left behind in a life of simplicity, forgiveness, joy, and love.

The spiritual journey creates a life and a love that sees no barriers, and this is the existence that God so desperately wishes for all creation. It is Jesus' agony and frustration that he knows all this is possible and also knows the steps to get there.

His early followers knew it, the early Quakers knew it, and the saints of all religions knew it. We each can be dimly aware of that seed planted in our innermost beings, for we feel it in our hearts even before we know what it is. And it is to our hearts we must retreat in order to understand the demands of love and be drawn deeper and deeper into this spiritual life, this different life, this wonderful life.

CHAPTER 14
CHURCH OF EQUALITY, HUMILITY, SERVICE, AND LOVE

The Washing of Feet

John's description of the Last Supper with his disciples does not establish a ritual Eucharist. He has discussed the significance of Jesus' flesh and blood (John 6) as the source of spiritual nourishment in a much broader context. John describes a very different sacramental act at the Last Supper. Although foot washing was a custom in ancient lands, in this context it is given a very fresh and clear meaning.[125]

> *He riseth from supper, and laid aside his garments; and took a towel, and girded himself. After that he poureth water into a bason, and began to wash the disciples' feet, and to wipe them with the towel wherewith he was girded. Then cometh he to Simon Peter: and Peter saith unto him, Lord, dost thou wash my feet? Jesus answered and said unto him, What I do thou knowest not now; but thou shalt know hereafter. Peter saith unto him, Thou shalt never wash my feet. Jesus answered him, If I wash thee not, thou hast no part with me. Simon Peter saith unto him, Lord, not my feet only, but also my hands and my head. Jesus saith to him, He that is washed needeth not save to wash his feet, but is clean every whit: and ye are clean, but not all. For he knew who should betray him; therefore said he, Ye are not all clean. So after he had washed their feet, and had taken his garments, and was set down again, he said unto them, Know ye what I have done to you? Ye call me Master and Lord: and ye say well; for so I am. If I then, your Lord and Master, have washed your feet; ye also ought to wash one another's feet. For I have given you an example, that ye should do as I have done to you. Verily, verily, I say unto you, The servant is not greater than his*

> *lord; neither he that is sent greater than he that sent him. If ye know these things, happy are ye if ye do them.* (John 13:4–17)

Jesus first discards his garments and comes in humility as one with nothing material to support him. He starts to wash the disciples' feet and wipe them dry with the towel. This is, for me, both an act of service and of intimacy. Presumably, each of them would have washed his hands before eating and probably his face on arrival. Feet are a different matter, for they are both dirtier and smellier and yet more personal. They gather the dust and dung along the roads, and yet we are not accustomed to people touching them. We might do the same for a sick relative, as another might for us. To clean another's feet is an act of addressing the lowest part of the body, the one closest to the ground, a part rarely touched by others. The feet are also sensitive, not so much the hardened soles as the tender uppers, and when our feet are injured or sore we feel it with every movement.

This must have been an unexpected act, given Peter's reaction. Might we feel the same? Peter has a wonderful impetuousness in his spiritual searching. This is the same Peter who jumped overboard into the water when he saw Jesus across the Sea of Galilee (Matthew 14:24–33). His spontaneous reactions might remind us of someone we know or of parts of ourselves. When challenged by Jesus to submit to having his feet washed, Peter responds immediately, "Then wash me all over!" Was Peter thinking of total immersion in water, the baptismal washing in the river performed by John and by Jesus' own disciples in earlier days? For me, Jesus is saying, "No, that is all behind you, think about what I am doing in mystical terms. This washing that I do of your feet is the touch of the Spirit that will cleanse you completely".

This interaction between Peter and Jesus also reveals the need for each of us to allow ourselves to be cleansed. We have to free ourselves from inhibitions and wariness and freely allow the Spirit to work within us. Many find that difficult. Perhaps we are not sure it is possible for us to be cleaned out; perhaps we still think we can do it ourselves if we take a bit more time; perhaps we are wary of what might happen and the things that might be asked of us; or perhaps we are nervous of what others might think, so we hold back from being completely open and relaxed and welcoming so the Spirit can work within us. So too did Peter want to "have it his way". The old habits of wanting to control had not yet been overcome.

The symbolism of external washing to represent inner cleansing would have been widely known through the work of John the Baptist. In addition, Hebrew history contains the story of Elisha sending the enemy soldier Naaman down to the river to wash and be cleansed of his leprosy. As a result of this miraculous healing, Naaman returns and admits to Elisha, "Now I know there is no God in all the world except in Israel" (2 Kings 5:15); the outer washing was matched by spiritual transformation.

Jesus acknowledges he is the Lord and Master, and yet he is able to come down to everyone else's level and wash their feet. However, this story is not one where Jesus gathers the group around him, handing out a few towels and a couple of basins and saying, "Now, what I want each of you to do is to choose one of your fellow disciples, perhaps one you do not know well, and go and wash his feet". This is no New Testament group therapy session. No, Jesus, the acknowledged spiritual leader and master, does the washing himself.

When Jesus comes to wash the disciples' feet, he first lays aside his garments. He comes bare, just with the towel that is required for the job. For those at the time, familiar with Jesus' teachings, they could easily contrast this with the parables of the *certain rich man, clothed in purple and fine linen* who feasted each day and refused to assist the beggar Lazarus at his door, poor and covered with sores (Luke 16:19-31) or with Jesus' advice to a certain ruler who was very rich (Luke 18:18-25). In each of these cases, God's gifts had been utilised for personal adornment and worldly self-indulgence, not for service. Jesus' example is completely the opposite. His ministry was performed without any personal adornment, without pretence of leadership, without any signs of authority or of higher office. May our own ministry every day be in the same spirit as Jesus has shown us.

Jesus does not just wash the feet of one or two of his followers as a demonstration; he washes 'their feet', all of them, all of them individually. My reading is that he also washes the feet of Judas Iscariot, for there is no mention otherwise, and later the disciples sense no break amongst themselves when Jesus indicates there is one who will betray him. Jesus does not give more or less to one than another. There is no weighing up of past transgressions.

What would this have felt like? What would each of the disciples have reflected upon, first as his turn came and then afterwards? So, what would it be like to have Jesus come and wash our feet? Would we each allow it to happen, remembering as Jesus said in John 13:8 that it is a necessary part of becoming linked to the divine? Or would we hold back? Spiritually, are we ready to sit, be still, and await the cleansing, purifying experience of the Light within? If we feel any resistance to this possibility, then that resistance is an expression of our spiritual resistance to Jesus and to the Light that seeks to change us and prepare us for the next stages of our journey. Whatever resistance is exposed within us, whatever wariness we feel, whatever hesitation is exposed at this moment by the Light, this is the next step to be overcome in our journey.

This teaching is sacramental. John describes an act that is the culmination of Jesus' teaching. The relationship with God is an intimate and a two-way affair; we have to be prepared to submit to the washing and the cleansing by the Light, and in return the divine power supports us in accepting God's ministrations and in our outer works of love and service. In our contemplative times, we have to be prepared to allow the Light to work within us so that in our active lives we will look after one another. We become a person through other people, in spiritually guided acts of service. Jesus is telling us to do this to each other; we are equals and we need to care for each other. In this sacramental washing of the disciples' feet, Jesus assures us he is with each of us every step of the way.

In Kahlil Gibran's words:

> Jesus said: "Now I will wash your feet. For I must needs free your feet from the dust of the ancient road, and give them the freedom of the new way."[126]

In contrast to church teaching based on the Synoptic Gospels and some of Paul's writings indicating that the Last Supper places Jesus on high, this teaching places Jesus as a servant. This is an example for us all.

The teachings of John 13 are commemorated in a church practice dating back to the Middle Ages, when a parish priest would wash his parishioners' feet in a special service on Maundy Thursday, the day before Good Friday. The term Maundy comes from the Latin *mandatum*, or 'commandment', the instruction given by Jesus at the Last Supper.[127] In England, the custom of washing the feet of the poor is said to have begun with St. Augustine of Canterbury in 597 CE and was performed in Westminster Abbey by the Catholic monarchs from Edward II until the death of James II in 1689. This has now been replaced by the ceremony of the 'Maundy money' in which the monarch distributes specially minted coins to a group of hand-picked elderly recipients at a cathedral in England, though not necessarily to the poor as was formerly done.

This deep teaching requires more than annual performances, more than coming down from on high for an hour from the pulpit or for a day from the throne. This is a sacramental lesson for all occasions. Having given the lesson, Jesus cautions us against any feeling of superiority. *Verily, verily, I say unto you, The servant is not greater than his lord; neither he that is sent greater than he that sent him. If ye know these things, happy are ye if ye do them.* He is very aware of our common failings. So he says, "If you know all these things, if you can hold them close with all your heart and not imagine this act places you in any superior place and let no glimpse of 'well done' intrude, then you can be happy you are following me on the Way towards the Presence of God".

Dismissing the Spirit of Betrayal

> *And when he had dipped the sop, he gave it to Judas Iscariot, the son of Simon. And after the sop Satan entered into him. Then said Jesus unto him, That thou doest, do quickly. Now no man at the table knew for what intent he spake this unto him. For some of them thought, because Judas had the bag,*

> *that Jesus had said unto him, Buy those things that we have need of against the feast; or, that he should give something to the poor. He then having received the sop went immediately out: and it was night.*
> (John 13:26–30)

Some commentaries find the inclusion of this section about Judas an interruption, perhaps a later editorial alteration, as it sits between Jesus' lesson on foot washing and his later instructions on the new commandment. For me, the Gospel According to John is a lesson in spiritual growth, and here again John shows he is a consummate spiritual guide and teacher.

During supper, the possible betrayal by Judas Iscariot has not been obvious to any of the assembled disciples, though Jesus has perceived what is in Judas' mind and heart (see also Matthew 26:23–26). Judas has made arrangements with the high priests to lead them to Jesus and to be paid thirty pieces of silver for his work.[128] Jesus has said, *Ye are not all clean* (John 13:11), and later, *One of you shall betray me* (John 13:21). What is not obvious to the world is always known to the Light. My own sense is that Jesus did not feel the time was ripe to make his final statements to his beloved disciples until the spirit of betrayal had been sent away.

We use the name Judas to refer to a traitor in any group. That leaves us comfortable because it is a term for that person over there, not ourselves. However, on the spiritual level, we each contain Judas. For what does Judas represent other than the need to control the outcome, the seeking of a reward for our efforts, the desire for approval, the deception of being of one appearance externally but harbouring corruptions inside?

Not until the betrayer has been dismissed can the disciples receive the final commandment—love one another. So it is for us; until self-centredness goes away, until the seeking of some reward such as another's approval or apology is abandoned, until we face and dispatch our own inner prejudices, until we cease to bargain with God, until all these are gone, we cannot unreservedly follow the new commandment. John has included this section to impress upon us the need to remove the 'Judas' from ourselves before we can fully enter the Presence of God. We all need the spiritual equivalent of foot washing, an inner cleansing that banishes these corruptions from our soul, for only then can we unconditionally love one another.

Love One Another

> A new commandment I give unto you, That ye love one another; as I have loved you, that ye also love one another. By this shall all men know that ye are my disciples, if ye have love one to another. (John 13:34-35)

When previously questioned by learned Jewish teachers, Jesus had nominated two ancient laws as the most important to follow: Love the Lord thy God with all thy heart, and with all thy soul, and with all thy mind, and with all thy strength. . . . And the second is like, namely this, Thou shalt love thy neighbour as thyself (Mark 12:30-31).[129] By identifying these two as the most important of all the vast number of laws and regulations in the Old Testament, Jesus used ancient teachings of his own Jewish tradition to confound the Pharisees. The second rule is commonly restated as "Do unto others as you would have them do unto you" (Matthew 7:12; Luke 6:31), which is modified by Jesus in John 13:15.

Jesus now adds a new commandment: Love one another (John 13:34). So simple, yet so difficult. Jesus cuts through to the essence of the matter. This instruction is significantly different, deeper, and more demanding than the Golden Rule, which asks that you do as you would like done to you. Jesus replaces any sense of self-interest by asking us to do as he would do. Then are we his disciples, living under a new law.

In this gospel, John has progressively introduced us to Jesus, describing several miracles as signs of Jesus' powers to heal physically and spiritually, showing examples of his mercy and forgiveness, yet making it clear he is ministering to all, for there are no barriers of age or class or race or gender. Jesus is universal in his ministry.

In chapter 13, John brings us to the very last act of Jesus' ministry, and it goes to the heart of his teachings. Unconditional love is the essence; all other laws and teachings are superfluous. Neither John nor Jesus allows us to dreamily accept that it will just happen magically. By inserting the example of Judas, we know we have to face and deal with our own inner corruption before we can fully show this love.

The will to love develops our relationship with God and with each other. This commandment became an abiding rule within the early Christian communities.[130]

Carlo Carretto's experience is, "You will be judged by your ability to love".[131] He advises us:

> Don't worry about what you ought to do. Worry about loving. Don't interrogate heaven repeatedly and uselessly saying "What course of action should I pursue?" Concentrate on loving instead. And by loving you will find out what is for you. Loving, you will listen to the Voice. Loving, you will find peace.[132]

The Spectre of Fear Within

> *Simon Peter said unto him, Lord, whither goest thou? Jesus answered him, Whither I go, thou canst not follow me now; but thou shalt follow me afterwards. Peter said unto him, Lord, why cannot I follow thee now? I will lay down my life for thy sake. Jesus answered him, Wilt thou lay down thy life for my sake? Verily, verily, I say unto thee, The cock shall not crow, till thou hast denied me thrice.* (John 13:36–38)

> *And Simon Peter followed Jesus, and so did another disciple: that disciple was known unto the high priest, and went in with Jesus into the palace of the high priest. But Peter stood at the door without. Then went out that other disciple, which was known unto the high priest, and spake unto her that kept the door, and brought in Peter. Then saith the damsel that kept the door unto Peter, Art not thou also one of this man's disciples? He saith, I am not. And the servants and officers stood there, who had made a fire of coals; for it was cold: and they warmed themselves: and Peter stood with them, and warmed himself.* (John 18:15–18)

CHURCH OF EQUALITY, HUMILITY, SERVICE, AND LOVE

> *And Simon Peter stood and warmed himself. They said therefore unto him, Art not thou also one of his disciples? He denied it, and said, I am not. One of the servants of the high priest, being his kinsman whose ear Peter cut off, saith, Did not I see thee in the garden with him? Peter then denied again: and immediately the cock crew.* (John 18:25-27)

For some time I was tempted to bypass this text in which Jesus reminds Peter that he would not stay as loyal and faithful as Peter expected he would. We know the story that Peter then denied Jesus three times before the cock crowed, though John does not recount the events till the story unfolds in chapter 18. Peter would not have understood the prophetic voice Jesus used in John 13:36, that he, Peter, would not be able to accompany Jesus through his trial and death, though 'afterwards' he does follow him very faithfully, defending Jesus very powerfully to the high priests (Acts 4:1-22) and becoming leader of the church in Rome before being martyred himself on a cross.

Later, John justifies his version of events by including an eyewitness statement. Although we cannot identify this 'other disciple' (John 18:15-16) for certain, the gospel implies it is John himself.[133] Mark notes that after the arrest in the garden, the other disciples fled, though Peter followed some way behind (Mark 14:50, 54). John supplies details of the situation inside the priest's courtyard.

John is clear on the sequence of events. Peter's first denial is before the interrogation (John 18:19-24), and his second and third are afterwards. Twice he denies the question, *Art not thou also one of this man's disciples?* Peter has succumbed to the fear of being exposed as one of Jesus' followers and probably to the fear that if he admits he is a disciple, he too will be taken in for questioning. He is not ready for this.

For me, this question is, in spiritual terms, "Do you believe in the Light and follow the light of Jesus?" For a disciple is one who learns; *discipulus* is Latin for 'pupil'. Even after a year of meditation and prayer with the gospel, I was not ready to publicly declare my submission to Jesus and his Light, not even to my own Quaker meetings, let alone in public. It was something I wanted to keep quiet about until I was more certain. I was fearful about declaring this because people might think me weird and also because I was afraid I would not be able to justify and speak clearly about it when questioned. Peter was in me, too.

Why does John insert this anecdote about fear immediately after Jesus gives the new commandment? It is because he knows that the opposite of love is not hate, it is fear. The destroyer of love is fear. Jesus often says in his ministry, "Do not be afraid".[134] John is well aware of our human frailties and uses this story of Peter to draw attention to the difficulties we will face on the journey. Some have commented that these verses are not very complimentary to Peter. Perhaps not, but let us not think that it is only Peter who has the problem. The problem is ours, too; we will all find ourselves praying for courage or faith.

The third denial is Peter's response to the question, *Did not I see thee in the garden with him?* This question places Peter not just as a follower and disciple but as a person who was part of the group close to Jesus, who was with him and knew where he could be found, in contravention of the high priest's instructions that people should let the religious authorities know where Jesus was (John 11:57). The danger is now much closer, for Peter might be interrogated not just as a follower but as an actual accomplice. No wonder Peter is scared to admit the relationship and denies it again.

In mystical terms, Peter has had to face within himself that he has not only been attracted to Jesus' ministry and followed him but has actually experienced being in Jesus' presence in the garden. He cannot admit to himself that Jesus is really the one he must acknowledge before all others. He has experienced and understands the power of the Light but is not able to put his other, worldly expectations and fears aside.

Then the cock crows—the instant of recognition, the awful recognition of what he has done, that dreadful moment when he recognises he has lived a lie. Have we not all felt this? Is this not the reason we have so much trouble living up to the new commandment? Where is the courage we need, the courage of Jesus, the courage of the early Christians and early Friends? Thomas Merton writes:

> But underlying all life is the ground of doubt and self-questioning which sooner or later must bring us face to face with the ultimate meaning of our life. This self-questioning can never be without a certain sense of existential "dread"—a sense of insecurity, of "lostness", of exile, of sin. A sense that one has somehow been untrue not so much to abstract moral or social norms but to one's inmost truth. "Dread" in this sense is not simply a childish fear of retribution, or a naïve guilt, a fear of violating taboos. It is the profound awareness that one is capable of ultimate bad faith with himself and others: that one is living a lie.[135]

Fortunately for us, the cock crows in the early morning as the herald of dawn. The spiritual day of light beckons us once we have come face-to-face with the darkness of our own inner denial.

CHAPTER 15
PRIESTLY INSTRUCTIONS FOR THE WAY TO LIFE AND PEACE

Jesus' prayerful summaries are impossible to fully understand, let alone make them a reality in our lives, without dealing with the issues that John has patiently taken us through in his gospel. We have to face the scale of change required in letting go of our own need to control, confronting our own material desires, escaping our reliance on habitual rituals, and surrendering our lives to the guidance of the inward Light.

> *Let not your heart be troubled: ye believe in God, believe also in me. In my Father's house are many mansions: if it were not so, I would have told you. I go to prepare a place for you. And if I go and prepare a place for you, I will come again, and receive you unto myself; that where I am, there ye may be also. And whither I go ye know, and the way ye know.*
> (John 14:1–4)

Let not your heart be troubled, believe in God—this is sound advice for all of us. Jesus focuses our attention on the real relationship to be pursued, that with God. Fortunately, there are many places or mansions, plenty of space, and we do not all have to be of exactly the same mould, because in the many rooms we all may find our place. There are many individual paths by which one comes to know God. In another sense, there are several stages along the spiritual path. Teresa of Avila listed seven mansions in *The Interior Castle*.

Thankfully, Jesus goes ahead to prepare the way and will return to receive us. We can follow the path secure in the knowledge that Jesus has prepared the way in front of us. This is the path towards God, not the path to worldly security and status. There are no guarantees of worldly safety and success. None of that is relevant.

I Am the Way

> *Thomas saith unto him, Lord, we know not whither thou goest; and how can we know the way? Jesus saith unto him, I am the way, the truth, and the life: no man cometh unto the Father, but by me. (John 14:5-6)*

"I am the way, the truth, and the life" are core words of Jesus' ministry. Often misunderstood, they have blocked many. Priests have mistakenly insisted on external creedal conformity, arguing that this is the only way and that all other churches and interpretations are wrong, cannot lead you to salvation, and in fact will lead you to damnation. I have known people living far more virtuous lives in other religious groups than I saw in suburban and national Christianity.

Now I am reconciled. For me, Jesus was absolutely correct. Keep his commandments, not just as abstract sayings but in practice in everyday life. The way he taught is the only way, and in that sense he is the Way.

For me, these words of Jesus mean: Do what I have done, follow what I have taught and shown you; there is no other way to enter the Presence of God.

Where do Jesus' teachings come from? They do not arise from his human side, and they do not come from any human ego. They come from his divine side, the "I Am", from his being the Christ, a manifestation of the Presence of God. This is not a statement of Jesus referring to his own ego. Jesus has made it abundantly clear he only works because of God flowing through him.

This "I Am", like the Light within, is in each of us, too. The only way is to act like Christ, following daily the Light within, drawing on that divine source within each of us, allowing that Light to transform us gradually into humility and holiness.

Jesus' statement that he is the only Way was very true within his own time and in his own generation. We know now of other teachers such as the Buddha who have also taught the same Christ-like path to enlightenment and salvation.

Many today, like the early Quakers, do believe that Jesus is the one and only Way, that the Light of Jesus alone has the power to save and redeem from sin. Why do we resist this notion?

> *If ye had known me, ye should have known my Father also: and from henceforth ye know him, and have seen him. Philip saith unto him, Lord, shew us the Father, and it sufficeth us. Jesus saith unto him, Have I been so long time with you, and yet hast thou not known me, Philip? he that hath seen me hath seen the Father; and how sayest thou then, Show us the Father? Believest thou not that I am in the Father, and the Father in me? the words that I speak unto you I speak not of myself: but the Father that dwelleth in me, he doeth the works.* (John 14:7–10)

Thomas and Philip, both of whom would later be very effective evangelists for Jesus, here at almost the last point before Jesus' death are still uncomprehending yet honest enough to say so. They cannot fully grasp the depth of Jesus' message. Is there a touch of frustration in Jesus' reply?[136] Thomas has not grasped what is required to travel the Way to God, and Philip has not grasped that Jesus is actually God in action.

Jesus reiterates his message: The Way is to follow his teachings and exercise love, gentleness, patience, mercy, compassion, and selflessness. For Philip, Jesus repeats that whatever signs and teachings he has done have been God's doing through him. For us, we are invited to follow Jesus, whom we experience as the inward Light.

If Ye Love Me, Keep My Commandments

> *If ye love me, keep my commandments. And I will pray the Father, and he shall give you another Comforter, that he may abide with you for ever; Even the Spirit of truth; whom the world cannot receive, because it seeth him not, neither knoweth him: but ye know him; for he dwelleth with you, and shall be in you. I will not leave you comfortless: I will come to you. . . . At that day ye shall know that I am in my Father, and ye in me, and I in you.* (John 14:15–18, 20)

> *Those who obey my commandments are the ones who love me, and those who love me will be loved by Abba God. I, too, will love them and will reveal myself to them. . . . Those who love me will be true to my word, and Abba God will love them; and we will come to them and make our dwelling place with them.* (John 14:21, 23–24 TIB)

As Jesus says: Any person who loves me keeps my words close at all times and does as they instruct. The result is that the Holy Spirit, the Comforter and Guide, will come to be present within us. This Spirit parallels the female voice of Wisdom, the Spirit of God that spoke to the prophets in the Old Testament. *The Inclusive Bible* also uses the feminine voice:

> *The Paraclete, the Holy Spirit whom Abba God will send in my name, will instruct you in everything and she will remind you of all that I have told you.* (John 14:26–27 TIB)

Many identify the Paraclete as the comforting presence of the Holy Spirit.[137] I find it also signifies the mystical presence of Jesus, who embodied the Spirit of Truth, the Light of Christ, returning to visit my soul.

Our experience is that "the Spirit dwelleth in us". When we hear or apprehend the words of the Holy Spirit, we know they are truthful. Do we follow them, modify them according to our own wishes, or even totally ignore them? If we choose to ignore them, we risk running from the Presence, out of the Light, and into inner darkness again.

However, if we do follow what Jesus instructs, we too experience closeness with God, for we are loved by God and by Jesus, and Jesus promises that *I, too, will love them, and will reveal myself to them* (John 14:21 TIB). This experience of sensing Jesus' presence has come to many people. It does not happen often to a particular individual, but it is unforgettable when it does. The early Quakers used the words, "Jesus has come to teach people himself".

Jesus is not teaching that the way to God is barely possible, with each of us in a state of sin against which we can never make much progress so that we risk dying and being condemned to hell for eternity. Jesus is teaching a way that involves receiving the spiritual comfort and guidance during this life, to bring us closer and closer to God. Our part is to keep the commandments God has given through him—to live in love and trust. We are not to be troubled or afraid. This is a life of deep intimacy with Jesus and God. The Spirit is divine teacher, Guide, and Comforter.

Thomas Kelly describes this developing contact with God, each abiding in the other, that is fostered by our desire for God and God's desire for each of us:

> It is the drama of the lost sheep wandering in the wilderness, restless and lonely, feebly searching, while over the hills comes the wiser Shepherd. For His is a shepherd's heart, and He is restless until He holds His Sheep in His arms. It is the drama of the Eternal Father drawing the prodigal home unto Himself, where there is bread enough and to spare. It is the drama of the Double Search, as Rufus Jones calls it. And always its chief actor is—the Eternal God of Love.[138]

Pope Gregory I explains how to prove one's love of Jesus as follows:

> If any one of you should be asked if he loved God, he would answer with entire confidence and complete conviction, 'I do'. But you heard at the beginning of the reading what Truth said: 'If anyone loves me, he will keep my word.' The proof of love is its manifestation in deeds.[139]

The new Way did not and does not require church doctrines. Jesus did not set up churches and doctrines; he set up a way of life and prayer. And that life and prayer is possible because the Spirit and the Light are present with us. It is our experience that the Spirit of Truth is within, waiting to be discovered and tapped.

Jesus offers peace, though not the peace of the world and not just lack of conflict with others (John 14:27). This peace is not to be gained by outward rituals. No longer is the sacrifice to God required of the burnt offerings of lambs, rams, and goats specified under Mosaic law.[140]

It is the peace that comes from giving up our own desires and surrendering to love, as Jesus did, making a personal and inner sacrifice. If there be any doubt about this relinquishment of his own agenda, Jesus makes it abundantly clear:

> *I won't speak much more with you, because the ruler of this world, who has no hold on me, is at hand; but I do this that the world may know that I love Abba God and do as my Abba has commanded.* (John 14:30–31 TIB)

It is the peace Jesus felt within himself, having done what was required of him, and he was ready to share it with his disciples. It is the incomparable inner peace experienced when we are reconciled to God, no matter what the surrounding worldly situation.

CHAPTER 16
THE SPIRITUAL COMMUNITY

The Vine—Intimate Union with Jesus and God

> I am the true vine, and my Father is the husbandman. Every branch in me that beareth not fruit he taketh away: and every branch that beareth fruit, he purgeth it, that it may bring forth more fruit. Now ye are clean through the word which I have spoken unto you. Abide in me, and I in you. As the branch cannot bear fruit of itself, except it abide in the vine; no more can ye, except ye abide in me. I am the vine, ye are the branches: He that abideth in me, and I in him, the same bringeth forth much fruit: for without me ye can do nothing. (John 15:1–5)

The verses *I am the true vine, and my Father is the husbandman. Every branch in me that beareth not fruit he taketh away: and every branch that beareth fruit, he purgeth it* are extraordinary statements in which Jesus freely admits that he himself is subject to God's ministrations. Jesus is clear that it is "my Father" who is removing "every branch in me" and who is doing the pruning. Jesus is clearly conveying his own experience, that he feels the pruning. This is a clear admission that Jesus is subject to God.

Jesus' analogy is that he is the vine and we are the branches, with God as the husbandman or gardener. Two separate actions are described: removal of unproductive wood and pruning of the fruiting wood. The plant grows more strongly if the diseased or dead wood, those unproductive parts of ourselves, are removed. Once the work for each season has been done, any excess growth is cut back.

The bearing branches are, in Jesus' word (in the KJV), 'purged'—that is, cleansed and emptied. In the vineyard, all the fruit is removed, the leaves die back and fall during autumn, and the gardener trims back the fruiting stems. In these ways, the vine is prepared for the new fruit that will grow the following year. Similarly, do we need pruning after each work undertaken in the guidance of the Spirit? Many who have given ministry or undertaken witness then feel empty and spend time quietly, allowing the Spirit to trim inwardly in preparation for the next work.

There is a time for every purpose under heaven, and when that purpose has been achieved, much as I might like to relax in the glow of the job well done, I always need to withdraw. The Light exposes any flourishing of self-satisfaction.

John 15:3 emphasises the 'word' again. A great spiritual teacher can enlighten a disciple with the right word at the perfect time. Is this what Jesus is saying? The text does not say that his listeners will become clean through his word or words but that they are clean already; they are purged and cleansed. Perhaps Jesus is referring to a prayer word, a single word, or maybe just supreme attentiveness, which he has taught them to use as a way into the Presence of God.

Those parts of ourselves that are no longer useful will be stripped away. A grapevine in winter is a very stark and bare skeleton. The glorious foliage and fruit from the previous season have been ruthlessly pruned off to prepare for new growth. For those involved seriously in the spiritual journey, we can expect a similar pruning of old habits or cherished items.

St. Bonaventure meditated extensively on this theme, explaining that the pruning was not just cutting out bits here and there.[141] Bonaventure notes that Jesus experienced the most severe pruning a human being is asked to endure. The home, possessions, and wealth we expect in life were cut from him, and he traveled with nothing to his name. He was pruned of almost all human support during his ministry, enduring constant antagonism from religion and state, and was deserted by almost all his supporters at his death. Even his clothes were taken, so he died alone, penniless, and naked. Yet the fruit of his life is abundant.

Eighteenth-century Quaker Luke Cock describes how his life changed as some of his habits were pruned:

> I remember when I first met with my Guide. He led me into a very large and cross [place], where I was to speak the truth from my heart —and before I used to swear and lie too for gain. 'Nay, then', said I to my Guide, 'I mun leave Thee here: if Thou leads me up that lane, I can never follow: I'se be ruined of this butchering trade, if I mun't lie for gain.'

> Here I left my Guide, and was filled with sorrow, and went back to the Weeping Cross: and I said, if I could find my good Guide again, I'll follow Him, lead me whither he will. So here I found my Guide again, and began to follow him up this lane and tell the truth from my heart. I had been nought but beggary and poverty before; and now began to thrive at my trade, and got to the end of this lane, though with some difficulty.[142]

The branch cannot bear fruit of itself, just as our life is barren without the presence of the Spirit. Our life bears fruit only because we are part of this vine, so that the sap of love and life enlivens our thoughts and words and actions. We are as intimately related to God as a branch is to the vine.

The mention of a vineyard would have recalled several teachings from the Old Testament for Jesus' hearers, for the vineyard was a common symbol of the Israelites as the community of God's people (Isaiah 5:1-7; Jeremiah 2:21). Yet in Jesus' hands these teachings are revealed not as a vine destroyed in punishment for sin but as a vine ready for growth and fruitfulness.

For me these verses are a teaching on spiritual community. Jesus does not say we are the plants in the field and he is the soil and water that enables each of us to grow. His analogy is of one vine. We are all connected, to each other and to the divine source of life, as a spiritual community. That is why we have to take great care with our own words and deeds and not introduce infections to the plant, lest they spread through the community.

Though each of the branches is separate, faces a different way, grows into a different shape, and produces its own bunch of fruit, yet each exists as part of the same vine. Some parts of each of us might want to be our own vine, maybe even a different plant, a special plant growing somewhere else, recognizable as an important individual plant. We are asked to lay aside this self-interest, to be part of a spiritual community, and to utilise fully our measure of the divine sap of life and love.

Abide in My Love

> *As my Abba has loved me, so have I loved you. Live on in my love. And you will live on in my love if you keep my commandments, just as I live on in Abba God's love and have kept God's commandments.* (John 15:9–10 TIB)

> *These things have I spoken unto you, that my joy might remain in you, and that your joy might be full. This is my commandment, That ye love one another, as I have loved you. Greater love hath no man than this, that a man lay down his life for his friends.* (John 15:11–13)

Jesus confirms that the love he dispenses comes from God. Previously he made it clear that he was instructed and empowered by God. Now he admits it is also God's love that flows through him.

This text summarises again (see John 14:15–23) the possibility of an extremely intimate and reciprocal relationship with Jesus and God. If any of us abides in another's love, as in marriage or between close friends, then we experience that love not only in tangible ways but also as a pervading presence in our lives. We are invited into that pervading presence with Jesus and God. Our part is to keep the commandments of love, and in so doing we receive Jesus' and God's love and support.

I understand abiding as a conscious wish and practice to be attentive to the Light within, whether each of us experiences that as the Holy Spirit, as the presence of Jesus, or as a turning to the unknowable God. The more we seek the divine presence, the more it is revealed to us. We live in it and it lives in us.

Abide in me, and I in you is not an esoteric description requiring a sophisticated philosophical explanation. This is a very real spiritual possibility; each of us may become one with God. God is in us, and all our actions are God operating through us as we seek to be completely merged with God. We have come home in the ultimate sense. The seeking, the struggling, the yearning is over. We are, finally, spiritually home.

> *Ye are my friends, if ye do whatsoever I command you. Henceforth I call you not servants; for the servant knoweth not what his lord doeth: but I have called you friends; for all things that I have heard of my Father I have made known unto you. Ye have not chosen me, but I have chosen you, and ordained you, that ye should go and bring forth fruit, and that your fruit should remain: that whatsoever ye shall ask of the Father in my name, he may give it you. These things I command you, that ye love one another.* (John 15:14-17)

Ye are my friends, that is, the friends of Jesus, is a statement of a mysterious and reciprocal relationship. It is potentially also the kind of relationship we have with each other, knowing each other in the things that are eternal, responding to that of God in each other.[143] Parts of our friendships with each other are easily explained and quite tangible, but other parts are far less easy to put in words. Exodus 33:7-11 describes the situation when Moses spent time in the tabernacle, the tent of meeting, and in this deeply sacred encounter, *The LORD would speak to Moses face to face, as one speaks to a friend* (NIV). In the Bhagavad Gita, Krishna begins to reveal the mysteries of the spiritual journey to divine union and assures the despondent Arjuna: "Today I am revealing to thee this Yoga eternal, this secret supreme: because of thy love for me, and because I am thy friend" (4:3).

There is no greater love than to lay down one's life for a friend, and we know Jesus is about to do this. Yet that decision happens also in reverse, for each of us has to lay down part of ourselves to be a friend of Jesus. Each of us has to allow our former life, focussed on worldly things, to die that we may be reborn spiritually.

Jesus is contrasting the roles of servant and friend. Service can result in a sense of duty. We know the value of service in the committed life—so what is Jesus saying here? His point is that our lives are no longer to be lived as service in the sense of a servant following instructions. We are instead to be friends to all and in so doing to be free of obligations and duty.[144] We act as friends, willingly placing another's needs high on our agenda, never cheating or harming or dishonouring another, and acting with honesty and love. In this we do service freely, without the overburden of duty.

Many of these verses repeat themselves, in slightly different forms or contexts, and Jesus' homily ends with his commandment *that ye love one another.* Surely this repetition related to love is simply because it is so important that we are asked to meditate on it repeatedly. How often do I make a decision or movement in life while forgetting to have done this?

To love one another is more than being a good neighbour, vital as that is. It means ensuring no petty jealousies or our need for self-recognition and self-justification invade our responses. We are asked to take great care not to place stumbling blocks and to have tender concern for another's soul. This is the spiritual community to which we are called, the blessed community. This community is where we can be as honest and plain and unhurtful with others as we are in our inner prayers with God.

> *When the Paraclete comes—the Spirit of Truth who comes from Abba God, whom I myself will send from my Abba—she will bear witness on my behalf. You too must bear witness, for you've been with me from the beginning.* (John 15:26-27 TIB)

The mutual path with God is finally emphasised when Jesus reiterates that we will receive the Holy Spirit as Paraclete, that we know also as Comforter and Guide. This Guide does in my experience recall the words of Jesus, passages from Scripture, at the time they are needed, whether they be words of solace or of reproof.

Our spiritual journey to salvation does not involve a lifetime of self-abasement to give us a chance of finally getting to God when we die. The spiritual journey outlined by Jesus is one of reciprocal and mutual love between God and us. Jesus is offering the possibility to become "children of God" in this way.

The Quaker poet John Greenleaf Whittier expressed his prayer for such a transformation:

> Clothe with life the weak intent,
> Let me be the thing I meant;
> Let me find in Thy employ
> Peace that dearer is than joy;
> Out of self to love be led... [145]

CHAPTER 17
COMFORT, GUIDANCE, AND HOPE

Promise of the Holy Spirit Again

> *They shall put you out of the synagogues: yea, the time cometh, that whosoever killeth you will think that he doeth God service. And these things will they do unto you, because they have not known the Father, nor me.* (John 16:2-3)

As he prepares for his own death and return to God, Jesus recognises the gulf that will be created and the difficulties his disciples will face. The worldly powers will harass his disciples just as they persecuted him. How will they cope when he is not there to reassure and guide them? How will they maintain commitment and hope?

Jesus repeats again (14:15-18, 25-26; 15:26-27; 16:7) the future gift of the Spirit as a Comforter and Guide. The Comforter will have three abilities: first, to recall and testify of Jesus and his teachings, second, to expose and reprove sin, and third, to provide comfort and solace.

> *Nevertheless I tell you the truth; It is expedient for you that I go away: for if I go not away, the Comforter will not come unto you; but if I depart, I will send him unto you.* (John 16:7)

> *When the Spirit of truth comes, she will guide you into all truth. She won't speak on her own initiative; rather, she'll speak only what she hears and she'll announce to you things that are to come.* (John 16:13 TIB)

Jesus knows he must go, as he showed physically when he departed up into the mountain after the feeding of the five thousand (John 6:15). He had to leave then to escape people's desire to put him on a worldly pedestal. Now near the end of his life, he reiterates the same message: He must go so that people will stop placing him in worldly kingship. His message and leadership is in the spiritual plane. Only when he is gone will people seek him spiritually and come to understand his real message. He also knows the Spirit will be needed to guide us into all truth. William Shewen wrote about this in 1683:

> It is a true saying which Christ spoke to his Disciples, when he said, *if I go not away, the Comforter will not come.* There is much in the words; many have read them, but have not understood what they read; for it is a blessed thing to know the going away of Christ after the flesh, and to be able to say, as one of old did, *know I him so no more.* They are those that know him come again in the Spirit as a comforter, as a prince of peace, and are witnesses of his peaceable government in their souls, and can say, *he is come, and we look not for another.*[146]

Jesus is telling us that, of all the spirits possible, it is the Spirit of Truth that is the true messenger from God. John in 16:13 is clear that the Spirit of Truth, the Holy Spirit, will convey what God has given to be said and shown. Yes, it will be a Comforter because it brings the comfort of God. Yes, a teacher and Guide, or Advocate (NIV), because the Spirit brings the guidance of God who knows all things and who does not need to be asked because God knows exactly what our spiritual welfare requires (e.g., Matthew 6:8). The Spirit is the messenger who brings comfort and words from God and is known only to the inward spiritual being, not to the outer worldly being. Elias Hicks put it as follows:

> In and under the gospel dispensation, the law and covenant is spiritual and universal—written in the heart of every rational being under heaven—and is therefore invisible to all the external senses and is only manifested by its fruits. And as the law and covenant are spiritual and internal, so likewise, the Messiah and the Comforter of the gospel dispensation are spiritual, and only internally and spiritually known and manifested—and is universally manifested to all the children of men the world over, and by whom the gospel is preached in every rational creature.[147]

Pray for Courage and Hope

> *And ye now therefore have sorrow: but I will see you again, and your heart shall rejoice, and your joy no man taketh from you. And in that day ye shall ask me nothing. Verily, verily, I say unto you, Whatsoever ye shall ask the Father in my name, he will give it you. Hitherto have ye asked nothing in my name: ask, and ye shall receive, that your joy may be full.* (John 16:22-24)

Jesus makes two promises. The first is that he will return, that he will see each of us again, and that we will feel joy in our hearts. This promise is made good initially for his disciples when he reappears to them in the closed room after his death and again a week later.

The second promise is that, if we are in need, we can pray to God for help and help will be given.

Jesus reflects on his own human struggle, the life of intense prayer and growing obedience:

> *These things I have spoken unto you, that in me ye might have peace. In the world ye shall have tribulation: but be of good cheer; I have overcome the world.* (John 16:33)

Those are the last words he says to the assembled disciples, and it is a conclusive statement—he has overcome the world. His example is the way to overcome all the difficulties and confusions we experience. He has actually done it. He has been able to count the world as nothing and follow the leadings of his *Abba*, his God. He has entered into suffering and has come out the other side.

In the modern sense, 'cheerful' conveys a sense of being in good spirits, stable, contented, and helpful, maybe even happy-go-lucky. The term 'of good cheer' is slightly different and means a frame of mind that is stout-hearted, courageous, and hopeful.

The latter term is used elsewhere, for example, by Paul as reassurance to those onboard when the ship was sinking and all were much alarmed (Acts 27:22). Paul knew this feeling from his time in Jerusalem when he was in danger of being assaulted and perhaps lynched, and yet God spoke to him saying be of good cheer for you are yet to go to Rome to be a witness (Acts 23:11). Jesus himself had used the term with his disciples who were afraid in the boat during a stormy night at sea (Mark 6:50).

In John 16:33, Jesus is saying, in different words, what he said in 14:27: *Peace I leave with you, my peace I give unto you: not as the world giveth, give I unto you. Let not your heart be troubled, neither let it be afraid.* His message here is, "Keep hope". In this, he comforts and reassures, recalling the great message at the end of Matthew's gospel: *and, lo, I am with you always, even unto the end of the world* (28:20).

CHAPTER 18
JESUS' OWN PRAYERS BEFORE GOD

Supplication, Vows, and Intercession

Jesus begins his priestly prayers, his final prayers to God, as he prepares to leave his disciples, and his prayers are addressed to his *Abba* (Father), his God. It is a prayer of self-dedication in that, having carried out his ministry, he now prepares for the final stage of his earthly life.

The ancient sequence of prayers involved four types: supplication, vows, intercessions, and thanksgiving.[148] Supplications are the acknowledgement of God as the source of all—as Jesus says, *all things whatsoever thou hast given me are of thee* (John 17:7)—and of our own need for mercy and support. The vows—or prayers, as they are sometimes specifically termed—are our own promises to do something. Intercessions are prayers for others, and thanksgivings are expressions of gratitude for spiritual and material blessings. Jesus' prayers have a sense of thanksgiving for God's love and support that has enabled him to fulfil the promises he made to care for his flock. His main prayers are of supplication and intercession.

Jesus says, in essence, "I have done all that you asked me to do on earth. But I know it does not stop here. I am ready for the next stage and to undertake whatever is required to unite me again with you, as we were before time began". This is a complete dedication of his remaining life to do whatever it takes to achieve that union with God. There is no holding back, no ifs, ands, or buts.

For me, the first verses are a very deep prayer of supplication, which says, in my words, "I recognise and admit that you, O God, are the source of all and the one to whom I long to return".

> *I have glorified thee on the earth: I have finished the work which thou gavest me to do. And now, O Father, glorify thou me with thine own self with the glory which I had with thee before the world was.*

> *I have manifested thy name unto the men which thou gavest me out of the world: thine they were, and thou gavest them me; and they have kept thy word. Now they have known that all things whatsoever thou hast given me are of thee. For I have given unto them the words which thou gavest me; and they have received them, and have known surely that I came out from thee, and they have believed that thou didst send me.* (John 17:4-8)

In saying "I have manifested", Jesus is confirming he has not just stood up and talked about God as a preacher, he has actually lived God's instructions and made them real for people. He has shown what God can do and what God wants of people. He also confirms that everything he has done was given to him by God. Nothing could be clearer than at this point Jesus is saying, "On earth I have done God's will, and I could have done not a thing of it without God".

> *I pray for them: I pray not for the world, but for them which thou hast given me; for they are thine. And all mine are thine, and thine are mine; and I am glorified in them. And now I am no more in the world, but these are in the world, and I come to thee. Holy Father, keep through thine own name those whom thou hast given me, that they may be one, as we are. While I was with them in the world, I kept them in thy name: those that thou gavest me I have kept, and none of them is lost, but the son of perdition; . . .* (17:9-12)

> *I pray not that thou shouldest take them out of the world, but that thou shouldest keep them from the evil. They are not of the world, even as I am not of the world. Sanctify them through thy truth: thy word is truth. As thou hast sent me into the world, even so have I also sent them into the world. And for their sakes I sanctify myself, that they also might be sanctified through the truth.* (John 17:15-19)

Jesus prays that God accept that he has fulfilled his vows, which leads into an intercession for his disciples, for those people who were drawn to him by the inward prompting of God. Having received them as his companions and followers, he has discharged his duty of caring for their spiritual lives and giving them what God gave him. He does not pray they be removed from worldly temptation and labour but that they be protected from evil.

> *Neither pray I for these alone, but for them also which shall believe on me through their word; That they all may be one; as thou, Father, art in me, and I in thee, that they also may be one in us: that the world may believe that thou hast sent me. And the glory which thou gavest me I have given them; that they may be one, even as we are one: I in them, and thou in me, that they may be made perfect in one; and that the world may know that thou hast sent me, and hast loved them, as thou hast loved me.* (John 17:20–23)

Vision of Unity with Jesus and God

Now Jesus prays as an intercession for the well-being of his followers, for their spiritual protection and sanctification. He prays for those in the future who will come to believe in him. Jesus understands only too well the immense struggle each person undertakes to follow faithfully the spiritual quest. The final aim of this quest is unity with each other and with God. This mystical situation is completely at odds with rational thought, completely at odds with an emphasis on strong individuality, completely at odds with desiring one's own ends rather than living for God.

> *Father, I will that they also, whom thou hast given me, be with me where I am; that they may behold my glory, which thou hast given me: for thou lovedst me before the foundation of the world. O righteous Father, the world hath not known thee: but I have known thee, and these have known that thou hast sent me. And I have declared unto them thy name, and will declare it: that the love wherewith thou hast loved me may be in them, and I in them.* (John 17:24–26)

Jesus continues his prayer for all those who follow him that they themselves will experience the love of God as he has experienced it and will experience Jesus' presence within them. That is, they will be united together in the love of God. This unity was one of the hallmarks of right decisions for early Friends. This unity is a hallmark of understanding and accepting God's will. It means there is no cause for friction, division, or discontent between Friends. It comes from all dwelling in the Light and experiencing the love of God.

There are times when I can feel those past, and Jesus in particular, praying me into existence.

Jesus is a heavenly man in the sense that his life is totally at one with God's will. In no place does he say "I am equal to God", though he does say he is one with the *Abba* and also that for those who keep his commandments, they too can become one with himself and *Abba* (John 17:11).

We know from other statements by Jesus that the Holy Spirit "whom I will send" is essentially a messenger, teacher, and Guide. Jesus' 'dream' as explained in John 17 is that we as humans may become one with himself and God, and the path is one of following divine leadings, of continuing faithfulness, of holy obedience, which he so perfectly modelled. The Light is the Guide for this journey.

It comes to me at times to ask, when faced with a dilemma of how to respond, what will bring unity, not necessarily unity with others, for that may just mean falling falsely into line, but what will bring unity with God—and in the company of committed Friends, this will bring unity amongst us too. George Fox had much to say on this:

> For all dwelling in the Light that comes from Jesus, it leads out of wars, leads out of strife, leads out of the occasion of wars, and leads out of the earth and up to God, and out of earthly mindedness into heavenly mindedness.[149]

> All they that are in the light are in unity; for the light is but one. . . . All who know the word, which is a mystery, are come to the beginning, are sanctified by the word, and clean through the word; . . . and this is a word of reconciliation, that reconcileth together to God, and gathers the hearts of his together, to live in love and unity one with another, and lets them see how they have been strangers and aliens from the life of God. . . . Abiding inwardly in the light, it will let you see one another and the unity one with another.[150]

CHAPTER 19
TRIALS AND CRUCIFIXION

Nonviolence, Submission, and Yielding in the Struggle between Light and Dark

We come now to the climax of the gospel, where John focuses our attention intensely on Jesus and the struggle between light and dark, between a life led by the Spirit and a life dictated by the demands of the world. There are no long discourses, and the events speak for themselves. If we feel emotionally involved and even in turmoil, that is acceptable. We are being drawn into this experience, and it is a shocking experience we would not like for ourselves nor ever wish on another. Yet it has been reality for many, and such suffering continues to the present day.

One of the extraordinary aspects is the anticipation and acceptance Jesus had of his death. He had alluded to it many times during the previous three years, sometimes directly (Luke 9:21-22, 43-45; 18:31-33; 22:1-6; John 10:31-33, 39; 11:8, 16), sometimes less directly (Luke 9:31; John 3:14). He was aware of the prophecies that the Christ would suffer and be killed (Psalm 22; Isaiah 53; Zechariah 13:7), and his later words on the road to Emmaus make it clear he knew he was the Christ (Luke 24:26). In contrast to many who fear death and do everything to evade it, which we link to natural animal instincts for survival, Jesus seemed to see his death as a natural and essential part of his life. He knew very deeply that *for this cause came I unto this hour* (John 12:27). Nicholas Peter Harvey writes that:

> Jesus' approach to his death as something desired, as something without which his destiny would be unfulfilled, left his friends in total disarray.... As the sense of death as desirable begins to emerge we are freed to live fully in the present rather than being trapped in the present.... Any failure to make Jesus' death central leaves us with a decentred theology, which may result in a preaching Jesus, an exemplary Jesus, a Jesus of

confrontation, a justice-and-peace Jesus, or a blandly resurrected Jesus. All of these ... make the mistaken assumption that the gospel is about some version of the good life rather than life with the living God. In thus distorting and diminishing Jesus we do drastically less than justice to ourselves and the possibilities of our own vocation.[151]

Jesus leads his disciples across the Kidron Brook onto the Mount of Olives and into the garden of Gethsemane, where he spends time in prayer, as is recorded in the other gospels (Mark 14:32-41; Luke 22:39-46). The Jewish authorities had not dared arrest him in daylight, fearing a strong reaction by the common people (Luke 19:47-48, 22:1-2; John 18:20-21). At night, out of the public eye, Jesus is identified by Judas Iscariot, arrested by a group of armed men sent by the high priest, and led away for questioning.

Later, Peter draws a sword and slices off the ear of the high priest's servant to defend Jesus from arrest, an act of misplaced protective violence and courage that Jesus immediately heals (John 18:10; Luke 22:50-51).

> *The high priest then asked Jesus of his disciples, and of his doctrine. Jesus answered him, I spake openly to the world; I ever taught in the synagogue, and in the temple, whither the Jews always resort; and in secret have I said nothing. Why askest thou me? ask them which heard me, what I have said unto them: behold, they know what I said. And when he had thus spoken, one of the officers which stood by struck Jesus with the palm of his hand, saying, Answerest thou the high priest so? Jesus answered him, If I have spoken evil, bear witness of the evil: but if well, why smitest thou me? (John 18:19-23)*

This interview with the high priest begins an extended interrogation of Jesus as the Jewish leaders try to pin on him an offence punishable by death. Asked about his disciples and doctrines, Jesus avoids giving any explanations that the priest can then seize upon, instead saying, "Ask some witnesses, everything I said was in the open, ask those who heard me". When struck by the officer, Jesus says, "Where is your evidence? Show me the witness that says I have done wrong". Justice is denied him. The powers of government, then as so often now, are interested in achieving their agenda, not in the truth. However, the Jewish leaders know they do not have the power to put Jesus to death, so early in the morning they take him to the Roman governor, Pilate. Pilate's role and dilemma are given full play by John. It is written drama.

> *Then led they Jesus from Caiaphas unto the hall of judgment: and it was early; and they themselves went not into the judgment hall, lest they should be defiled; but that they might eat the passover. Pilate then went out unto them, and said, What accusation bring ye against this man? They answered and said unto him, If he were not a malefactor, we would not have delivered him up unto thee. Then said Pilate unto them, Take ye him, and judge him according to your law. The Jews therefore said unto him, It is not lawful for us to put any man to death: That the saying of Jesus might be fulfilled, which he spake, signifying what death he should die.* (John 18:28-32)

Pilate initially goes out to talk with the Jewish elders, who will not enter the Roman-occupied building in case they transgress one of their religious laws. The irony, the hypocrisy is obvious; the priests will scruple to observe the law but have no scruples about putting a person to death unjustly if it suits them. Again, how commonly have we seen our own powers of government fabricate or exaggerate an excuse to repress or kill individuals while professing to uphold some law or traditional value? The evil intent is very obvious in 18:29-31. Pilate asks, "What is the charge?" The Jews cannot provide one, so they answer, "We would not have gone to the trouble of arresting and bringing him here if he had not done something wrong". Pilate answers directly, "Well, deal with him yourself". The Jews reply, "But we are not allowed to put a man to death". Roman rule stripped that legal responsibility away from colonised peoples; only the Roman governor could sanction the death penalty.

> *Then Pilate entered into the judgment hall again, and called Jesus, and said unto him, Art thou the*

TRIALS AND CRUCIFIXION

> *King of the Jews? Jesus answered him, Sayest thou this thing of thyself, or did others tell it thee of me? Pilate answered, Am I a Jew? Thine own nation and the chief priests have delivered thee unto me: what hast thou done? Jesus answered, My kingdom is not of this world: if my kingdom were of this world, then would my servants fight, that I should not be delivered to the Jews: but now is my kingdom not from hence. Pilate therefore said unto him, Art thou a king then? Jesus answered, Thou sayest that I am a king. To this end was I born, and for this cause came I into the world, that I should bear witness unto the truth. Every one that is of the truth heareth my voice. Pilate saith unto him, What is truth?*
> (John 18:33–38)

The Jerusalem Bible translates the last section of 18:36 as *but my kingdom is not of this kind*, emphasising the message of the previous sections of that verse. My own meditations take the KJV words more literally, and maybe that is the spirit discerned in earlier times: "My kingdom is actually *now*, right here inside you, not something to be fought for and to become a reality in the future". Jesus is not interested in whether he is classified as a king or not. His words are clear—he came to bear witness for the truth; that is the reason he was born.

Pilate returns inside and interviews Jesus, for he is puzzled by the ferocity of the Jewish elders who wish to put Jesus to death since they make no accusation of any crime. The parallels with government powers that mount propaganda campaigns based on no true evidence to whip up public antipathy are obvious. Pilate asks if Jesus is the king of the Jews, and Jesus' reply is noncommittal, asking only if Pilate is willing to own that question himself. Pilate replies, perhaps in sarcasm or perhaps in frustration, "Don't ask me—I'm not a Jew. What have you done?" At this point Jesus takes the opportunity to tell Pilate that he has no interest in the kingdoms of this world; his life has been to show the way to Truth; his is a spiritual quest.

Pilate's parting remark may be sarcastic. "What is truth?" is a question that has flummoxed philosophers for centuries. It may also be a very real statement of the difficulty faced in any court to determine what is really true in the face of conflicting evidence.

What is Truth? The answer is standing in front of Pilate, and he is too blind to see it, for the Light shineth in the darkness and the darkness comprehendeth it not. Subsequent events show Pilate does not link truth and justice very closely. In the presence of Jesus, in the presence of Truth and Light, Pilate is clearly convinced this man has done nothing wrong. Yet when he goes outside into the world again, into darkness, his judgment falters.

> *And when he had said this, he went out again unto the Jews, and saith unto them, I find in him no fault at all. But ye have a custom, that I should release unto you one at the passover: will ye therefore that I release unto you the King of the Jews? Then cried they all again, saying, Not this man, but Barabbas. Now Barabbas was a robber.* (John 18:38-40)

> *Then Pilate therefore took Jesus, and scourged him. And the soldiers platted a crown of thorns, and put it on his head, and they put on him a purple robe, And said, Hail, King of the Jews! and they smote him with their hands. Pilate therefore went forth again, and saith unto them, Behold, I bring him forth to you, that ye may know that I find no fault in him. Then came Jesus forth, wearing the crown of thorns, and the purple robe. And Pilate saith unto them, Behold the man! When the chief priests therefore and officers saw him, they cried out, saying, Crucify him, crucify him. Pilate saith unto them, Take ye him, and crucify him: for I find no fault in him. The Jews answered him, We have a law, and by our law he ought to die, because he made himself the Son of God.* (John 19:1-7)

The Jewish crowd demands Jesus' death and asks Pilate to free the robber Barabbas. One of the great ironies is that Barabbas means 'son of the Father' or 'son of God' (*Bar Abba*). In the event, the one named 'son of the Father' is set free and the one who is son of his *Abba* is murdered.

Pilate cannot silence the clamour of the Jewish elders and their mob, so to appease them he orders Jesus to be scourged, whipped cruelly, and then physically beaten and humiliated, presumably hoping that this punishment will appease the crowd. When Jesus is brought forth to show the effects of these beatings, the crowd still clamours, "Crucify him". Three times Pilate has said Jesus is innocent. Yet now he says, "Well, do it anyway, it is on your heads, because I can find nothing for which to punish him further". The Jewish leaders do not want to take the responsibility themselves; they still want to manipulate the situation so that Pilate has to make the judgment.

Realising their first line of propaganda has failed, they change tack and broach the crime of blasphemy, that Jesus has called himself the Son of God. This does not work either. Pilate is sufficiently affected by this proposal that John records that *he was the more afraid* (19:8). Perhaps made anxious by his wife's dream (Matthew 27:19) and by his own sensitivity to the power of gods, Pilate stalls and returns inside to talk again with Jesus.

> *When Pilate therefore heard that saying, he was the more afraid; And went again into the judgment hall, and saith unto Jesus, Whence art thou? But Jesus gave him no answer. Then saith Pilate unto him, Speakest thou not unto me? knowest thou not that I have power to crucify thee, and have power to release thee? Jesus answered, Thou couldest have no power at all against me, except it were given thee from above: therefore he that delivered me unto thee hath the greater sin. And from thenceforth Pilate sought to release him.* (John 19:8-12)

Jesus is not prepared to enter into a debate on his divinity; perhaps also he was exhausted from the sleepless night and the punishments. As Jesus knew, the Scriptures do in fact allow for us all to be sons (children) of God! He does not speak until he replies that Pilate can only do what he has been given authority to do. Whether Pilate takes this simply as a recognition of the power delegated to him by Caesar or whether he recognises that all life and power come from God is not clear. Pilate recognises the truth of this statement in one form or other, and also he knows that there is still no clear crime for which to execute Jesus. Again Pilate seeks to release Jesus.

The Jewish leaders make a third and last argument, now that their first two have failed. They propose that Jesus has spoken of himself as a king and hence is in opposition to Caesar. The comment that if Pilate lets this man go *thou are not Caesar's friend* is code for Pilate not being politically loyal to his superior, not having looked after the emperor's interests as a friend would. This is really blackmail. They could well say Pilate has not done his duty in defending Caesar. Here is the way out of Pilate's dilemma; he has a reason to execute Jesus and so placate the Jewish mob. He has no need to vacillate any further. He goes to the judgment seat and exclaims to the crowd, "Behold your king". The crowd asks for their king to be crucified. The worldly manipulation, the way of darkness, has succeeded.

> *But the Jews cried out, saying, If thou let this man go, thou art not Caesar's friend: whosoever maketh himself a king speaketh against Caesar. When Pilate therefore heard that saying, he brought Jesus forth, and sat down in the judgment seat in a place that is called the Pavement, but in the Hebrew, Gabbatha. And it was the preparation of the passover, and about the sixth hour: and he saith unto the Jews, Behold your King! But they cried out, Away with him, away with him, crucify him. Pilate saith unto them, Shall I crucify your King? The chief priests answered, We have no king but Caesar. Then delivered he him therefore unto them to be crucified. And they took Jesus, and led him away.*
>
> *And he bearing his cross went forth into a place called the place of a skull, which is called in the Hebrew Golgotha: Where they crucified him, and two others with him, on either side one, and Jesus in the midst. And Pilate wrote a title, and put it on the cross. And the writing was, JESUS OF NAZARETH THE KING OF THE JEWS. This title then read many of the Jews: for the place where Jesus was crucified was nigh to the city: and it was written in Hebrew, and Greek, and Latin. Then said the chief priests of the Jews to Pilate, Write not, The King of the Jews; but that he said, I am King of the Jews. Pilate answered, What I have written I have written. Then*

> *the soldiers, when they had crucified Jesus, took his garments, and made four parts, to every soldier a part; and also his coat: now the coat was without seam, woven from the top throughout.* (John 19:12-23)

So Jesus is led out and crucified, a brutal, agonising, and drawn-out death.[152] From elsewhere we know the two men crucified with him are convicted criminals. One is penitent, the other not. Such is also our choice in the presence of the Light. Do we ourselves continue to justify choices and actions that the Light has shown us are in error, or do we admit the errors?

On the cross is pinned the notice of the crime for which the prisoner has been executed. In Jesus' case it reads "King of the Jews". When the Jews request Pilate change the notice to say just that Jesus said he was king of the Jews, Pilate refuses point-blank. That is the final accusation on which Pilate proclaimed the death sentence. The Jewish leaders have been forced into a blasphemy themselves because they know that God is their king, and yet they have lied that "Caesar is our King" and then succeeded in having Jesus, the man they have had killed, in the end labelled as their king. They have murdered a child of God. There is no escaping the truth shed by the Light. When we come face-to-face with the Light, all is shown for what it really is, not the false impressions we may like to give.

Jesus was crucified naked. Each of the four gospels records that his garments were taken from him and shared amongst those present. Pictures and statues typically show him with a piece of cloth draped across his body to suit our modest tastes, but the truth is he had nothing to cover him and was left completely exposed. Nothing of this world remained. The drama of the trials and execution show an alternation of light and dark. Much of this may have taken place in the early morning, perhaps barely daylight, with the Jewish groups outside while Jesus is inside in a room that was presumably lit by candles. When Pilate is inside with Jesus, in the presence of the Light and Truth, he finds him innocent. When he is outside with the Jewish elders and mob, in the world of darkness, he becomes confused, cannot remain steadfast, and lapses into condemning an innocent man to die. His measure of the Light was so small that he was not able to maintain the clarity of his leading when he went outside into the world and its darkness. Pilate's vacillating to and fro between the opposing demands of the Spirit and the world are part of us, too. Meditation on these passages can be a painful and revealing exercise.

We have not yet reached the resurrection. John, the writer of the gospel, knows very well the struggle that remains to be faced by each of us.

Jesus refuses to be drawn into any of the worldly arguments set by Pilate and the Jewish leaders. Jesus continues to defend his role in establishing a different kingdom, the Presence of God. His ministry has taught that there is a life for people who are centred on God, one in which love is the driving force and where the present barriers erected by petty regulations, by gender, by race, and by wealth have no part to play. Jesus is saying this is all possible if we believe and do what he has taught us, if we follow the Truth.

However, there is to be no coercion. This is not a kingdom as people have normally envisaged it in the world. It is not to be made by fighting with outward weapons. This is made with the path of nonviolence. William Dewsbury wrote about his discovery of spiritual versus physical weaponry:

> At that time did the wars begin in this nation. . . . Then I was willing to give my body to death, in obedience to my God, to free my soul from sin, and I joined with that little remnant which said they fought for the gospel, but I found no rest among them. And the word of the Lord came unto me and said, 'put up thy sword into thy scabbard; if my kingdom were of this world, then would my children fight', which word enlightened my heart and discovered the mystery of iniquity, and that the Kingdom of God was within, and the enemies was within, and was spiritual, and my weapons against them must be spiritual, the power of God. Then I could no longer fight with a carnal weapon against a carnal man, and returned to my outward

calling, and my will was brought in subjection for the Lord to do with me what his will was.[153]

Before starting his ministry, during his long retreat fasting in the desert, Jesus had faced three ways the worldly Self seeks to control an individual (Matthew 4:1-11; Luke 4:1-13). The first temptation was to make bread and thus symbolically receive all that could provide for his appetite and lust; the second was the temptation to see over the vast kingdoms of the world, that is, to have immense power of worldly rule. And the third was the temptation to throw himself off a pinnacle of the temple, that is, to have control of natural events in the manner of God, the delusion of being God. If Jesus had accepted these tempting offers, he could not have succeeded on earth in his spiritual quest. In each case, Jesus, using quotes from the Old Testament, rejected these offers and honoured God as the supreme authority. He came to completely understand and embody the spiritual insight that surrender of his own life was what God was asking of him. If he attempted to establish his spiritual leadership in any other way, it would be false and would fail. As William Temple notes,

> Every one of these conceptions contained truth. Yet if all of these are taken as fully representative of the Kingdom, they have one fatal defect. They all represent ways of securing the outwards obedience of men apart from inner loyalty; they are ways of controlling conduct, but not ways of winning hearts and wills. He might bribe men by promise of good things; he might coerce men to obey by threat of penalty; he might offer irresistible proof; [but] all these rejected methods are essentially appeals to self-interest; and the kingdom of God, who is love, cannot be established that way. . . . The new conception which takes the place of those rejected is that the Son of Man must suffer. For the manifestation of love, by which it wins its response, is sacrifice. The principle of sacrifice is that we choose to do or suffer what apart from our love we should not choose to do or suffer.[154]

Suffering and Sacrifice

So Jesus has brought us face-to-face with a critical act in the spiritual journey—self-sacrifice. Jesus was aware of the hatred against him and knew he would be killed sooner or later, as have been many prophets who challenged the established worldly powers.[155] Justin Martyr, Mohandas Gandhi, Oscar Romero, Martin Luther King Jr., Rachel Corrie, and Tom Fox were also aware of the evil forces ranged against them.

Jesus had foretold this end to his disciples, and he said it again after the resurrection in his conversation with the two disciples on the road to Emmaus: *Ought not Christ to have suffered these things, and to enter into his glory?* (Luke 24:26) It was not a matter of God's predestined will that Jesus should die on the cross; it was Jesus' supreme act of faithfulness. His example is that a life lived in obedience to the Spirit can only be done with some sacrifice. Thank heavens we are not all asked to go through a sacrifice at this horrifying level. However, some level of sacrifice is always required on the journey along the Way. Many who know better than I have written on suffering. My own experience is that suffering happens, for it is part of life. Pain and misfortune and grief have a way of awakening us to our mortality and dependence upon God. Suffering seriously damages the Self (ego), and if we open ourselves to God, we will be comforted.

One of the seven vices Mohandas Gandhi identifies is Worship without Sacrifice. There is no denying the advice of those who have really travelled the path, and Gandhi considered the following traits to be the most spiritually perilous to humanity:
- Wealth without Work
- Pleasure without Conscience
- Science without Humanity
- Knowledge without Character
- Politics without Principle
- Commerce without Morality
- Worship without Sacrifice

It is not that suffering is sent by God to benefit us, no more than any parent would wish a child to be bullied for their benefit. It is that suffering is part of life, a result of natural events and disasters or of the thoughtlessness or malice or evil of others. The Presence of God is always with us, and it is a matter of staying close to the stream of Life that we may know God's Presence whether in joy or in suffering.

Acknowledging the Presence of God in all things is a helpful practice in the good times for then it also can be found in the more difficult events. We learn not to be wise in our own eyes but rather, as Jesus did, to follow in trust the Guide, the Light within. Marcelle Martin puts it this way:

> Jesus did not want to be crucified, but he was willing to surrender his own will, and he carried out a ministry that led to the cross. For Quakers today, to "live in the cross" is to make sacrifices that our limited human will would prefer not to make, and to do so for God's greater purposes.[156]

Nowhere does John in this gospel justify Jesus' crucifixion by referencing the Old Testament, as is done, for example, in the Letter to the Hebrews (9:11-14, 23-28; 10:1-3) comparing the shedding of Jesus' blood to the ancient Hebrew animal sacrifices. This letter does affirm Jesus' commitment to doing what God asks of him (Hebrews 10:7). Nor does John introduce the concept that Jesus was sent to die for our sins.[157] John's point is that Jesus' surrender to death is love—an example of doing what is loving to all people. John is clear that God sent Jesus, teacher and healer, to heal and lead souls to salvation (3:16).

I am sure Jesus knew deeply that what he was about to do would have permanent effects on his disciples and on all those who came after and believed in him. This was the reason for Jesus' instructions and his own prayers recorded in John 14 and John 17.

For me, Jesus was not sent to die for our sins in some prearranged pact with God. Jesus surrendered his earthly life as the final act, consistent with living in the hands of God who only asks us to do good, to reject violence, to love, to be merciful, to be compassionate. Jesus always did what was good, irrespective of what the world around him thought was sensible or fitted their previous notions. His way of dying was the same.

Similarly, our lives are deeper if we do not justify our lives in terms of our caring for others or saving those people over there or changing this law but instead surrender into God's work of having brought us to face these needs and injustices and then follow up by doing what is asked of us, no matter how demanding. We are doing God's work, not ours. As Elias Hicks wrote,

> For if it was the purpose and will of God that he [Jesus] should die by the hands of wicked men, then the Jews, by crucifying him, would have done God's will, and of course, would all have stood justified in his sight—which could not be. But it was permitted so to be, as it had been with many of the prophets and wise and good men that were before him, who suffered death by the hands of wicked men for righteousness sake, as examples to those who come after, that they should account nothing too dear to give up for Truth's sake, not even their own lives.[158]

Jesus, after following God faithfully, found himself rejected by the leaders of his own faith who then accused him falsely and had him executed. He was both an earthly man and a heavenly man. His earthly man yielded in love, mounting no resistance, confronting evil with goodness, speaking only truth, and offering himself as a sacrifice against the darkness of worldly power. Jesus' perfect sacrifice, offered in complete humility, replaces all others, and many have experienced that it is effective. The heavenly man, the Christ within himself, was released so that in some eternally mysterious, inexplicable way, it is available to all those who believe in him. An awful human experience that God enabled him to sanctify enables us to experience release from worldly falsity, fears, and past sins and to open ourselves to the Presence of God within us.

Jesus is not necessarily leading us to sacrifice our own lives. Rather, we are invited to follow his example by sacrificing our own wills and worldly desires, listening for God's Word in the silent depths of our hearts and taking that as our only Guide.

Having been through the process of suffering and sacrifice himself, Jesus is able to confirm his invitation:

> *Come unto me, all ye that labour and are heavy laden, and I will give you rest. Take my yoke upon you, and learn of me; for I am meek and lowly in heart: and ye shall find rest unto your souls. For my yoke is easy, and my burden is light.* (Matthew 11:28-30)

This was very important for the early Christians enduring persecution and for life in general because they recognised that Jesus had gone through it all himself and could truly commiserate with them. As was written in the Letter to the Hebrews (2:18), Jesus himself suffered when he was tempted and is able to help those who are being tempted.[159]

In the Old Testament, the yoke typically referred to a heavy burden.[160] Jesus is calling people to bring their suffering and burdens into his presence. Learn from him, for his yoke is light and his way leads to peace and rest. It is not always so simple, yet with practice we can learn to hold our suffering, our pain, our anger, and our resentments more gently and to bring them in our prayers and lay them before the Light. This is not to say we do not struggle against injustice or work for peace. It says we do God's work while also committing our suffering and negative thoughts to Jesus. The same advice is given by Thich Nhat Hanh in his commentary on the Buddha's teaching:

> Without suffering, you cannot grow. Without suffering, you cannot get the peace and joy you deserve. Please don't run away from suffering. Embrace it and cherish it. Go to the Buddha, sit with him, and show him your pain. He will look at you with loving kindness, compassion, and mindfulness, and show you ways to embrace your suffering and look deeply into it. With understanding and compassion, you will be able to heal the wounds in your heart, and the wounds in the world. The Buddha called suffering a Holy Truth, because our suffering has the capacity of showing us the path to liberation. Embrace your suffering, and let it reveal to you the way to peace.[161]

CHAPTER 20
RESURRECTION

Jesus Appears after His Death to His Disciples

Jesus' disappearance from his tomb and then his reappearance after his death must have been the ultimate miracle. His earlier miracles seem minor compared to this extraordinary event. The impact is clearly stated in John 20:8 when John, the "other disciple", on seeing the empty tomb, "saw, and believed".

> The first day of the week cometh Mary Magdalene early, when it was yet dark, unto the sepulchre, and seeth the stone taken away from the sepulchre. Then she runneth, and cometh to Simon Peter, and to the other disciple, whom Jesus loved, and saith unto them, They have taken away the Lord out of the sepulchre, and we know not where they have laid him. Peter therefore went forth, and that other disciple, and came to the sepulchre. So they ran both together: and the other disciple did outrun Peter, and came first to the sepulchre. And he stooping down, and looking in, saw the linen clothes lying; yet went he not in. Then cometh Simon Peter following him, and went into the sepulchre, and seeth the linen clothes lie, And the napkin, that was about his head, not lying with the linen clothes, but wrapped together in a place by itself. Then went in also that other disciple, which came first to the sepulchre, and he saw, and believed. (John 20:1-8)

Mary is recorded as being among the first to come looking for Jesus' body early in the morning, before dawn on the third day, which would be our Sunday. As the Passover is on the full moon, there would have been plenty of moonlight before dawn. Mary continued to stay near the tomb, feeling the great loss yet being drawn to sit in her grief awaiting what would come next. First the messenger angels appeared. Then Jesus himself returned and gave her the job of the first preaching of his resurrection. This example of waiting patiently for the coming of the Light is one to ponder.

> *But Mary stood without at the sepulchre weeping: and as she wept, she stooped down, and looked into the sepulchre, And seeth two angels in white sitting, the one at the head, and the other at the feet, where the body of Jesus had lain. And they say unto her, Woman, why weepest thou? She saith unto them, Because they have taken away my Lord, and I know not where they have laid him. And when she had thus said, she turned herself back, and saw Jesus standing, and knew not that it was Jesus. Jesus saith unto her, Woman, why weepest thou? whom seekest thou? She, supposing him to be the gardener, saith unto him, Sir, if thou have borne him hence, tell me where thou hast laid him, and I will take him away. Jesus saith unto her, Mary. She turned herself, and saith unto him, Rabboni; which is to say, Master. Jesus saith unto her, Touch me not; for I am not yet ascended to my Father: but go to my brethren, and say unto them, I ascend unto my Father, and your Father; and to my God, and your God. Mary Magdalene came and told the disciples that she had seen the Lord, and that he had spoken these things unto her.* (John 20:11–18)

John recounts four times when Jesus appeared to his disciples after his death: to Mary in the garden outside the tomb on the first day of the week, the third day after his crucifixion (20:14–17); to the assembled disciples locked in the room that same evening (20:19–23); eight days later when Thomas was present (20:26–29); and finally to seven of the disciples on the shore of the Sea of Tiberias (21:1–23). The first three took place in Jerusalem and the fourth in Galilee, where the disciples had evidently gone, fearful of the Jews after the traumatic events of the trial and crucifixion. Luke alone records the appearance to the two disciples on the road to Emmaus (Luke 24:13–35), which is followed immediately after by a description of Jesus' presence in the midst of the eleven apostles.

Probably the same three appearances are mentioned by Mark (16:9–18): to Mary, to the two on the road, and to the assembled group. Matthew records a brief appearance outside the tomb and then later on a mountain in Galilee

(Matthew 28:9–10, 16–20). Five of these are described in detail: the Emmaus story in Luke and the four in John.

First Gift of the Holy Spirit and Call to Discipleship

> *Then the same day at evening, being the first day of the week, when the doors were shut where the disciples were assembled for fear of the Jews, came Jesus and stood in the midst, and saith unto them, Peace be unto you. And when he had so said, he shewed unto them his hands and his side. Then were the disciples glad, when they saw the Lord. Then said Jesus to them again, Peace be unto you: as my Father hath sent me, even so send I you. And when he had said this, he breathed on them, and saith unto them, Receive ye the Holy Ghost: Whose soever sins ye remit, they are remitted unto them; and whose soever sins ye retain, they are retained.* (John 20:19–23)

Jesus returns to show them he can still be even physically present, for up to this point the disciples have known only that his body disappeared, though Mary has seen and heard him, and, if the Emmaus story in Luke's gospel refers to this same day, then the two disciples have returned and presumably told their news of having had Jesus walk and talk with them. Now Jesus is in their midst, and he declares it is time for them to start their own ministry: *as my Father hath sent me, even so send I you.*

What is the requirement implied in the words *as my Father hath sent me*? It is in this same way we are to be sent forth. We are to go forth in the imitation of Christ, and the implications of this give me pause to breathe carefully. Can I, can we, become like Jesus, seeking and depending on God's guidance moment by moment, following so that we say and do just what God asks of us, completely faithful, with trust and courage and simplicity and vulnerability and love, just as Jesus did?

To enable the first disciples to do this, to undertake such ministry, Jesus breathes on them, saying: *Receive ye the Holy Ghost.* Jesus uses the word 'receive'. He does not say, I give you the Holy Spirit. The disciples, and each one of us, have to make a conscious decision to receive the gift. We can refuse it.

> *But Thomas, one of the twelve, called Didymus, was not with them when Jesus came. The other disciples therefore said unto him, We have seen the Lord. But he said unto them, Except I shall see in his hands the print of the nails, and put my finger into the print of the nails, and thrust my hand into his side, I will not believe.*

> *And after eight days again his disciples were within, and Thomas with them: then came Jesus, the doors being shut, and stood in the midst, and said, Peace be unto you. Then saith he to Thomas, reach hither thy finger, and behold my hands; and reach hither thy hand, and thrust it into my side: and be not faithless, but believing. And Thomas answered and said unto him, My Lord and my God. Jesus saith unto him, Thomas, because thou hast seen me, thou hast believed: blessed are they that have not seen, and yet have believed.* (John 20:24-29)

Unfortunately for Thomas, he was absent the first time Jesus came to the assembled disciples and is told of the Lord's appearance by the others. Many have slighted him as 'doubting Thomas' for his response. I find it not so difficult to sympathise with him. After all, he has been a very loyal member of the group, and when Jesus decided to return to the tomb of Lazarus it was Thomas who had the courage to say, "Let us go with him to Jerusalem, even if it does mean we suffer death also" (John 11:16). I detect a great desire in Thomas to believe yet also a great fear of the disappointment if it turns out that Jesus' reappearance after his physical death is not really true. Some of us may be scared of believing too much; it will be too painful if it turns out to be wrong. We need a sign to reassure us. That is what Thomas is asking for.

A week later, his desire is granted. Thomas, after his episodes of doubt and his previous incapacity to fully understand, enunciates his final acceptance of his relationship with Jesus, a relationship we may each one day attain, by saying, *My Lord and my God*. Here we are at the end of the gospel, having been shown all of Jesus' ministry, and some of us will have come to trust in Jesus, the Light, at an earlier point, convinced by the examples of his teaching or miracles. It is not until we are brought directly into inner contact with Jesus or the Light in our prayers that we finally, finally accept the Lord and God part. Although the words may offend some because of their previous church experiences or male overtones, I invite you to consider understanding 'Lord' as spiritual leader and 'God' as spiritual source.

These disciples were devout men who were being asked to give up most of the religious training they had lived by. They were to give it up to be the leaders of a new religious path, a way that would clearly have to be forged against widespread opposition in their own culture. They would not have others to be their teachers; they had to do it themselves with the inner support of Jesus, a man who had just been crucified, though they had just had the amazing experience of seeing and hearing him after his death.

It is perhaps hard for us, nearly two thousand years later, to accept and understand this concept that Jesus actually reappeared many times, in person and in spirit, to his followers after his death.[162] Yet, as it was for John on the third day when he entered the tomb, so for many others later, the fact of the resurrection was the key issue for the early Christians—it totally convinced them. Did they just accept it intellectually, or did many of them have mystical experiences in which Jesus entered them and redeemed them in a spiritual sense?

We have records from throughout the last two thousand years that confirm such visions and inner cleansings do happen. Many people have written about such experiences, and I have had one myself. Paul described such an experience in his Letter to the Romans: And if *the Spirit of him who raised Jesus from the dead is living in you* (8:11 NIV).
Jesus came through that painful death without bitterness. No recriminating against his persecutors, no recounting of their bad deeds. All was washed away in the love of God. Such too is the effect of the coming of the Christ within each of us.

Many times in his earthly ministry Jesus had healed people who placed their faith in him, saying, "Your sins are forgiven, go forward and sin no more". They had been redeemed and released from past iniquity. That measure of Light and Life, gifted within from birth yet previously imprisoned, was liberated and resurrected within them.

In some eternally mysterious and inexplicable way, the Christ released from Jesus at the crucifixion is still available to redeem those who believe in him. Although not as full or perfect in us as in Jesus, a measure of Christ's Light is still there in each of us. The more we own the Light and witness to it, the more the measure grows, changing and leading us.[163]

This is not a rationally understood experience; it is a spiritual experience, and when it happens, it is more real than anyone might expect. It does not guarantee future perfection—it simply releases the weight of the past and provides a new foundation, a new Way. George Fox describes his own experience:

> And when all my hopes in them and all men were gone, so that I had nothing outwardly to help me, nor could tell what to do, then, Oh then, I heard a voice which said, 'There is one, even Christ Jesus, that can speak to thy condition', and when I heard it my heart did leap for joy.[164]

Francis Howgill writes:

> Wait in patience for the judgment, and let the Lord's work have its perfect operation in you; and so as you turn to him who has smitten and wounded you; he will bind up and heal. And give up all to the great slaughter of the Lord, to the Cross . . . And as the earth comes to be plowed up, the seed which is sown comes up; and the rocks broken, the water gushes out. You so will see . . . hope in the midst of calamity.
>
> As you own the gift which Christ has given you, that is repentance, you will see to life, and then you will see something arising and shine in you. . . . And as you come to be redeemed from the bondage of sin, . . . and the pure principle lives in you, there will be a delight to do the will of the father, who has redeemed you.[165]

CHAPTER 21
DISCIPLESHIP—A LIFE OF FAITHFULNESS AND HOLY OBEDIENCE

Jesus Confirms the Benefits of a Life of Obedience to the Spirit

The disciples stayed together in Jerusalem at least for the week following the Passover, and, fearful of the authorities, they kept the doors of their room closed. Now we find seven of them have returned to Galilee, perhaps still in fear, most likely amazed and traumatized by the events, but surely still overwhelmed by Jesus' reappearances.

> *There were together Simon Peter, and Thomas called Didymus, and Nathanael of Cana in Galilee, and the sons of Zebedee, and two other of his disciples. Simon Peter saith unto them, I go a fishing. They say unto him, We also go with thee. They went forth, and entered into a ship immediately; and that night they caught nothing. But when the morning was now come, Jesus stood on the shore: but the disciples knew not that it was Jesus. Then Jesus saith unto them, Children, have ye any meat? They answered him, No. And he said unto them, Cast the net on the right side of the ship, and ye shall find. They cast therefore, and now they were not able to draw it for the multitude of fishes. Therefore that disciple whom Jesus loved saith unto Peter, It is the Lord. Now when Simon Peter heard that it was the Lord, he girt his fisher's coat unto him, (for he was naked,) and did cast himself into the sea. And the other disciples came in a little ship; (for they were not far from land, but as it were two hundred cubits,) dragging the net with fishes.*
> (John 21:2-8)

Have the disciples taken up the ministry Jesus bequeathed to them, have they made use of the Holy Spirit he breathed upon them, have they gone forth as he sent them to do? No, they have not. What have they done? They have returned to the familiar places of their home country. What do many men do when they have been stressed and are uncertain? Go fishing![166]

After being out in the ship all night and catching nothing, they make towards the shore as dawn approaches. In the dim light they see a person on the shoreline, though not who it is. The stranger asks, in the manner of someone older and in authority, *Children, have ye any meat?* That is, "Lads, did you catch anything? No? Well, throw the net out from the right side of the ship". I can imagine Peter and the others thinking, "Maybe the man saw the water ruffled by a shoal of fish over there; let's give it a go". They are not able to draw in the net because it is so full and heavy with fish. Given the result, they are almost certain to have looked to see who it was that had hailed them. Perhaps the light is a little brighter now. John realises the stranger is in fact Jesus, probably the last person they would ever imagine would be there.

> *As soon then as they were come to land, they saw a fire of coals there, and fish laid thereon, and bread. Jesus saith unto them, Bring of the fish which ye have now caught. Simon Peter went up, and drew the net to land full of great fishes, an hundred and fifty and three: and for all there were so many, yet was not the net broken. Jesus saith unto them, Come and dine. And none of the disciples durst ask him, Who art thou? knowing that it was the Lord. Jesus then cometh, and taketh bread, and giveth them, and fish likewise. This is now the third time that Jesus shewed himself to his disciples, after that he was risen from the dead.* (John 21:9–14)

Peter, in his usual impetuous fashion, was the first to suggest going to sea and is the first to abandon ship to go to the Lord. He drops what he is doing and directs his being to the Lord. The rest of the disciples work to bring the catch ashore; it seems they cannot haul it aboard so they row in with the dinghy, dragging the net into shallow water where they can beach it by hand. When they get there, Jesus has food ready for them: fish laid upon the coals, and bread.

The symbol of bread and fish as food recalls the feeding by the Lake as told earlier by John (6:1–13). In the prior event,

Jesus fed people as a human being living on earth, and now by the same lake he provides food as a divine spirit. The meaning of the number of fish, specified as 153, is not clear to us, although it may have had symbolic meaning in the times the gospel was first told and written.

Onshore, the seven disciples are confronted by an amazing sight. They each knew Jesus and had been with him for three years—maybe more if they had known him in childhood. They knew he had been crucified and died. And yet here he is, again, in front of them. It is he.

John mentions this is the third time Jesus appeared to his disciples, and he must mean the third separate day on which such an event happened, since the first two appearances (to Mary in the garden and later that night to the disciples assembled in the closed room) happened on the same day, albeit in different places.

Then there was the second appearance a week later in the same room when Thomas was present, and finally this third reappearance in Galilee. John does not mention Jesus' appearance on the road to Emmaus nor the one that same evening, though this may also have been the time when Thomas was present a week later. John seems to be limiting his discussion to appearances to this smaller band, in that Jesus showed himself to his disciples (John 21:1).

Before eating, Jesus tells them to bring the fish, so Peter returns and, with his strength, the net is drawn up onto the beach. There are a large number of fish, and the catch includes great fish, not just minnows. Yet the net is not damaged. The allegory is the spread of the gospel to reach many peoples, remembering that Jesus had much earlier predicted he would make these disciples "fishers of men" (Mark 1:17).

On a deeper level, for ourselves, it is apparent that, having decided to follow Peter and go fishing, the disciples have been out all night and, despite their long experience as fishermen, have caught nothing. Yet when Jesus is present and they follow his instructions, their net is filled to overflowing, though it does not break. Such is the spiritual lesson of following the lead of the Spirit and not just trying to do it all alone. The bounty of the Spirit can fill us completely but does not do us damage.

The helpful message comes from an apparent stranger, a friendly stranger, who they only discover later is Jesus. The implication is that we too can often receive Light unexpectedly; we should accept the Light from whatever quarter it comes. In this case, the Light brings two blessings. The first mentioned is the fish upon the coals with bread, that is, food to sustain them immediately.

The second blessing is the net full of fish, more than they could possibly use, especially since they had no refrigeration. Clearly this bounty is for their next meal, but more especially it is to be shared with their family and friends and, given there is so much fish, with others in the community. Such is the nature of the spiritual blessings we each receive; some is for our own spiritual nourishment yet is also meant to be shared around.

These verses are worthy of meditation, of imagining these traumatized and troubled people who had been at sea all night and came ashore at dawn to find needed sustenance.

Reconciliation and the Call into Ministry

> *So when they had dined, Jesus saith to Simon Peter, Simon, son of Jonas, lovest thou me more than these? He saith unto him, Yea, Lord; thou knowest that I love thee. He saith unto him, Feed my lambs. He saith to him again the second time, Simon, son of Jonas, lovest thou me? He saith unto him, Yea, Lord; thou knowest that I love thee. He saith unto him, Feed my sheep. He saith unto him the third time, Simon, son of Jonas, lovest thou me? Peter was grieved because he said unto him the third time, Lovest thou me? And he said unto him, Lord, thou knowest all things; thou knowest that I love thee. Jesus saith unto him, Feed my sheep. Verily, verily, I say unto thee, When thou wast young, thou girdedst thyself, and walkedst whither thou wouldest: but when thou shalt be old, thou shalt stretch forth thy hands, and another shall gird thee, and carry thee whither thou wouldest not. This spake he, signifying by what death he should glorify God. And when he had spoken this, he saith unto him, Follow me.* (John 21:15-19)

After they had dined, Jesus focuses his attention on Peter, who would become the leading apostle for the early Church. Peter is asked whether he loves Jesus. Initially the question is whether Peter loves Jesus more than the others, and the second and third times, whether he loves Jesus irrespective of others—in other words, absolutely. Three times the question is asked, each time giving Peter the opportunity to resolve within himself any further doubts or hesitations in his love or fear of doing so.

The three affirmations that Jesus brings forth from Peter can be seen as responses to the three times Peter denied Jesus the night before his crucifixion. In this way, Jesus is allowing Peter to answer and make amends for his previous three denials and to reconfirm his faith. This is an occasion of complete forgiveness; there are no recriminations, and the relationship is taken up as if the previous denials had not happened and no longer matter. There is reconciliation.

What is important is to start here and now and to look to the future. Jesus' words in John 8:12 are explicit: "Whoever follows me here and in the present shall have the Light of life from here on". Yet it is also an act of free choice—Peter was free to say no. Obedience is not to be imposed by an external authority with threat of punishment; it is an act of personal willingness and love.

For me, Jesus' request that Peter feed his sheep and lambs is not just an instruction. Repeated three times, it is the sealing of a very deep understanding and commitment between Peter and Jesus. Jesus then says "Follow me", and as Peter then turns and follows Jesus, apparently away from the rest of the group, I am left with the sense of Peter finally understanding what this relationship with Jesus is all about. It is one of total commitment on his part to what Jesus asks, and this is mirrored completely by the total commitment of Jesus to Peter's spiritual well-being. The love between them is both total and reciprocal.

If any of us have ever said to others or in our own meditations, "Yes, I love God", yet have to admit we are not fully living the way we have been shown, we too are in Peter's shoes. We will be asked again. We will be asked until we come to the point of commitment and trust in God, just as Peter had to do.

So also for another reason is it three times that Jesus asks if Peter loves him, and three times Peter is told to feed Jesus' lambs and sheep. In other words, Jesus wants Peter to care for and nourish his flock. Jesus is emphasising that all the teaching that was given, plus the gift of the Holy Spirit, are not for nothing. There is work to be done. It is not sufficient to go back home and go fishing.

Though focussed on Peter, this conversation recalls the wider message in Jesus' words from John 20:21: *As my Father hath sent me, even so send I you.* The relationship with Jesus and the gift of the Holy Spirit require a life of working to bring God's peace and justice and healing, at whatever level we are individually called to. The inner transformation and reconciliation with God are preparation for ministry.

In the words of Matthew, who also described Jesus' reappearance in Galilee, albeit on a mountain: *Go ye therefore and teach all nations. . . . Teach . . . them to observe all things whatsoever I have commanded you, and, lo, I am with you always, even unto the end of the world.* (28:19-20).

We know now that Peter did just that. Peter, an unlearned fisherman, a man who is characterised by enthusiastic love and leadership mixed with the human frailties of acting before he thinks and of periodic fear, becomes, by following Jesus, a wonderful teacher and defender of the Way to a life with God. John also has Jesus allude to Peter's death. Peter was martyred upside down on a cross ca. 64 CE, his fate well known to all the early Christians, and this happened well before John's gospel was finally written down. By then the other leading disciples had died, and John was the only one remaining.[167]

> *Then Peter, turning about, seeth the disciple whom Jesus loved following; which also leaned on his breast at supper, and said, Lord, which is he that betrayeth thee? Peter seeing him saith to Jesus, Lord, and what shall this man do? Jesus saith unto him, If I will that he tarry till I come, what is that to thee? follow thou me. Then went this saying abroad among the brethren, that that disciple should not die: yet Jesus said not unto him, He shall not die; but, If I will that he tarry till I come, what is that to thee?* (John 21:20-23)

The verses in which Jesus says simply "Follow me and do not worry about the others" remind me of the parable of the labourers in the vineyard. Our job is not so much to worry about the behaviour of other people and their journey. Jesus says: What is it to you? Worry about your own path. In fact, concentrate on following me. Thomas à Kempis has much the same advice, that we are not to mind greatly who is for or against us, but that we take good care God is with us in everything we do.[168]

The story of this Gospel According to John is ended.

> *This is the disciple which testifieth of these things, and wrote these things: and we know that his testimony is true. And there are also many other things which Jesus did, the which, if they should be written every one, I suppose that even the world itself could not contain the books that should be written. Amen.* (John 21:24-25)

Presumably the 'we' who collated and ensured these teachings were preserved were the elders and leading members of John's community at Ephesus. John confirms he has given only a few examples of the teachings and signs performed by Jesus, and we know much more is contained in the other three gospels. John has selected particular events with a clear purpose in mind—to lead us to the belief that Jesus can guide us to God and to a fully divine life.

> *And many other signs truly did Jesus in the presence of his disciples, which are not written in this book: But these are written, that ye might believe that Jesus is the Christ, the Son of God; and that believing ye might have life through his name.* (John 21:30-31)

CHAPTER 22

THE SPIRITUAL JOURNEY WITH JOHN

Sequence of Teachings in the Gospel According to John

The narrative of Jesus' ministry in the Gospel According to John forms a very clear teaching about the spiritual life. For many, this sequence parallels the spiritual lessons and changes we each go through.

Chapter 1 of the gospel presents Jesus as the Christ, the Word, the Light, and the Life—a breathtaking vision of creation and ongoing revelation. Jesus is introduced as a human being into the culture of his time. The first disciples are called. They, and we, yearn for a richer spiritual life, and here is a guide into such a life. This call comes in two stages—first the call by a messenger that makes us aware we need to change, and second a direct call by the one who can show us the Way.

Chapter 2 describes the miracle of changing the water into wine at the wedding feast in Cana and the clearing of the temple. These early examples show that Jesus is capable of effecting miraculous change and that we must prepare ourselves to undergo serious yet wonderful changes within ourselves. We start this journey when we confront our material desires. As a result, our perception of the world around us changes, and we begin to feel the rising of Life within us.

Chapter 3 records the story of Nicodemus and the need to be reborn spiritually to enter the Kingdom of God. The scale of the change is surprising, even daunting at first, and we need time to alter our mental and spiritual frameworks. We are reassured that Jesus is not here to punish all our misdeeds but to effect forgiveness and encourage us to begin anew, now. Humility is essential. The movement from dark to light has begun in earnest.

Chapter 4 contains the stories of the Samaritan woman at the well and of the healing of the nobleman's servant. Jesus' ministry crosses religious, cultural, class, and gender barriers. He has previously taught the need for change, and now at the well in Samaria he asserts he is the source of Life to make those changes. Responding perfectly, the woman immediately welcomes and accepts the Light that brings healing. For the first time, Jesus confirms that the sustaining power in his life is to do "the will of the One who who sent me, and to complete this work".

The spiritual journey begins in earnest as we allow our faults to be revealed and healed in the Light. We have reached the place where we need to make an effort to travel the road. Jesus institutes the new covenant of worshipping God in Spirit and in Truth. Although he is harsh on hypocrites, Jesus does not excoriate genuine seekers for past sins. Instead, he brings healing and says, "Open yourselves to change. Move on". The spiritual journey is in the here and now, a continuing revelation, and for every moment into the future "the hour cometh and now is".

Chapter 5 describes the Sabbath healing of a lame man at the pool of Bethesda. Jesus has established that the work of the Spirit can occur anywhere, for instance, in Galilee, in Samaria, or by the roadside. The day of visitation of the Light may come without warning, and we do well to be alert and attentive to it. Jesus confirms that the work of the Spirit is not subject to human cultural or religious timetables. It is accessible anytime! Jesus again confirms he is doing God's work on earth. He of himself can do nothing. The real power is God—he, Jesus, is but the agent.

Chapter 6, the last narrative from Galilee, tells of the feeding of the five thousand, another example of God's bountiful blessings, and of the miraculous walking on water as Jesus reappears out of the darkness to calm his frightened disciples, an enduring gift. Jesus also discusses his body and blood, which other gospel writers and Paul presented as a ritual Eucharist.

However, John places accepting Jesus as the source of spiritual food in a much broader context, a mystical appreciation at all times of the sustaining and unifying presence of the Eternal Christ. The spiritual journey has moved to a new level. Many follow Jesus. Others, unwilling to change or affronted by the idea of "eating" his flesh and "drinking" his blood, do leave Jesus.

Chapter 7 brings us to face our own resistance. Jesus has been teaching and working miracles for a year and a half across the region. He reiterates in Jerusalem that his teachings are not his own but those of the One who sent him. His ministry has divided the community; some believe, but some resist the changes required for the new Way. It is the same for most of us who have embarked on the spiritual journey. After a period in which we have experienced a few internal miracles and the opening of our inner eyes, parts of ourselves are ready to follow the Light, but other parts cling to our established habits. It is the same for our communities, where the new ways for peace and justice have to struggle with old patterns based on entrenched habits, self-centredness, fear, and greed.

Chapter 8 describes the balanced life that is both contemplative and active. Jesus goes to the mountain to pray at night and to the towns to teach and to heal during the day. The effects of this balanced life are exemplified in his mercy towards and forgiveness of the woman caught in adultery. There is no harsh punishment. He advises her to go and sin no more. The dependence of righteousness on external laws is replaced by the requirement that all our deeds and judgments be answered truthfully before God in our own hearts. We are called to worship and to act "in spirit and in truth". Jesus confirms again his dependence on his *Abba*, his God.

In chapter 9, John introduces the curing of a blind man with its parallel to the curing of our own inner blindnesses. The Pharisaic voices are still present and need to be rejected in favour of the voice of the Spirit. Jesus had to deal with them continually, and so do we. That is part of doing God's work in the world.

In chapter 10, Jesus confirms that he is the good shepherd who knows and cares for his flock both in good times and in danger, and the sheep who know his voice follow him in trust. The good shepherd was predicted and awaited by the ancient Israelites. It is the yearning we all feel, the yearning for a true guide who will lead us out of the spiritual and emotional turbulence we constantly feel, out of the darkness of confusion and into a life of sureness and peace. Like the disciples and Jesus, we are free to follow or not.

Chapter 11 brings us to the lesson that Jesus not only heals and restores sight but also gives life itself. Lazarus is raised from the dead in answering the call of Jesus to come forth, come out of the darkness of the tomb and into the light of life. Much of our present existence has to die for the new life to be instilled. Yet darkness may still be present within each of us.

Chapter 12 concludes Jesus' earthly public ministry, and Jesus reminds us he is the Light. On Palm Sunday he enters Jerusalem, where people are joyously anticipating that he will be a worldly king and saviour. Jesus knows he cannot fulfil this role. Our worldly aspirations have no relevance to this spiritual journey, as will become dreadfully apparent. The Way is more by self-denial, suffering, and sacrifice than worldly comfort—surrendering ourselves to God's purpose and service.

In chapter 13, at the Last Supper Jesus teaches the sacrament of caring for each other as equals, the washing of the feet, a lesson in humility, equality, service, and love. Such are the principal requirements for the spiritual journey. In the first twelve chapters, his ministry has been about healing the blind and lame and identifying the new way to Life towards God. By this stage, Jesus and John are assuming we have understood these teachings, though we may need to keep practising them, and in the Last Supper Jesus begins to pay serious attention to how we overcome fear and become a blessed community of seekers.

In chapter 14, Jesus gives his priestly instructions for the spiritual journey—"I Am" the Way; follow the Light I am giving each of you; follow my commandments; these are the way to a life with God. Jesus promises, "To help you I will make sure the Spirit, the Comforter, the Guide is sent to you". When we follow inner promptings and leadings, we are led closer and closer to God and experience Jesus, the Christ, the Light within, in our own lives. Jesus is ready to return, a second coming, an inner resurrection that is possible in this life. The wonderful peace of being reconciled to God is possible.

In chapter 15, John is directing our attention again to being part of a spiritual community. The allegory of the vine means that we are all connected to Jesus as the source of life and love, and yet we are also all connected to each other in the spiritual community. If we are cut off from either, we die. The hallmarks of this community are friendship and love.

In chapter 16, Jesus is ready to leave his disciples and, acknowledging their sorrow, provides reassurance and hope. Jesus promises again the gift of the Spirit as Guide, teacher, and Comforter. The Spirit will help recall Jesus' sayings and, moreover, will later say the things that we cannot bear to hear now. That is, we are brought gradually into a closer relationship with God as parts of ourselves are progressively stripped away. We need to be prepared for this stripping; it would be too painful if it happened all at once, and we might flee the journey rather than stay engaged with the Spirit.

Chapter 17 contains Jesus' priestly prayer for his followers. He acknowledges it is God alone who has enabled him to undertake his ministry and that he has faithfully done so, not just by talking about God but by making God's presence a worldly reality through his teachings and healings. Jesus also prays for disciples and for those who come after, finally praying that those who follow him will experience the wonderful union with himself and God, the unity for which he yearns and has lived his life.

Chapters 18–19 contain Jesus' arrest, trial, crucifixion, and burial, in a struggle between Light and darkness. Jesus yields himself in love. The Jewish leaders finally have their way, with the assistance of the indecisive Pilate, who when he is in the presence of the Light can see Jesus is innocent but cannot maintain that judgment when he is exposed to the darkness of the Jewish elders and mob. Pilate's dithering is symbolic of much in ourselves and in the community. The radical witness of Jesus' eventual crucifixion makes it clear that the way to God involves love and sacrifice, including parts of our life that were dear to us.

In chapter 20, miraculously, Jesus reappears to Mary and to the disciples after his death. The gospels record several more appearances until the final one forty days later (Acts 1:3–8). When Jesus reappears to his disciples in the closed room, he breathes on them, passing to them the Holy Spirit.

Forty days later, at Pentecost, this gift of the Holy Spirit is repeated. The Light has survived the murdering efforts of darkness and is available *even unto the end of the world* (Matthew 28:20).

Chapter 21 is not just an add-on; it is a teaching to maintain our faithfulness and holy obedience in the spiritual life. John recounts the appearance of Jesus to a group of disciples fishing on the Sea of Tiberias. This is an example of Jesus continuing to reach out to us, even when we have been frightened off the path. Jesus' attitude is one of forgiveness without recrimination. He provides the food and sustenance, and he gives Peter the chance to make amends for his previous denials, to reconfirm his faith and his willingness to follow. Jesus emphasises that the disciples need to use their spiritual gifts to undertake the work he has left them, and he singles out Peter as the leader. Peter's job, above all things, is to care for the flock and to continue the work Jesus has done in his own ministry, repairing the wanton neglect of the Hebrew priests so castigated by the earlier prophets. The gift of the Spirit brings with it the call to all of us into ministry. We are changed that we may be of use.

Jesus Acknowledges God as Far Greater Than Himself

John records that Jesus testified many times he is not God; that he comes *from* God; that he does what God, his *Abba* (Father), asks and empowers him to do; and that he could do none of this without God's instructions and power.[169] This is the case for all of us, as Jesus tells Pilate: *Thou couldest have no power at all against me, except it were given thee from above* (John 19:11).

God is the source of all spiritual energy and goodness. As Jesus says, *Be ye therefore perfect, even as your Father which is in heaven is perfect* (Matthew 5:48); *Why callest thou me good? there is none good but one, that is, God* (Matthew 19:17). James makes the same point: *Every good gift and every perfect gift is from above, and cometh down from the Father of lights, with whom there is no variableness, neither shadow of turning* (James 1:17).

Luke's gospel is clear that Jesus returned from his baptism in the Jordan filled by the Spirit and was then led by the

Spirit into the wilderness (Luke 4:1-2). Next, in the power of the Spirit Jesus returned to his village and taught with authority (Luke 4:14-22). The other gospels also mention this. John makes this teaching an overwhelming testimony of Jesus—that all goodness and love and guidance comes from God and that not even he, Jesus, could do anything without this source. By his own admission, Jesus is the Christ, full of the Presence of God, but he is not God.

This omnipresent God is testified in many other deep spiritual faiths: there is one God, an ultimate, unknowable source of all. Jesus felt the same Spirit of God working through him.

> Supreme Brahman, Light supreme,
> and supreme purification, Spirit divine eternal,
> unborn God from the beginning,
> omnipresent Lord of all.[170]

Consider the many times John records that Jesus emphasised God's greater being:

> *"My food," said Jesus, "is to do the will of him who sent me and to finish his work." (John 4:34 NIV)*

> *Then answered Jesus and said unto them, Verily, verily, I say unto you, The Son can do nothing of himself, but what he seeth the Father do: for what things soever he doeth, these also doeth the Son likewise. (John 5:19)*

> *For as the Father hath life in himself; so hath he given to the Son to have life in himself; (John 5:26)*

> *I can of mine own self do nothing: as I hear, I judge: and my judgment is just; because I seek not mine own will, but the will of the Father which hath sent me. (John 5:30)*

> *For I came down from heaven, not to do mine own will, but the will of him that sent me. (John 6:38)*

> *And he said, Therefore said I unto you, that no man can come unto me, except it were given unto him of my Father. (John 6:65)*

And the Jews marvelled, saying, How knoweth this man letters, having never learned? Jesus answered them, and said, My doctrine is not mine, but his that sent me. (John 7:15–16)

So you think you know me and my origins! Yet I haven't come of my own accord—I was sent by One who is true, whom you don't even know. But I do know this One, because those are my origins, and by this One I was sent. (John 7:28–29 TIB)

"But the One who sent me is truthful and what I have learned I now declare to the world." They didn't grasp that Jesus was speaking about Abba God. Jesus continued, "When you have lifted up the Chosen One, then you'll know that I AM and that I do nothing of myself; I say only what Abba God has taught me." (John 8:26–28 TIB)

Therefore doth my Father love me, because I lay down my life, that I might take it again. No man taketh it from me, but I lay it down of myself. I have power to lay it down, and I have power to take it again. This commandment have I received of my Father. (John 10:17–18)

If I do not the works of my Father, believe me not. But if I do, though ye believe not me, believe the works: that ye may know, and believe, that the Father is in me, and I in him. (John 10:37–38)

Jesus cried and said, He that believeth on me, believeth not on me, but on him that sent me. (John 12:44)

For I have not spoken of myself; but the Father which sent me, he gave me a commandment, what I should say, and what I should speak. (John 12:49)

Don't you believe that I am in Abba God and God is in me? The words I speak are not spoken of myself; it is Abba God, living in me, who is accomplishing the works of God. (John 14:10 TIB)

Jesus answered... and the word which ye hear is not mine, but the Father's which sent me. (John 14:23-24)

I go unto the Father: for my Father is greater than I. ... that the world may know that I love the Father; and as the Father gave me commandment, even so I do. Arise, let us go hence. (John 14:28, 31)

If ye keep my commandments, ye shall abide in my love; even as I have kept my Father's commandments, and abide in his love. (John 15:10)

But when the Comforter is come, whom I will send unto you from the Father, even the Spirit of truth, which proceedeth from the Father, he shall testify of me. (John 15:26)

I have manifested thy name unto the men which thou gavest me out of the world: thine they were, and thou gavest them me; and they have kept thy word. Now they have known that all things whatsoever thou hast given me are of thee. For I have given unto them the words which thou gavest me; and they have received them, and have known surely that I came out from thee, and they have believed that thou didst send me. (John 17:6-8)

That they all may be one; as thou, Father, art in me, and I in thee, that they also may be one in us: that the world may believe that thou hast sent me. And the glory which thou gavest me I have given them; that they may be one, even as we are one: I in them, and thou in me, that they may be made perfect in one; and that the world may know that thou hast sent me, and hast loved them, as thou hast loved me. (John 17:21-23)

Jesus acknowledged that he came and did as God commanded and empowered him; he did not do it just of himself. He was a faithful servant. As Jesus said in slight exasperation to Philip (John 14:9-10), he does as God instructs, so if you watch, you will see God at work; you will see God. He made the same point to the Pharisees (John 8:19). Is it really a problem that Jesus can say these things while still admitting he is in union with God, a child of God—or, to use the ancient Hebrew term, a Son of God? Not for me.

The early Christian communities understood this relationship very well. They accepted that Jesus surrendered in obedience (Philippians 2:8). As the Letter to the Hebrews put it, drawing on Psalm 40:7-8: *Here I am—it is written about me in the scroll—I have come to do your will, my God* (10:7 NIV).

George Fox fully accepted Romans 5:18, convinced that Jesus brought us out of the sin that had existed since Adam's time. The fall from grace that had characterised people for thousands of years could now be forgiven, for in the apostles' time there was knowledge and presence of the Spirit that overcame the fallen state.

The words and deep understandings of the early apostles have been a beacon for others to follow for centuries. Their behaviours, their gifts of prophecy and of healing, their triumph over sufferings, their radiant obedience to the Spirit—these were all clear evidence of the Spirit's presence and of the extraordinary life that can be lived on earth.

George Fox believed he had found again that same type of life that had been lost since the apostles' days. The original Quakers were convinced it is possible for all of us to recover that life. It is possible for the "old person" to die and for new life to be resurrected in this lifetime. The process often involves our own suffering as parts of us are melted or "burnt away in the refiner's fire". For Fox, that was Jesus' message, and that is the message of John as well.

Among the early Quakers, as there has been in other individuals, there was an extraordinary, sometimes radiant, spiritual presence that enabled them to convince others, to undertake radical works, to suffer gladly, and to bring to reality a way of living that many had thought impossible. However, this rebirth depended on their full acceptance of Jesus and the Word he brought and on their willingness to accept without reserve the nature of their shortcomings as revealed by the Light and to be healed by the Light. Jesus, by being completely obedient to God, had become one with

God. In such a way, we too could become fully one with that of God in each of us.

Are we able to accept this vision of Fox's?

John's Gentle Corrections of Earlier Gospels

The Gospel According to John takes care to correct several matters recorded in the earlier gospels.

1. The period of Jesus' ministry is set over three years, not one year as in the Synoptic Gospels.
2. The first gift of the Holy Spirit was on the first Sunday after the crucifixion (John 20:19-22), not at Pentecost (Acts 2:1-4), which was seven weeks later.
3. There is no mention of the instituting of the sacrament of the Eucharist. John refers to the body and blood of Jesus in a universal context, and the main sacrament instituted by Jesus the night before his death is that of humble service, as exemplified in the washing of the disciples' feet. John may well have been concerned that the Eucharist was already becoming a ritual habit for people rather than their seeking the transformed life so clearly required by Jesus.
4. Supreme authority in the Christian community is not given to one person (Matthew 16:18-19), such as a monarchical bishop. The supreme authority is God (John 3:19-21; 9:4-5; 12:44-46, 49-50), with the Holy Spirit the messenger, reprover, Comforter, teacher, and Guide (John 14:16-17, 26; 15:26; 20:22-23).[171]
5. John emphasises the possibility for all to become one with Jesus and God, the idea that salvation is possible in this life (John 1:9, 14:23, 17:11). Not much credit is given to the idea of salvation only after death. The Eternal Christ so perfect in Jesus is also within each of us and striving to perfect each of us. This Spirit is accessible if we faithfully follow Jesus, the inward Light, the Word—no matter what our culture, class, race, or gender.
6. John emphasises that Jesus came as a servant of God and is also the spiritual Light, the Word, and the Truth, as bestowed on him by God, his *Abba* (Father).

The Change Required

To enter into the Way to God we must each be prepared for major change. As Jesus told Nicodemus, we must be reborn. This is a clear statement that it is not enough to make minor adjustments and retain all that we desire as personal comforts and indulgences. The turning of water into wine at Cana is a physical example of the scale of inner change required. Peter and Nicodemus are examples of what can happen.

We remember many examples of such changes. Moses was called from being a shepherd in the desert to lead the greatest journey of escape from slavery in recorded history. Francis of Assisi relinquished a life of wealth and pleasure to become a mendicant friar and spiritual leader. Catherine McAuley used her considerable Quaker inheritance to found the Sisters of Mercy and led a life of poverty, chastity, and obedience. Jane Addams used her prosperous background and education not to further her own position but for the betterment of poor women and children and to campaign against war. Mohandas Gandhi relinquished his ambition and training as a well-mannered British lawyer and his personal comforts and possessions to become a servant of the poor of India. Margaret Fell let go of her comfortable existence on a large manor to mother the despised early Quakers, and she lost property and spent time in prison for her faithfulness. Oscar Romero walked away from the safety and prestige of a bishopric among the rich and powerful, choosing to speak continually on behalf of the poor. There are countless examples in our own communities of people who have made such changes on all scales.

Finally, Jesus reminds us that the peace he provides, and the inward peace that we seek, is "not of this world". There is no promise of happy times and worldly peace day after day. The journey will involve some sacrifices and suffering, although the extent and type varies for each of us. The examples of others show us that external peace is replaced by a wonderful internal peace, a trust and joy that are unassailable.

Being born is in itself the start of a spiritual journey.

Struggle between Light and Dark on the Way

The purpose of John is stated at the end of Jesus' ministry:

> *But these are written, that ye might believe that Jesus is the Christ, the Son of God; and that believing ye might have life through his name.* (John 20:31)

The miracles are signs of Jesus' power, a measure of which power is sent to us in the form of the Spirit. Jesus physically made the blind see; he healed and made people whole; he brought people Life. Parallel signs can be effected spiritually for us by the Light, which early Quakers knew as the Light of Jesus Christ. Whatever this inward Light or Word asks of us is the way of Truth. This healing energy is still available; it did not die out with Jesus' death. If we avoid the Light, our hearts become darkened and the Light much more difficult to perceive.[172] As George Fox wrote:

> Many of the people stayed and I turned them to the light of Christ by which they might see their sins and see their saviour Christ Jesus, who was their way to God and their mediator that made their peace betwixt them and God.[173]

It normally takes time. The path is one of learning to follow the Light and relegate the dark. The voice of God is Light, and we have to learn to follow this while disregarding whatever the Spirit asks us to discard. Jesus taught that the path to the Presence and union with God, to becoming at peace with God, is travelled by showing love. His example is a balance of contemplative prayer and active ministry. His teaching is simple and does not require an understanding of sophisticated doctrines.

Instead of being entangled in mental frustrations, it is better to allow the Spirit to show us what to do. Our endless mental gymnastics and arguing cannot solve all our problems. In that way of life, we are easily confused. That is the way of the law and the letter, for *the letter killeth, but the spirit giveth life* (2 Corinthians 3:6). The real life is a willing obedience to the Spirit, a life that leads to peace with God.

Jesus has replaced the outward signs and rituals with a new covenant, an inward covenant. The spiritual quest is now and is a matter of being; it is not a matter of following certain rules but of focussing on the life of the Spirit. The important time is now, not in past memories or future musings; the place is here, not over there somewhere but right here; and the task is this one in front of us.

Since God is a Spirit, in spirit must God be worshipped. A personal and communal worship of God is possible in ways that surpass rehearsed prayers. Worship occurs within the silence of the temple of our own hearts, directly with God.

Forgiveness, Not Condemnation

Jesus came not to judge or condemn but to save (John 3:17). His behaviour with the Samaritan woman at the well (John 4:5-30) and with the woman taken in adultery (John 8:3-11) both show that Jesus is not concerned with judging past sins and meting out the requisite punishment. Jesus meets people where they are and shows them the way out of sins and the way to Life. He often says, "Follow me. Do as I have done", encouraging all to a new beginning. Guilt is un-necessary.

Jesus' ministry is the fulfilment of a wonderful prophecy of Jeremiah, a belief echoed as an experience of the early Christians in Hebrews 8:8-12 and 10:15-18. According to Jeremiah:

> *But this shall be the covenant that I will make with the house of Israel; After those days, saith the LORD, I will put my law in their inward parts, and write it in their hearts; and will be their God, and they shall be my people.* (Jeremiah 31:33)

> *No longer will they need to teach one another or remind one another to listen to YHWH. All of them, high and low alike, will listen to me, says YHWH, for I will forgive their misdeeds and will remember their sins no more.* (Jeremiah 31:34 TIB)

These words describe a relationship with God that we know or come to know. We may start off as children and young adults learning the Ten Commandments and having others teach us. With grace we find the laws that are written inside us, and the Light makes them clear to us. They are no longer written on tablets of stone; they are written in our hearts.

This is a new, personal, and intimate relationship with God in which the high priests are no longer required to dictate the law to us. Each one of us is to pay attention inwardly.

Jesus spoke on many levels, always with great concern for people's spiritual and earthly welfare. He spoke

- with great tenderness to children, the sick, the uncertain, and the marginalised;
- with compassion and directness to the blind and the lame;
- with deep understanding and humour to the troubled souls who sought him;
- with passion and sometimes frustration to those who saw his miraculous signs but refused to believe in him; and
- with courage and authority when he confronted the powerful and the hypocrites.

Jesus does not say, "Go, attend church regularly and memorise all the laws". He says, "Go and sin no more" (John 5:14). His message is not that we are damned to hell for our errors but that we are called to a much fuller life, a life of continuing goodness, abundance, and joy, an everlasting experience of the Life within. Further, Jesus is calling us to that life as part of our earthly existence, not just postponing it till a day of judgment. Any judgment is made by the Light within us, in this lifetime. Are we are willing to accept it?

George Fox wrote:

> For the Lord God alone will teach his people; and he is coming to teach them, and to gather his people from idols' temples and the customary worships, which all the world is trained up in.[174]

James Nayler experienced this fuller life:

> There is a spirit which I feel delights to do no evil, nor to revenge any wrong, but delights to endure all things, in hope to enjoy its own in the end. Its hope is to outlive all wrath and contention, and to weary out all exaltation and cruelty. . . . It sees to the end of all temptations . . . for its ground is the mercies and forgiveness of God.[175]

Jesus and the Union with God

Some commentaries on the Gospel According to John make much of the tension between Jesus' statements that he is "one with the Father" and that his Father is "greater". Can we allow, in meditation and prayer, for the Spirit to move us from the head to the heart to deepen our understanding? If we are determined to remain in the head until it is all clear and worked out, then we are in for disappointment. If we allow the Spirit to instruct us, the seeming tension may resolve.

Jesus provides a model and a guide for us to resolve the difficulty. It is in acknowledging God's greater being, in leading a life of holy obedience, that we become closer and closer to God, with the prospect of becoming one, of being in union with God. Jesus refers specifically (John 14:11, 20-23; 15:7; 17:21-23) to the mystical union between God, himself, and ourselves. See, for example, John 14:23: *Those who love me will be true to my word, and Abba God will love them; and we will come to them, and make our dwelling place with them* (TIB). The message and promise of Jesus is that we can come to experience the relationship Jesus experienced himself.

Early Friends allowed themselves to follow the Light regardless of the personal costs, and they found remarkable power to do so. As Marcelle Martin has written, early Friends knew that "the power they sought was not their own, but was God's".[176] That power would not come simply by subscribing, however fervently, to a set of beliefs or doctrines. It was only attained by actions of love and by relinquishing, or in their language by sacrificing or inwardly crucifying, their personal ambitions and agendas.

Their model was Jesus, who said, "I can do nothing except by the Father". Early Friends were in the mould of the first Christians, the people of the Way, the children of the Light,[177] obedient to the Light that guided them so they could justifiably feel themselves a 'people of God'.

Love Always

Jesus calls us to love in all circumstances, in ways that test our limits every day. We are required to love our enemies, bless those who curse us, do good to those who hate us, and pray for those who persecute us.[178] It is not sufficient to love only those who do good to us. We are to love those who criticise us, who are antagonistic or even aggressive towards us. Such is the extraordinary world Jesus envisaged, a life that he taught is possible.

We are to love one another with no excuses so that our lives may become more Christ-like. We find our love is the love of God made available to us. Jesus confirms this new covenant is to love one another that we may abide in him and he in us. The love of his being, the Eternal Christ, can then flow through us.

Charles Freer Andrews writes:

> In setting forward this standard, . . . we are clearly claiming a sovereign faith in what George Fox called "that of God in every man," which, as it is led from within by the Spirit of God, is bound to respond to the supreme appeal which we make to love and truth. In such a faith and trust we are surely following Christ's own example, and we may do so with perfect confidence. For if anything is clear from the Gospel story it is this, that, knowing the evil that was in the world and in the heart of man, He [Jesus] yet retained His own unbounded faith that goodness would in the end prevail. He saw this goodness, still a flame beneath the surface, in Mary Magdalene, out of whom he cast seven evil spirits, and in the woman 'who was a sinner' who came to him at the house of Simon. . . . For He saw right through to the inner man or woman and won them back to goodness by his own faith in them when everyone else condemned them and treated them as outcast.[179]

Chapter 23
I AM

"I AM" Is the Name of God; "I Am" Refers to the Presence of God

This book uses the term "I am" in three ways. "I AM" (fully capitalized) is the name of God (Exodus 3:14). "I Am" (with capital 'A') indicates the link to God rather than the human ego and refers to the Presence of God manifested in each of us and in all creation. "I am" (lowercase 'a') is used for personal behaviour, as in "I am saying . . ." Although the Bible uses "I am" for these last two meanings, I differentiate them, for it is crucial to understand that when Jesus says "I am" he is not referring to human ego but to the Presence of God as the mystical Christ within him. I use Light (capitalised) to refer to the mystical, inward Light, the Light of Christ.

I AM WHO I AM is clearly stated to Moses as the name of God when Moses is working as a shepherd for his father-in-law Jethro (Exodus 3:13-14 NIV). Moses is drawn to a bush that is burning with fire yet is not consumed. God speaks and instructs him to go to the Pharaoh of Egypt to bring forth the Israelites from bondage and the afflictions of Egypt. Moses knows the Israelites are unlikely to accept the words of a desert shepherd and will ask who sent him. God tells Moses *I AM WHO I AM* and asks Moses to tell the Israelites that *I AM has sent me to you*. Thus, I AM is the name of God.[180] Similar mystical statements in the Bible are:

> *Thus saith the LORD the King of Israel, and his redeemer the LORD of hosts; I am the first, and I am the last; and beside me there is no God.* (Isaiah 44:6)

> *Hearken unto me, O Jacob and Israel, my called; I am he; I am the first, I am also the last. Mine hand also hath laid the foundation of the earth.* (Isaiah 48:12-13)

> *I am Alpha and Omega, the beginning and the ending, saith the Lord, which is, and which was, and which is to come, the Almighty.* (Revelation 1:8)

"I am" as a statement of divine being, supreme, unknowable yet approachable, occurs in many sacred texts, including the Bhagavad Gita: "I am the beginning and the middle and the end of all that is. Of all knowledge I am the knowledge of the Soul. Of the many paths of reason I am the one that leads to Truth".[181] The Qur'an writes similarly: "Inform my servants that I am the Forgiving, the Merciful".[182] It is a statement of is-ness, of being, of the creative force that pervades the entire seen and unseen universe. We can know God *is*, but we cannot know *what* God is.

We experience the working of God's Presence within us, the "I Am". This is not a name for God but refers to the Presence of God in all things and beings, which is normally an unconscious presence yet with meditation, attentiveness, and prayer can become a conscious presence. "I Am" is statement of being in the present, for that is when we experience the Presence. "I Am" is about our spiritual selves, that of God within us, when our actions and words bear witness to that of God working within us. The Presence of God is the Way, the Truth, and the Life. In the Presence of God is holiness, as expressed by Peter referencing Leviticus 11:45: *Be ye holy; for I am holy* (1 Peter 1:16).

John quotes Jesus using the words "I am" several times. The "I am", as in *I am the Way*, is not an ego statement. It is very important to free ourselves from any thought arising from our Self that the "I am" represents a statement by Jesus referring to himself in praise. Many have mistakenly rejected the statements of Jesus, saying, "How can he be so egotistical as to think he is the only way?" As I realised for myself, this thinking is really my own ego projecting itself and my wish to be the judge of the facts. The "I am" is a mystical statement, in the sense of "I Am", and has nothing to do with the ego.[183]

The "I Am", the Presence of God, is the bread, the water, the Light of Life, the restoration of life, our spiritual sustenance and guidance. Jesus was so perfectly faithful that he was and is the "I Am", the Presence of God, the Christ. Into this Presence are we invited, into a life that some call the higher Self, the true Self, the universal Self—the Self beyond the reach of worldly ego, error, and evil.

Joel Goldsmith puts it this way:

> One of the most important statements in the New Testament is the passage, "I am the way". The incorrect interpretation of these few words has kept the world in spiritual darkness for seventeen hundred years. On his understanding of that one passage hinges man's spiritual darkness or his spiritual enlightenment. . . . When you personalise those words of Jesus and believe that they refer to a person, you are in spiritual darkness. Did not Jesus say, "I can of mine own self do nothing"? . . . Rightly interpreted, the words "I am the way" mean what they say. The way, the truth, and the life more abundant are to be found in *I*—the *I* that I am, the *I* that you are, for you have been told you and your Father are one. It is in that oneness you find spiritual freedom, spiritual harmony, and spiritual grace, a life "not by might, nor by power, but by my spirit." . . . It is in this word *I* that you find the entire secret of the spiritual message given to the world by Christ Jesus, a message that is destined to set men free and break from them all shackles and all limitations, that they may live as children of God, completely free, under the domination of no man, under the domination of no circumstances or conditions, and under the grace of God alone.[184]

When Jesus uses "I am", it is in recognition of his spiritual nature as the Christ who fully embodies the eternal Presence of God, a presence that has always been and will always be. This is the unchangeable divine presence. That is why he could say, *Verily, verily, I say unto you, Before Abraham was, I am* (John 8:58). Christ has been present forever and will persist forever, difficult as that appears to our rational minds.

There is one God. God is one being, one light, one word, one life, one bread, one way, one resurrection, irrespective of the variety of religious beliefs, images, and rituals, and the Presence of God is "I Am" and you see it fully in me. That is what Jesus came to say.[185]

Jesus and God: I Am

In this gospel, Jesus speaks of his close dependence on God, and as the gospel unfolds, Jesus speaks of and is a manifestation of seven things (using "I Am" as just explained):

- I Am the bread of the spiritual life—the daily bread and sustenance for those feeling faint, confused, or lost (6:35, 48).
- I Am life, the vine, the true vine, the giver of life, and the sap of the spiritual life (1:4; 15:1–10). My teachings are a source of living waters (4:13-15; 7:38) for the spiritually parched.
- I Am the light of the spiritual journey—the wisdom, the teacher, that shows us what we need to do and the path to follow out of darkness (1:4-5; 8:12; 9:5).
- I Am the truth (14:6)—the infallible and unchangeable counsel.
- I Am the way (14:6), the door or gateway (10:9) —the one to follow in wonderful safety.
- I Am the good shepherd (10:11)—the leader, bishop, and priest whom you can trust to lead you into safe and nourishing spiritual pastures.
- I Am the resurrection, the restoration of that which is dead to that which is alive, not at some distant day of judgment but in our lives now (11:25; 12:39-44; 14:6; 15:1, 5).

In the sense that Jesus fully manifests the Eternal Christ, yes, he is the Way, the Truth, and the Life, not because of his human Self, or imagined ego but because he is living as the Christ. John does not report Jesus saying "I am the Word". John identifies Jesus as the Word in living form, though Jesus does not make that claim for himself. In the sense that Jesus does exactly what he hears from God, he becomes that Word, that teaching in action. So I can understand why John identified Jesus as the Word, though Jesus did not claim this for himself.

I find it helpful to focus on these statements as issues for ourselves in our everyday lives. Each of these "I am" statements is not a call to total belief in a creed or doctrine but is an invitation to each of us to watch for the Light within us, to listen for the Word, to become aware of that Presence of God rising softly within us, every moment and everywhere

The "I Am", the Presence of God so fully manifested in Jesus, is also within each one of us. The ground has "I Am", the trees have "I Am", the air has "I Am", and we have "I Am". The "I Am", that of God in me, can recognise the "I Am" in you. The Presence of God, the One, the Light, the Love is within me, within you, and within all things.

I Am the Bread of Life

> *And Jesus said unto them, I am the bread of life: he that cometh to me shall never hunger; and he that believeth on me shall never thirst.* (John 6:35)

> *I am that bread of life. Your fathers did eat manna in the wilderness, and are dead. This is the bread which cometh down from heaven, that a man may eat thereof, and not die. I am the living bread which came down from heaven: if any man eat of this bread, he shall live for ever.* (John 6:48–51)

I am the bread of life—but which life? Certainly not just our mortal existence. In 6:35 the words are reminiscent of the Sermon on the Mount: *Blessed are they which do hunger and thirst after righteousness* (Matthew 5:6). These words recall our yearning for God. The spiritual life can be a long and difficult journey despite the joys and consolations. Dry periods, loneliness, disappointment, and even depression occur. Each of us can experience times of being spiritually alive and periods of spiritual darkness, confusion, or emptiness. We know what sustains our bodily needs. What sustenance is there for our spiritual hunger and thirst?

Jesus refers to the manna that Moses showed to the wandering Israelites in the desert wilderness on their journey to the promised land (John 6:49).[186] Is Jesus speaking in a humorous, ironic way to engage his listeners? Is he saying, "You all know about the manna that came down from the sky overnight with the dew, that manna which kept your forefathers alive in the desert for forty years"? Heads would be nodding around the group. "Well, folks, they have all been dead for centuries. What do you make of that? What is there to sustain you and lead you to an ongoing spiritual life that persists forever and does not die?"

Those with Jesus, familiar with the Hebrew Scriptures, could recall texts, such as Deuteronomy 8:3, that remind us that God tries us in our own wildernesses to show us and help us understand that we do not live just on manna but by the Word of God.[187]

What underpins our gifts of intelligence and what do we rely upon in times of spiritual exhaustion? The answer, Jesus says, is the Presence of God, the "I Am", manifested in himself. All our gifts come from God. When we are spiritually at a loss and feeling faint, we can take some of Jesus' words and sit with them in meditation and prayer, waiting patiently for the life and power to return to us. Jesus will not fail us. Such a relationship is spiritual communion.

I Am the Life, the Vine, and the Living Water

> *I am the true vine, and my Father is the husbandman. Every branch in me that beareth not fruit he taketh away: and every branch that beareth fruit, he purgeth it, that it may bring forth more fruit.* (John 15:1-2)

I am the true vine, not a false vine that will wither or produce bad fruits, of which there are many on offer in the world. The vine of "I Am" does not wither because it is sourced in God, and it does not produce evil fruit because it can only produce the goodness of God. We can only grow while connected intimately to the sap rising through the vine. Every day we need to stay connected. Complete faithfulness is the aim.

Yet Jesus also warns us who become part of this vine with the sap of life and love, that the unfruitful parts of ourselves will be stripped away. As the vine is cleared of dead or infected wood, we too can experience the healing of inner wounds and inner illnesses, just as the lame man at Bethesda was enabled to rise and walk.

Whatever bears fruit will be pruned to make it more fruitful. We need to be prepared and not become alarmed if we feel serious changes within us whereby some previously cherished parts are now left behind. We may find ourselves tearful, as the vine weeps. If God is doing the pruning, we will be the better for it. After winter, the spring of life brings new growth.

"Living water" assuages a parched soul. The inner life requires this heavenly moisture, which may be experienced as inner dew, as light rain, or even as a flowing stream. For some it is the experience an inner fountain, upwelling with life and love.

I Am the Light

People who live by the truth come out into the light, so that it may be plainly seen that what they do is done in God. (John 3:21 TIB)

The next time Jesus spoke to them, he said, "I am the light of the world. Whoever follows me won't walk in darkness, but will have the light of life." (John 8:12 TIB)

As long as it is day, we must do the works of him who sent me. Night is coming, when no one can work. While I am in the world, I am the light of the world. (John 9:4–5 NIV)

Believe in the light while you still have the light. Only then will you become children of light. (John 12:36 TIB)

When Jesus says *I am the light of the world*, he is confirming he represents the Light of God.[88] The Light is in each of us, and it illumines that of God within us, that which is pure, unchangeable, and full of Truth and Love. It shows us the path towards God, leading us up to God, a path trod by Jesus as Christ in that he followed whatever God told him to do or say. Jesus said that if you watch him you see God working, you see God's Presence. That is why the life of Jesus can illumine our Way to live a more Christ-like life ourselves.

We become closer to this Presence when we live in the present, seeking to love God alone, and to do only as God would have us do. The Light of Christ within is at various times inspiring, comforting, revealing, guiding, reproving, and healing. Daily discernment is assisted by following Jesus' example. Effort and practice are needed because our own self-centred fears and desires have a way of obscuring this path and leading us astray. The Light within, however, is an ever-reliable source of Truth.

Rarely is the whole path laid out, and we have to be content to be shown a step at a time. The Light may be dim at first, arising in our conscience. As we begin to follow it, come to love it as the leading of God, and use it as the guiding principle in our lives, our measure increases. We receive more inner strength to resist the temptations of our own desires and self-centredness.

Rex Ambler has rendered George Fox's description of an experience he had in 1653 into modern English:

> So the first step to peace is to stand still in the light—the light that reveals whatever is opposed to it. And standing still there you will receive the power and strength to resist that part of you which the light has exposed. Because this is where grace grows, where God alone is seen to be glorious and powerful, and where the unknown truth—unknown to the world out there—is revealed. The truth then liberates what has been held in prison, and in the course of time it revives it, leading it in time to the God who is beyond time.[189]

This is a process of engagement with the divine, with that of God within us, where each tiny step of loving surrender on our part deepens our relationship with God. The Light within can never be accessed by our own thoughts or efforts, for it comes as a gift and typically with faithfulness and holy obedience. Isaac Penington writes about faith and obedience exercised:

> In waiting on the light for the leadings in the law of life, and then subjecting to the leader; being content with all his dispensations therein; with the time he chooseth for standing still, and with the time he chooseth for travelling on; with the proportion of light and leading that he judgeth fit, with the food and clothing which he prepares and preserves; with the enemies he sees fit to have avoided or encountered with. Hereby thy own

wisdom, thy own will, thy own strength, thy own desires, thy own delights, with all the murmurings, weariness and discontents, which arise from the earthly part, are by degrees worn out, and pure vessel prepared for the pure birth to spring up and appear in.[190]

Elias Hicks describes his experience of the gradual arising of the Light:

A great power of darkness seemed so to prevail . . . but as I patiently submitted to the baptism and willingly became baptized with and for the death— as it is only through death that the resurrection from death can be witnessed—a little glimmering light appeared, in which I felt the necessity of standing up, but with the utmost caution to mind the stepping stones. For my way (for a time) was like passing through a miry bog, enclosed with mist and darkness, with just enough light to see the way—and that composed of stepping stones, and but one visible at a time. And when I had taken one step and found it to be solid and sure, I had then to look carefully for the next. And as I thus proceeded, keeping my eye single to the light that led the way, the light more and more arose out of obscurity.[191]

Jesus was sure of his role, saying, *I am come a light into the world, that whosoever believeth on me should not abide in darkness* (John 12:46). Does Jesus mean we must believe all the doctrines later formulated to underpin church authorities and structures? I do not think so. I am sure Jesus meant "believe on me" in a far simpler and deeper sense, a sense independent of doctrines, a sense any one of us can have without ever having been in a church or knowing anything about bishops and creeds. In fact, much of the doctrine was formalised some three hundred years after Jesus' earthly life and ministry.

These words can be understood exactly as the earliest apostles understood them. Jesus means believe in the sense of "Yes, I can rely on you totally and not have to resort to other gods. Nor will I rely on myself, a process that so commonly has undone me. I will trust your teachings implicitly. What you show me to do, this I will do. I will rely on you utterly".

To believe in the Light is to accept totally its guidance for living a holy and productive life, no matter who you are or what your station in life. It is to accept the Light within as Guide, not relying on your own thoughts and machinations. As Isaac Penington put it:

> When the invisible life is felt and known, do not disdain to follow it into whatever visible thing it leads. Let not thy wisdom be judge what the life will lead into, or what the life is to be followed into, or what the life is to be followed in; but let the life itself be the judge: and let the child, which is born of the life, follow it singly.[192]

George Fox felt the life and power from the Presence of God that was before the fall,

> So live in life, and the love, and the power of God, which was before man and woman fell; in that power you are kept over all outward things, that have been set up, and are set up in the fall, which cause pride, and contention, and strife; which, if lived in, keeps out of the power, in which is the saints' everlasting fellowship, that stands and remains, and is everlasting, for ever and ever. In which power the living seed lives, and the living babes are preserved; in which power they have their food from the God of life, which is living, which nourishes the immortal babes up to the immortal God, with the immortal food; through which they come to be the living stones, that build up the spiritual household (1 Peter 2:5), who are the church in God; who are brought out of the state, where Adam and Eve with their sons and daughters are drove from God, up to God again by Christ, the power of God (1 Corinthians 1:24).[193]

The Universal Nature of the Light

The early Quakers were sure the Light of Christ within is universal, available to every person, no matter whether or not each knew the Scriptures or had heard the gospel preached.[194] This did not sit well with the mainline churches in the 1600s.

William Penn wrote in *Some Fruits of Solitude* (1693) that "The humble, meek, merciful, just, pious, and devout souls are everywhere of one religion; and when death has taken off the mask they will know one another, though the divers liveries they wear here makes them strangers."[195]

It is significant that the Buddha is described as reaching 'enlightenment', a description of what many have experienced. The Qur'an, too, refers to the Light:

> Turn to God with sincere repentance; in the hope that your Lord will remove from you your ills and admit you to Gardens beneath which Rivers flow, . . . Their Light will run forward before them and by their right hands, while they say, "Our Lord! Perfect our Light for us, and grant us forgiveness: for You have power over all things".[196]

The experience of divine Light is also recorded in the ancient Bhagavad Gita of India:

> He who remembers the Poet, the Creator, who rules all things from all time, smaller than the smallest atom, but upholding this vast universe, who shines like the sun beyond darkness, far, far beyond human thought; . . . But beyond this creation, visible and invisible, there is an Invisible, higher, Eternal; and when all things pass away this remains for ever and ever. . . . This Spirit Supreme, Arjuna, is attained by an ever-living love. In him all things have their life, and from him all things have come. . . .These are the two paths that are for ever: the path of light and the path of darkness. The one leads to the land of never-returning: the other returns to sorrow.[197]

And in the words of a modern Quaker:

> I saw the love of God streaming through the universe for each and every one of us— endlessly, ceaselessly, cascading as a benign flood.[198]

On rare occasions, this Light may be an experience overwhelming in its presence and power, as it was for the three disciples, Peter, James, and John, who were present at the transfiguration (Mark 9:2-8). For some, the Light is a total reproof, such as the Light that, at its most powerful, temporarily blinded Saul on the road to Damascus (Acts 9:3-9).

Very rarely do people receive such strong mystical visions. The Light is present with us all the time if we choose to notice it, and provides guidance moment by moment. We feel it first, in a small measure, the gift of God. Our task is to follow these small glimmerings and gradually bring our life more and more into the guidance of the Light of Christ.[199]

This covenant of Light, implanted in the depths of our hearts, was known to the prophets of old, for they had anticipated and hoped for it. Many have justified Jesus as the Christ in terms of these ancient prophecies or of knowing Jesus through the Gospels.[200] However, it is not necessary to know of or believe in these connections, for the Light is experienced by many who have never known the Hebrew or Christian Scriptures.

I Am the Truth

The Truth, infallible and unchangeable, is known from ancient times. God talking to Balaam says: *God is not human, that he should lie, not a human being, that he should change his mind* (Numbers 23:19 NIV; also 1 Samuel 15:29). Humans are fallible and liable to change their minds, in contrast to the truthfulness and constancy of the Word of God.

Jesus affirms that in the Presence, the "I Am", we can know the truth of God. Jesus was in this Presence, and his teachings and example are so truthful that they are sure guides in our spiritual journey towards God.

For me, Truth embodies everything that Jesus taught, and he did not teach anything that was not in the Truth. Early Quakers used phrases such as "loving Truth", "be faithful to Truth", "die for Truth".

This usage was also common in early Christian thought and belief. For example, Gregory the Great comments on Jesus' words in John 8:47: *He that is of God heareth God's words: ye therefore hear them not, because ye are not of God.* I read the following words by Gregory and my heart responds to God.

> If one who is of God listens to the words of God, and one who is not of him cannot listen to his words, let each of us ask himself if he perceives the words of God with the ears of his heart. Then he will understand from where he is. Truth commands us to desire our heavenly home, to trample underfoot our physical desires, to turn away from the world's praises, not to covet what belongs to another. . . . They do not hear the words of God who refuse to put them into practice in their deeds. Call your life before the eyes of your hearts, dearly beloved. After you seriously reflect on it, take alarm at what you hear from Truth himself.[201]

I Am the Way and the Door

> *The truth of the matter is, I am the sheep gate. All who came before me were thieves and marauders whom the sheep didn't heed. I am the gate. Whoever enters through me will be safe—you'll go in and out and find pasture.* (John 10:7–9 TIB)

> *Jesus told him, "I am the Way, I am Truth, and I am Life. No one comes to Abba God but through me. If you really knew me, you would know Abba God also.* (John 14:6–7 TIB)

These texts say in essence, "There is no other way than the way I have shown you". In other words, "If you think you can skirt around by the back door, or muscle your way in, you are mistaken. Those who have come before pretending to show you the way have merely stolen what you had to offer and left you little in return; but those who come with me [Jesus] will find safety and real food for the soul. Consider what you see in me, for in those you also see and know *Abba*, God".

The Way recalls an ancient spirituality, not the self-serving God here to conquer other tribes but a much deeper personal spirituality. In the words of Psalm 86:11, for example: *Teach me thy way, O LORD; I will walk in thy truth: unite my heart to fear thy name.*

It seems that the followers of Jesus understood they had become followers or children of the Way. For example, Mark records Bartimaeus's response: *And immediately he received his sight, and followed Jesus in the way* (10:52). This means more than just following Jesus down the road. Jesus taught his followers how to travel spiritually and practically in the Way.

When we feel unsure, confused, or depressed, perhaps these words *I am the way* can be a pointer. We cast our inner view towards Jesus or the Light that shows the temptation or confusion. We pray quietly to Jesus or the Light till confusions and temptations dissipate.

Some have said, "There is no way to peace; peace is the way". That is similar to what Jesus is stating when he says he is the Way. This process starts with an intermittent mental application of Jesus' gospel teachings, growing into a life committed to the Way exemplified by Jesus and to the prayerful state where a living relationship with God changes and reorders both the individual's and the community's life.

Contemporary Quaker Sandra Cronk writes:

> Gospel order was the phrase early Friends used . . . to denote the personal and cosmic dimensions of God's new order. . . . 'Gospel' does not refer primarily to the intellectual content of faith or a religious message. It is the actual life, power, and reality of the relationship with God. . . . the term 'order' refers to the characteristics of daily living which flow from God's life and power and which allow the community to maintain and deepen its relationship with Christ.[202]

I Am the Good Shepherd

In ancient Palestine, the shepherd walked in front of or beside his sheep, leading them rather than driving them from behind. In this way, he met danger first and negotiated difficult pathways and crossings. He found pasture and water, caring for and protecting his sheep. The shepherd might be with the flock for years, not just a few days like the hired hand. The true shepherd knew each of his sheep. The young lambs got special help, even being carried in places where they could not keep up with the adult flock. The sheep in each flock knew the distinctive voice of their own shepherd, and it would be him they followed. Jesus' final instructions to Peter were "feed my sheep, feed my lambs". That is, be their pastor (the Latin *pastor* means 'shepherd'); be the caregiver for the flock.

The teachings and example of Jesus are the reliable shepherd for our own spiritual journey. The "I Am" is waiting in each of us to remove our fear and give us confidence and courage in facing the rigours of the spiritual journey, whatever actions may be required of us.[203]

I Am the Resurrection, the Giver of Life

> *Jesus said to her, "Your brother shall be raised up and restored to life." "I know," Martha told him, "that he will be raised up and restored at the end of time when all are restored." Then Jesus said to her, I myself am both Life and the restoration of life.* (John 11:23–25 TIB)

Martha refers to the general Hebrew belief in the resurrection of the dead in the spiritual afterlife. On this day when the Messiah comes to initiate the perfect world of peace and prosperity, the righteous dead will be brought back to life and experience the perfected world that their righteousness helped to create.[204]

Jesus debated elsewhere the issue of resurrection following a provocative remark from the Sadducees (Mark 12:18–27; Matthew 22:23–32; Luke 20:27–38). It may be that these aristocratic, well-versed, and educated elders of Jerusalem were trying to poke fun at Jesus, who was in their eyes a country hick, a Galilean peasant. The traditionalist Sadducees spurned the concept of resurrection. The Essenes believed in spiritual survival but rejected the reunification of body and spirit after death, which is the essential notion of bodily resurrection.[205]

In contrast to such emphasis on a future possibility, Jesus replies that whoever believes in him and what he is saying can experience the inner change from death to life in the living present (John 11:25). This rebirth, experienced as the coming of the Presence of God, is stated as "I Am". Jesus is concentrating on the present, not on some imagined heavenly state after a judgment day at "the end of time". His words *he that believeth in me, though he were dead, yet shall he live* mean that those of us and those parts of each of us that are spiritually dead and dark may come alive.

Jesus is contrasting Martha's plan to let it happen in the future with his insistence on the here and now. Jesus refers to himself as the embodiment of the source of real life, of spiritual existence for the life we have been given: *I am come that they might have life, and that they might have it more abundantly* (John 10:10).[206]

Although the worldly Self desires a bodily resurrection visible with outward eyes, this is not worship in the Spirit. The resurrection is spiritual and inward and occurs when those parts of our Self that have lived in darkness die; when we are transformed and find ourselves living in the present, in the Presence of God, the "I Am".

Gradually a new being is resurrected within us in the image of Christ. When each of us is ripe, the risen Jesus arrives and is spiritually present, as experienced by many people over the centuries.

The resurrection is true even now, two thousand years later, for people still experience Jesus. They experience the effect of his Light and words in their hearts.[207] The worldly powers did not succeed. Jesus is still present as the Eternal Christ, living as a spiritual reality, enabling us to lead lives centred on God. Jesus was both human and divine and is capable of leading us from dark to light so that we experience a resurrection in this life, an inward dying and a rebirth. This resurrection comes as a gift, in God's own time.

EPILOGUE

For me, John has achieved his stated aim. I have come to understand Jesus' teachings and now believe he is the Way. Yet it was not until Easter 2015 that Jesus visited me and I handed over my warm heart in a vision, after eight years of responding to the call of the shepherd seeking my soul. Not till another year had passed was I ready to talk about it much to others.

This certainty in Jesus does not mean I ignore all other spiritual writings, for many of these have had profound spiritual benefits for me, as they have had for thousands of others. The same spirit of God, the same Christ, speaks through these other writings also. However, Jesus not only provides statements that are spiritually valid; he has also left us the enduring values of his parables and miracles and, finally, his continuing Presence and Light.

One night the seed of new Life appeared to me and I learnt of the Light. My shame is that I did not stay close but wandered into paths of my self-centred thinking. Light-centred listening is required. Yet the seed continued to germinate in the darkness, and my committedness and attentiveness were fostered. I am so far from perfection it does not bear thinking about, yet there is peace in this journey and hope that more might be my portion in the end.

And it is the Light of Christ that has wrought this work, for without the Light none of it would have happened. The change that was made was made by the Light, and without the Light no change could have been made that was made.

If what I have written helps others on their journey, all praise to God.

Open our hearts, O God, to the Light of Christ.

APPENDIX 1

Historical Background

The ancient Hebrew people established themselves in the land of Canaan, now Palestine and Israel, in the period 1100-900 BCE, with continuing campaigns of warfare and territorial domination of the native tribes, as chronicled in the Hebrew Scriptures (the Christian Old Testament).[208] After their exodus from enslavement in Egypt, the ancient Hebrews in turn dominated, murdered, and enslaved the inhabitants of Canaan. The feudal system they had learned and suffered in Egypt became their own pattern.

This was the nature of the ancient world. Agrarian communities who lived on a subsistence level became dominated by wealthy landowners, and these landowners also assumed practical, religious, and cultural control of those peasant communities. For the ancient peoples of this region, wars and violence were common as each elite ruler sought to dominate and extract wealth from surrounding tribes or nations. Defeat meant death for the defeated elite, with enslavement and taxation of the people. The Hebrew peoples similarly took their own opportunities to expand control and garner power and wealth when possible. There was a millennium of the building and fall of foreign empires as well as cycles of Judaic nation building and cultural destruction. This pattern of unholy behaviour continues in the present world.

The Bible chronicles five invading empires, and is supported by modern archaeological research. These invasions subjugated the Hebrews and took away their independence for over 750 years (see appendix 2):

- Assyrians rule from 722-605 BCE (2 Kings 15:19)
- Chaldeans (Babylonians, now modern Iraq) rule from 605-539 BCE (Jeremiah 24:1, 34:1, 39:1-10, 52:1-26; Daniel 1:3-6)
- Persians rule from 539-334 BCE (Daniel 5:31, 6:1)
- Greeks rule from 334-166 BCE
- Jews are independent under the Maccabees and Hasmonean kings from 166-63 BCE

- Romans rule from 63 BCE to after 135 CE (Luke 2:1–3; John 11:48)

During one period (597/587 to 538 BCE), much of the Hebrew population was exiled to Babylon (2 Kings 24:14) until the Persians allowed their return to Jerusalem (see the book of Ezra). The Hebrew prophets portrayed these losses as God's punishment of an unfaithful people, and there was always a struggle for justice, peace, and compassion against the harsh policies of powerful and wealthy leaders.

Ancient Palestine, although a centre of traditional Judaic religion and culture, was in reality a multicultural and multilingual region with immigrant communities who maintained their own cultures and languages. Aramaic, Greek, and Roman cultures were inserted into the Hebrew nation.

The Aramaic language of the ancient Assyrians was the international trade language of the ancient Middle East beginning around 600 BCE and was the language of government administration under Assyrian and Babylonian rule of the Near East and also under the Persian Empire that stretched from India to the Mediterranean Sea.[209] Aramaic is a Semitic language closely related to Hebrew and was the general language in Palestine at the time of Jesus. Around 700 CE, Aramaic was replaced by Arabic.

The gospel of Mark records Aramaic words spoken by Jesus six times (Mark 3:17; 5:41; 7:11, 34; 14:36; 15:34), indicating that the gospel is the graphic report of an eyewitness upon whom the local language had made a deep impression. For example, in a miraculous curing of hearing and speech, Jesus uttered *Ephphatha*, the Greek form of a Syro-Chaldaic or Aramaic word that is translated as "be opened" (Mark 7:34; see also Isaiah 35:5). Mark's gospel is characterized by his use of Aramaic words that fell from Jesus' lips. Jesus' utterance on the cross of *Eli, Eli, lama sabachthani* is similarly of Aramaic origin. Although Hebrew was the official language of Judaism, it seems both Aramaic and Hebrew were used by Jesus during his ministry.[210] Paul uses the term *Abba* (Romans 8:15; Galatians 4:6), and the Aramaic words of prayer *Maran tha* (Come, O Lord) at the end of his first letter to the community at Corinth (1

Corinthians 16:22), indicating that these Aramaic words were used in the spiritual life of the early Christian communities.

Greek communities remained in the area after the invasion by Alexander the Great (334 BCE) and the subsequent imposition of Greek rule and culture by Alexander's general Seleucus. This period falls between the histories of the Old and New Testaments and so is not chronicled in either. Even after the Hebrew Maccabean revolt against this colonisation, Greek communities remained under Hasmonean rule, and Greek became the widespread language of commerce across the Mediterranean and eastern regions.[211] Reference to "Greeks" in the New Testament makes clear the presence of these language communities (e.g., John 12:20; Acts 18:4, 19:10, 17; 1 Corinthians 1:24).

The Old Testament is based on ancient Hebrew scrolls and on the Septuagint, a Greek translation of the Hebrew Scriptures prepared in Alexandria between 300-200 BCE. The Septuagint was widely used by Greek-speaking Jews and allowed foreigners who did not speak Hebrew some understanding of the ancient Judaic Scriptures. There are also ancient Masoretic and Syriac texts. It is not known if there were written Aramaic, Hebrew, or Latin versions of the gospels, for the earliest extant manuscripts of the gospels and letters of the followers of Jesus are in Greek.

Roman rule (Luke 2:1-3; John 11:48) began with the subjugation of Palestine by Ptolemy in 63 BCE. Latin, the language of the Romans, was used for their official administrative speech and records and also presumably spread into more general use. The Romans established new Roman cities and renamed local geography to suit their colonising agenda; for example, the Sea of Galilee became the Sea of Tiberias. There was seething resentment among the common people against Roman rule and taxation, anger at the polluting of Judaic sacred sites, and mixed contempt for and fear of Jewish collaborators and of the elite who profited from the colonial rule.

Luke is clear that Jesus was born during the reign of Caesar Augustus (27 BCE-14 CE) and the rule of Herod the Great (Luke 2:1, see also Matthew 2:1), about six months after his cousin who became John the Baptist (Luke 1:35-56). King

Herod the Great, appointed by the Roman Senate, ruled Palestine 37-4 BCE and was a fearsome individual. Herod started to rebuild the temple at Jerusalem (19 BCE), amongst many other important public works, yet he also murdered his wife, three sons, and other relatives and reportedly ordered the massacre of all boys under the age of two near Bethlehem in an effort to kill Jesus, who had been labelled as King of the Jews (Matthew 2:16).

John the Baptist's ministry started *in the fifteenth year of the reign of Tiberius Caesar* (Luke 3:1), which was 29 CE, and John was later imprisoned and beheaded by Herod Antipas (Luke 3:19-20; 9:9). Jesus' ministry started while John the Baptist was still preaching (John 1:15-34) and lasted for three years before he was crucified.

The first seventy years of Christianity developed under the rule of the Romans, who were wary of the new sect and in many cases deliberately persecuted it (see appendix 4). The established leaders of the Judaic religion were also opposed to the Christian sects. Roman rule, commonly with the manipulation or encouragement of the Jewish high priests, was responsible for the deaths of most of the important early leaders. Only the Apostle John seems to have still been alive a full two generations after the crucifixion of Jesus.

APPENDIX 2

Significant Dates in Palestine Based on the Old Testament

HEBREW JUDGES AND KINGS

ca. 1400 BCE	Israelites enter Canaan (Palestine) following exodus from Egypt
1025–930 BCE	Hebrew kings Saul, David, and Solomon establish kingdom of Israel and Judah
960 BCE	Solomon's temple completed in Jerusalem
930 BCE	Split of the kingdoms of Israel (Samaria) and Judah
738 BCE	Invasion of Israel by the Assyrians (2 Kings 15:19); Aramaic language dominant

BABYLONIAN (CHALDEAN) RULE (605–539 BCE)

605 BCE	Nebuchadnezzar destroys the Egyptian army at Carchemish (Jeremiah 46:2), besieges Jerusalem (Jeremiah 34:1, 39:1–10) takes Daniel to Babylon in present-day Iraq (Daniel 1:3–6)
597 BCE	Ten thousand Jews exiled to Babylon (present Iraq) by Nebuchadnezzar (2 Kings 24:14; Jeremiah 24:1).
586 BCE	Destruction of the temple at Jerusalem by Nebuchadnezzar following revolt by the appointed Jewish king Zedekiah; king executed, more Jews exiled (Jeremiah 52:1–26).

PERSIAN RULE (539–334 BCE)

539 BCE	Darius of Persia (559–530 BCE) captures Babylon and frees the Jews, who with permission from Cyrus return to Jerusalem (538 BCE) with the temple treasures (Ezra 1) to practise their own culture; many Jews remain behind (Esther); Aramaic mandated

	as the *lingua franca* from the Mediterranean to India
516 BCE	Temple rebuilding at Jerusalem is finally completed by permission of the Persian king Darius (Ezra 6:7-8, 15-18), despite bitter conflicts with the Samaritans
458 BCE	Jewish community in Jerusalem strengthened by the return of Ezra (458 BCE) and Nehemiah (438 BCE), supported by King Ataxerxes of Persia

GREEK RULE (332-166 BCE)

332 BCE	Alexander the Great conquers Palestine, having already subdued lands further east, and decrees a world united by Greek language and culture. The division between Jews who accepted the possibilities of Greek culture and those who resisted the idolatry and damage to Judaism becomes a lasting source of conflict and political wrestling in Palestine and Asia Minor
323 BCE	Death of Alexander; Greek Empire divided amongst his generals; Ptolemy takes Egypt, Seleucus rules Syria and Mesopotamia, and Ptolemy is the initial and considerate ruler of Palestine
250 BCE	Ptolemy Philadelphus sponsors Jewish scholars to produce a Greek translation of the Hebrew Scriptures at Pharos Island off Alexandria; this translation, the Septuagint, becomes the Bible of Jews outside Palestine
198 BCE	Seleucids wrest control of Palestine; Antiochus IV Epiphanes (175-164 BCE) later forcibly promotes Greek culture and the eradication of Judaism

MACCABEAN-HASMONEAN PERIOD (166–63 BCE)

166 BCE	Mattathias and family revolt against Greek Seleucid rule and the oppression of Judaism
166–164 BCE	Maccabean Revolt against Greek influence led by Judas, who established Hasmonean rule in Palestine with hereditary "high priesthood"
134–63 BCE	John Hyrcanus continues conservative Judaic Hasmonean rule in Palestine; beginning of the Sadducee and Pharisee sects; destruction of the Samaritan temple on Mount Gerizim ca. 128 BCE; from 104 BCE, a succession of Hyrcanus sons, who were less devout Jews and had Greek sympathies, undermined the Judaism of the former Maccabean leaders

ROMAN RULE (63 BCE–after 135 CE)

63 BCE	Roman general Pompey invades Palestine, intervenes in Hasmonean family rivalry and, after a three-month siege, massacres the priests in Jerusalem and subjugates Judea; provincial government of the Roman colony is entrusted to local princes
37 BCE	Herod the Great (a non-Jew) gains control of Jerusalem after a six-month siege; Herod honours Judaism and extends his empire and, though a typically ruthless, murderous ruler and Roman collaborator, also undertook major building programs, including a new temple starting in 20 BCE

Sources: *NIV Study Bible* (2011); Strauss, *Four Portraits, One Jesus*; Pfeiffer, *Between the Testaments*.

APPENDIX 3

Brief Background of the Gospels

The gospels known as Mark, Matthew, and Luke are termed the Synoptics—they see the events through the same eyes.[212] They were probably written in the period 50–70 CE, a period of conflict with the Roman occupiers (see appendix 4). In 70 CE, Jerusalem was sacked by the Roman general Titus, followed by the burning of the temple and the genocide of the Judaic community. The gospels might have been written with a sense of urgency, in these traumatic times, to preserve the oral records, to rally the early Christians, and to proclaim Jesus as a prophetic voice within Hebrew religious culture. Early followers of Jesus, the believers (Acts 4:32, 5:12), operated within the Judaic culture and synagogues (Luke 24:53; Acts 3:1–10, 5:20–21, 42), but this work to reinvigorate Judaism did not last. With the destruction of the temple at Jerusalem in 70 CE, Christians split from Rabbinic Judaism.

The Gospel According to John was written later (85–90 CE), perhaps twenty to thirty years after the other gospel narratives and two generations after the crucifixion of Jesus, when many converts had little idea of the Judaic context of Jesus' ministry. Much had happened to the early Christian communities in those decades. The policies of the Roman dictators and the fierce antipathy of the Sadducean high priests ensured persecution of the Christians for decades (1 Thessalonians 2:14).[213] However, communities of people believing in Jesus had been established across much of the northeastern Mediterranean following the missionary work of Paul and Peter. These communities were mainly Gentile with some local Jewish converts and early followers of the Way who had fled the persecution in Jerusalem.

Only a few years after the crucifixion, the followers of Jesus, referred to as Christians in Antioch probably by 40 CE,[214] were recognised as a separate religious group. Christians lived both as separate groups and also as Jewish Christians within the synagogue communities. The Letter of James, apparently written by the first bishop of these Jewish Christian communities and dating from around 45–49 CE, is an exhortation to live boldly the new Way in troubled times.

APPENDIX 3

However much of the traditional Jewish leadership stuck loyally to their Torah and would not countenance Jesus as the Christ. About 85 CE, a formal anathema was inserted in the synagogue liturgy that the Nazarenes and heretics be destroyed and removed from the Book of Life.[215]

The early Christian leader Stephen was stoned to death on the orders of the Jewish high priest in 35 CE.[216] John's brother James was beheaded by Agrippa 1 in Jerusalem in 44 CE. James, Jesus' brother and leader of the Christian community in Jerusalem, was stoned to death in 62 CE on the orders of the high priest Annas during a brief interlude between Roman procurators. Peter too was killed, probably in Rome during Nero's reign in 64 CE or shortly afterwards. Andrew was martyred in Greece in 69 CE.

By 68 CE, Paul was also gone, for he had been executed in Rome in 67/68 CE. Paul was close in age to Jesus and the disciples. He was born ca. 5 BCE and studied the Hebrew religion under Gamaliel (Acts 22:3). Paul was present at and approved the stoning of Stephen (Acts 7:54-59) and later embarked on serious persecution of Jesus' followers (Acts 9:1-2; Galatians 1:13-14; Philippians 3:5-6). Paul may have been an eyewitness to Jesus' ministry. Although he fiercely opposed Jesus at first, he became a devout apostle, entering into a mystical union with the Eternal Christ (Romans 8; Colossians 1:27; Philippians 2:1-8).

By 68 CE, of the three most intimate with Jesus,[217] James and Peter were both dead and only John was left. By 70 CE, Andrew and Paul were also dead. The Jewish leadership had been complicit in the deaths of Jesus, Stephen, and both James, as well as the persecutions of Peter and Paul. John was the last major apostle alive.

John's gospel is set over three or four years rather than the compressed narrative of one year in the other three gospels. John includes the Jewish festivals that Jesus attended and mentions that Jesus went openly into the synagogues to teach his radical message. The Torah required men to *appear before the LORD thy God* on three mandatory festivals: the Feast of Unleavened Bread (Passover), the Feast of Weeks, and the Feast of Tabernacles (Deuteronomy 16:16). The festivals provide a religious and seasonal time frame to explain Jesus' teachings in terms of the Hebrew traditions.

This intertwining places the events in their social Judaic context. It particularly explains the situation of early followers to the Way, Greek and otherwise, who were not familiar with Jewish customs. See, for example, John 6:4, *And the passover, a feast of the Jews, was nigh,* or John 19:40, which notes the burial practices of the Jews.

John is explicit why he wrote this gospel: *that ye might believe that Jesus is the Christ, the Son of God; and that believing ye might have life* (John 20:31). Jesus performed signs and delivered a message from God for the path to salvation, not only for the Jews but also as a universal ministry. John is very clear and logical about what is happening and why.

Although modern researchers debate the issue, the early church writers were clear that John's gospel derives from the authority of John the apostle, one of the two sons of Zebedee, a cousin of Jesus, one who was present with Jesus. The date of its writing is unresolved. Some modern scholars have suggested 50–70 CE. Ancient writers and early Christian traditions, drawing on the writings of Eusebius *(The Ecclesiastical History* 6.14.7, ca. 325 CE) suggest later, perhaps 90–100 CE, in Ephesus towards the end of John's life.[218]

It is unlikely that the Apostle John actually drafted and edited the text, considering the evidence in Acts 4:13 that both Peter and John were unlearned men. William Barclay argues that it was probably authored by John the Elder, a very gifted man who was close to John the Apostle at Ephesus. William Temple takes much the same view. Raymond Brown notes evidence from St. Irenaeus (ca. 180 CE), who had known Polycarp, who in turn was supposed to have known John. Brown suggests reasons to suspect the author was not the apostle, though he acknowledges the author was a "beloved" disciple and an actual witness of Jesus' life (John 13:23; 19:26; 20:2; 21:7, 20, 24). Whitacre considers three possibilities: a single source later edited, multiple sources, and composition within a community of those who had heard the teachings first-hand.[219]

John's authorship is supported by the similar wording and theology of the letter 1 John, which early Church fathers (Irenaeus, ca. 185–253; Tertullian. ca. 150–222; Clement of Alexandria, ca. 155–215; and Origen, ca. 185–253) agreed was authored by the Apostle John. Eyewitness statements (especially 1 John 1:1-4) giving evidence of a close relationship with Jesus and the tone of spiritual authority in the text support the apostolic origin of 1 John.

I accept that the internal assertions of the author's presence in the gospel are truthful (19:26, 35; 21:20, 24), for I cannot understand why the author would fabricate these details. The depth of detail in terms of places and times, the familiarity of the author with the Jewish "scene" in Palestine, and the fact it is carefully written to extend over the three years of Jesus' ministry instead of an artificially compressed storyline within one year (as in the Synoptics) all convince me that John knew the full story and was present with Jesus. In this appendix I refer to the author as John while recognising there may have been other inputs, and I hope to show just how coherent this work is. It would not surprise me at all if future scholars came to the conclusion that the Gospel According to John is indeed the record of John who walked with Jesus.

The Gospel According to John is the oral and perhaps written record of someone who was very close to Jesus and was imbued with Jesus' spiritual teachings, and it contains many eyewitness statements of Jesus' life and death. Yet this gospel is much more than a historical record. It is a teaching on the spiritual life, and it is very clearly organised and written to that end (John 20:31). I can imagine John talking with a new enquirer who came to live and learn from him in the Ephesus community. John could start at the beginning and then talk about the miracle at Cana. When the disciple had grasped that, John would tell the next story, gradually deepening the disciple's understanding of Jesus and his or her spiritual life at the same time.

John is also deeply emotional, deeply evangelical about the messages of Jesus' life and ministry, very disparaging of contemporary Jewish religious and business leadership, and passionate in his advocacy of a life of spiritual renewal and dependence on God. John talks about what Jesus' life meant, and he does it in a way that steps outside the Jewish culture to provide a version with far more universal appeal. Most of all, John addresses the contemplative life as opposed to the active life expressed in the Synoptic Gospels. John is about the spiritual essence.

John makes no pretence of writing a complete version of all that Jesus did, and he deliberately notes that there were many other signs *which are not written in this book* (John 20:30; see also 21:25). John seems to assume his readers will be familiar with Jesus' teaching and ministry, which had been taught orally and also recorded in the Synoptics. This gospel is both a recital of events and a commentary on Jesus—a record of Jesus' ministry and also a teaching by John about that ministry. It is an organised narrative of the journey of Jesus' disciples over three years and thus a series of steps for each of us in the journey of our own discipleship.

John rarely uses parables, though he does recount specific miracles, or signs of the Spirit, to highlight points in his narrative. There are repeated references to the many miracles that Jesus performed (John 2:11, 23; 7:3, 31; 10:19-21, 25; 11:47-48; 20:30). John selects nine examples, most of them new, as signs of Jesus' divine power. He chose these to bring his listeners and readers to mentally and spiritually accept Jesus as Christ. Only the miracles of Jesus' reappearance on the third day and the feeding of the five thousand are also in the other gospels:

- Changing the water into wine (2:1-11)
- Healing the official's son (4:46-54)
- Healing the lame man at the pool of Bethesda (5:1-15)
- Feeding of the five thousand (6:5-14)
- Walking on water (6:16-21)
- Giving sight to the man born blind (9:1-34)
- Raising of Lazarus from death (11:1-44)
- Jesus' resurrection and appearances on the third day to Mary and to the disciples (20:10-16, 19-22) and a week later to the disciples when Thomas was present (20:26-28)
- Jesus' reappearance with fish for breakfast beside the Sea of Galilee (21:1-14)

John's narrative style parallels Jesus' way of asking his audience a question, commonly with an ironical twist. John's teaching strategy is to quote Jesus to the people around him, initially drawing comments of puzzlement or ignorance and gradually bringing out a realisation of the spiritual weight of his teachings. The interaction with Nicodemus (John 3:1–15) is a good example. John shows clearly that Jesus was an excellent public speaker and teacher.

One of my favourite examples of Jesus' rhetorical style, though not from John, is his humorous but very serious response when people asked him about John the Baptist: "When you went out into the wilderness, what did you go for? Did you go out to see a reed waving in the breeze?" (Matthew 11:7–9).

Some may well have gone to the wilderness curious to know what might be there, having heard of this strange man preaching repentance. Was anyone spiritually daring enough to reply to Jesus? None is recorded. He raises another question to help them understand: "So what did you go out into the desert to see? Obviously not the grass waving in the breeze, so, what? A man in fine robes?" I hear the amusement in his listeners, it being well known that John was clothed in a raiment of camel hair and living off locusts and honey. Jesus scoffs at the idea: "Of course not. Those who wear soft clothing are in king's houses; they don't live in the desert".

I am sure that Jesus, like most great spiritual teachers, was very humorous. If we read this section and imagine what is happening, or better still have one friend read the role of Jesus and another react like the crowd, the humour of Jesus' teaching method becomes delightfully apparent. Then Jesus, having engaged the crowd with humour, becomes serious and replies to his own questions: "You went to see a prophet, and indeed more than a prophet—you went to see the messenger, the messenger who prepared the way".

And sometimes that is how it is, even for ourselves when we are drawn to an occasion and it turns out we hear the messenger. The messenger is just that, the preparer and pointer of the Way, not the Word itself, not the inner change, for that change is wrought quickly afterwards within us and is the work of the Spirit. But the messenger is more than a prophet who voices concerns about the state of the world; the messenger is the voice that brings us to the point of change. We never forget the messenger who brought us to that point.

The Holy Spirit continues to speak to me through the words John was given to say and write nearly two thousand years ago. For me, John is one of the messengers.

APPENDIX 4

Significant Dates in Early Christianity Based on the New Testament

7/6 BCE	John the Baptist born, six months before his 'cousin' Jesus of Nazareth (Luke 1; 2:1–3; Matthew 1:18–25).
6/5 BCE	Birth of Jesus. Birth (?) of Saul, later a pupil of Gamaliel the Elder (Acts 22:3).
4 BCE	Death of Herod the Great at Jericho, replaced by Archelaus. Palestine divided into four areas (Tetrarchs) controlled by three rulers: Herod Phillip II, Herod Antipas (Galilee), and Archelaus (Samaria, Judea, and Idumea).
5/7 CE	Jesus in the temple, aged twelve (Luke 2:41–52).
6 CE	Revolt in Judea against Roman taxation led by Judas the Galilean suppressed by the Romans with assistance of the high priests. Emperor Augustus exiles Archelaus to Gaul, and imposes Roman military rule and taxation. Judea becomes a procuratorial province under Roman rule with capital at Caesarea Maritima. Jewish Sanhedrin, dominated by hereditary (Sadducean) high priests Annas, Eleazar, and Caiaphas, collaborates with the Romans to be in effective social control and garner great wealth.
14 CE	Tiberius becomes Emperor (14–37 CE) upon the death of Augustus. Appoints as prefects (i.e., Roman administrators, judicial agents, and revenue collectors) Valerius Gratus, 15–26 CE, and then Pontius Pilate, 26–36 CE.
20 CE	City of Tiberias founded in 20 CE on the western edge of the Sea of Galilee in honour of the Roman emperor, and the colonial name Sea of Tiberius replaces the native name Sea of Galilee.

29 CE	John the Baptist undertakes a strong public ministry (fifteenth year of the reign of Emperor Tiberius, Luke 3:1). Jesus' baptism in the Jordan by John the Baptist (Luke 3:1) in 29 CE (spring?), and then John and Jesus are both teaching (John 3:22-24). Jesus' first disciples are drawn from the followers of John the Baptist (John 1:35-42). John the Baptist imprisoned for criticizing Herod Antipas and later beheaded (30-31 CE) early in Jesus' ministry.
30 CE	Jesus starts public ministry in the late summer (John 2:20) after John the Baptist arrested (Mark 1:14). Atmosphere of growing revolt against Roman taxation, military force, and desecration of religious culture by Pontius Pilate.
33 CE	Crucifixion of Jesus occurs on Passover eve, 14th of Nisan (Friday 3 April), Herod Antipas ruler and Pontius Pilate prefect. 7 April 30 CE is the alternative date.
34/35 CE	Martyrdom of Stephen ordered by the Sadducean high priests, persecution of the apostolic communities in Jerusalem and elsewhere, led by Saul (Acts 9:1-2, 26:9-11; Galatians 1:13). Believers of the Way scattered (Acts 9:2). Conversion of Saul in Damascus (Acts 9:3-19).
37-44 CE	Herod Antipas banished 39 CE. Caligula emperor (37-41 CE) and then Claudius (41-54 CE), who concedes kingship of Galilee (39 CE), then Judea and Samaria (41 CE), to Herod Agrippa I following the recall of Pilate.
44 CE	James the Great, apostle, brother of John, beheaded by Herod Agrippa I before the Passover, and then Peter imprisoned (Acts 12). Agrippa dies and Roman rule and taxation re-established under corrupt procurators.
45 CE	Famine in Judea (Acts 11:28-30)

APPENDIX 4

45–49 CE	Possible writing of Letter of James, if by James the brother of Jesus and first bishop in Jerusalem, before he was murdered in 62 CE.
48–53? CE	Paul's Letter to the Galatians from Syrian Antioch.
49–50 CE	Council of Jerusalem confirms the growing religious complexity and abandonment of Judaic rituals by early Jewish and Gentile Christians (Acts 15).
51 CE	Paul's letter 1 Thessalonians (from Corinth?), followed by 2 Thessalonians in 51/52 CE.
54 CE	Nero emperor 54–68 CE, with persecution of Christians.
55 CE	Paul's letter 1 Corinthians, written probably in Ephesus. Second Corinthians was written later, ca. 56 CE, in Macedonia.
57 CE	Paul's Letter to the Romans, probably from Corinth or nearby.
58–60 CE	Possible writing of the gospel of Luke at Caesarea during Paul's imprisonment there. Luke does not mention the death of James in 62 CE.
60–61 CE	Paul's Letters to the Ephesians, Colossians, Philemon, and Philippians while under house arrest in Rome.
60–70 CE	Probable dates for gospels of Matthew, Mark, and Luke.
62 CE	James, brother of Jesus, head of the Judaeo-Christian community, is stoned to death on orders of Jewish high priest the younger Annas, with no Roman procurator present.
63–65 CE	Paul's first letter to Timothy from Macedonia, and to Titus probably from Philippi.
64 CE	Temple completed in Jerusalem. Great Fire in Rome, for which Nero persecutes Christians.
66–67 CE	Second Timothy written by Paul while imprisoned by Nero in the Mamertime dungeon near the end of his life (2 Timothy 4).

66–74 CE	Jewish revolt, initially suppressed by the Roman governor Vespasian. Vespasian emperor 69–79 CE. Destruction of Jerusalem during the Passover by Titus 70 CE. Temple burnt, walls destroyed, end of the Sadducees, genocide of the Jews with people killed, sold into slavery, or condemned to hard labour. Disintegration of Jewish culture. Final suppression of Jewish revolt and massacre of the Jewish outpost at Masada in 74 CE.
67–68 CE	Letters of Peter. Peter martyred in Rome just before Nero's suicide. Paul's trial and execution probably 67/68 CE.
81–96 CE	Domitian the Roman emperor, again with heightened conflict with Jews.
85–95 CE	Writing of gospel and letters of John.
90–95 CE	John exiled to Patmos, and writing of final text of Revelation.
Ca. 100 CE	Death of John at Ephesus, early in rule of Roman emperor Trajan (98–117 CE).
130–135 CE	Bar Kokhba Jewish revolt in response to Emperor Hadrian setting up a temple to himself and Zeus. Expulsion of Jews from Jerusalem. Complete split of Christianity from Rabbinic Judaism. In 135 CE, city of Aelia Capitolina built on the site of Jerusalem by Hadrian.

Sources: Barnett, *Bethlehem to Patmos*; *NIV Study Bible*; Chadwick, *The Early Church*; Pfeiffer, *Between the Testaments*.

ACKNOWLEDGEMENTS

Although I aspire to understand and practice the ways of the early Quakers, I know my limitations. How can I acknowledge all the messengers who have helped me to this point? The patience and mercy of God to continue drawing me onward are more than I can understand.

Certainly the written works of the Quakers George Fox, Margaret Fell, Robert Barclay, Stephen Crisp, Sarah Jones, James Nayler, William Penn, Isaac and Mary Penington, William Dewsbury, Joseph Pickvance, William Shewen, Elias Hicks, Rex Ambler, Lewis Benson, Hugh Barbour, Michael Birkel, Paul Buckley, Sandra Cronk, Gerry Guiton, Douglas Gwyn, Richard Foster, Marcelle Martin, Janey O'Shea, John Punshon, Arthur Roberts, Dan Seeger, Bill Taber, Frances Thorsen and Terry Wallace are prominent in my grateful mind. Many other writers are referenced in this book.

Ian Grant introduced me to the writings of Joel Goldsmith and has been a regular companion on this journey. Many participants in the retreats I have led on John's gospel have enriched my own journey.

My wife Patricia has allowed and accompanied me in my extended silences, her questioning has encouraged my surrender, and her suggestions have improved my writing.

Charles Martin introduced me to the extracts quoted from William Shewen and has been a friendly companion on this writing journey. Kathy McKay has also eldered me by checking that the words coming through me are clear and accountable.

Grateful acknowledgement is made to the following publishers and authors for permission to reproduce excerpts from the publications listed below:

To Acropolis Books, Inc., for excerpt from Joel S. Goldsmith, *The Mystical 'I'*. © 1971 Emma Goldsmith.

To Darton, Longman and Todd Ltd of London for excerpts from Thomas Merton, *Contemplative Prayer*, © 1973 The Merton Legacy Trust; from Carlo Carretto, *Letters from the Desert*, 1972; and from Nicholas Peter Harvey, *Morals and the Meaning of Jesus: Reflections on the Hard Sayings*, originally published by Darton, Longman, and Todd, Ltd., London, as *The Morals of Jesus*, © 1991 Nicholas Peter

Harvey; and with Wm. B. Eerdmans (USA Rights) for excerpts from *God of Surprises* © 1985 Gerard W. Hughes SJ.

To Farrar, Strauss & Giroux, and Curtis Brown Ltd, for excerpt from "The Road Ahead" from THOUGHTS IN SOLITUDE by Thomas Merton. Copyright © 1958 by the Abbey of Our Lady of Gethsemani. Copyright renewed 1986 by the Trustees of the Thomas Merton Legacy Trust. Reprinted by permission of Farrar, Straus and Giroux. Reprinted by permission of Curtis Brown, Ltd.

To Foundation Publications for excerpt from Patrick J. Burns and Terry H. S. Wallace, eds., *The Concurrence and Unanimity of The People Called Quakers As Evidenced By Some of Their Sermons*, 2010.

To HarperCollins for brief quote from p. 51 of *A Testament of Devotion* by Thomas R. Kelly. Copyright 1941 by Harper & Row Publishers, Inc. Renewed 1969 by Lois Lael Kelly Stabler. New Introduction Copyright © 1992 by HarperCollins Publishers Inc.

To Inner Light Books for excerpts from William Shewen, *Counsel to the Christian-Traveller: Also Meditations & Experiences* © 2008 Inner Light Books; from Paul Buckley, *The Essential Elias Hicks* © 2013 Paul Buckley; from David Johnson, *A Quaker Prayer Life* © 2013 David Johnson; and from Marcelle Martin, *Our Life Is Love: The Quaker Spiritual Journey* © 2016 Marcelle Martin.

To Liturgical Press for excerpts from Thomas Merton *Contemplative Prayer* (US Rights); and from Gregory the Great, *Forty Gospel Homilies*, translated by David Hurst, Cistercian Studies 123, © 1990 by Cistercian Publications, Inc., © 2008 by Order of Saint Benedict, Collegeville, Minnesota.

To Paraclete Press for excerpts from *The Imitation of Christ*, translation © 2008 The Community of Jesus.

To Pendle Hill Publications for excerpts from Hugh Barbour and Arthur O. Roberts, *Early Quaker Writings, 1650–1700*, 2004; from Howard H. Brinton, *Guide to Quaker Practice*, 1955 (reprinted 1993); from *Gospel Order: A Quaker Understanding of Faithful Church Community*, 1991, original © Sandra L. Cronk; and from Marcelle Martin, *Invitation to a Deeper Communion*, 2003.

ACKNOWLEDGEMENTS

To Penguin Books of England for excerpts from *The Bhagavad Gita*, translation © 1962 Juan Mascaró and reproduced by permission of Penguin Books Ltd, and to Penguin Random House for excerpt from Kahlil Gibran *Jesus Son of Man*, originally published by William Heinemann.

To Peter Kearney for verse 1 of "To See the Light" from the CD *Make Me a Song*, © 1986 Peter Kearney. Available through http://www.peterkearneysongs.aradium.com.

To Quaker Books for excerpts from *Truth of the Heart: An Anthology of George Fox 1624–1691*, © Britain Yearly Meeting and Rex Ambler 2001; from *Light to Live By: An Exploration in Quaker Spirituality*, © Britain Yearly Meeting and Rex Ambler 2002; from *Journey into Life: Inheriting the Story of Early Friends*, © Gerald Hewitson 2013; and from *Knowing the Mystery of Life Within: Selected Writings of Isaac Penington in Their Historical and Theological Context*, © Britain Yearly Meeting, Melvin Keiser and Rosemary Moore 2005.

To the Religious Society of Friends (Quakers) in Australia for excerpts from the Backhouse Lectures 2008 and 2016.

To the Yearly Meeting of the Religious Society of Friends (Quakers) in Britain for excerpts from *Quaker Faith and Practice*, 2nd ed., 1999; and from *The Journal of George Fox*, edited by John L. Nickalls, 1975.

To Rowman & Littlefield for excerpts from *The Inclusive Bible*, © Priests for Equality 2007, all rights reserved.

All other excerpts involve less than 250 words, comprise less than 1 percent of the original book, and so have been reproduced as 'fair use'.

BIBLIOGRAPHY

Abbott, Margery Post. *Everyday Prophets*. The James Backhouse Lecture 2016. [Kenmore, Queensland]: The Religious Society of Friends (Quakers) in Australia, 2016.

Ali, Abdullah Yusuf. *The Meaning of the Holy Qur'an*. Pulau Pinang, Malaysia: Secretariat for Asia Assembly of Ulama', 2005.

Ambler, Rex. *Light to Live By: An Exploration in Quaker Spirituality*. London: Quaker Books, 2002.

———. *Truth of the Heart: An Anthology of George Fox 1624–1691*. London: Quaker Books, 2001.

Andrews, C. F. *The Sermon on the Mount*. New York: Macmillan Co., 1942.

Barbour, Hugh, and Arthur O. Roberts. *Early Quaker Writings, 1650–1700*. Wallingford, PA: Pendle Hill Publications, 2004.

Barclay, William. *The Gospels and Acts*. London: SCM Press, 1976.

Barnett, Paul W. *Bethlehem to Patmos: The New Testament Story*. Rev. ed. Milton Keynes, UK: Paternoster Press, 2013.

The Bhagavad Gita. Translated by Juan Mascaró. Harmondsworth, Middlesex, England: Penguin Books, 1962.

Birkel, Michael L. *Silence and Witness: The Quaker Tradition*. London: Darton, Longman & Todd, 2004.

Braithwaite, William C. *The Beginnings of Quakerism*. London: Macmillan and Co., 1912.

———. *The Second Period of Quakerism*. London: Macmillan and Co., 1919.

Brinton, Howard H. *Guide to Quaker Practice*. Pendle Hill Pamphlet # 20. Wallingford, PA: Pendle Hill Publications, 1955 (reprinted 1993).

Brother Lawrence. *The Practice of the Presence of God: Being Conversations and Letters of Brother Lawrence* [1692]. 5th impression. London: A. R. Mowbray & Co., 1977.

Brown, Raymond E. *The Gospel and Epistles of John: A Concise Commentary*. Collegeville, MN: The Liturgical Press, 1988.

Buckley, Paul. *The Essential Elias Hicks*. San Francisco: Inner Light Books, 2013.

Burns, Patrick J., and T. H. S. Wallace, eds. *The Concurrence and Unanimity of The People Called Quakers As Evidenced By Some of Their Sermons* [1694]. Camp Hill, PA: Foundation Publications, 2010.

Carretto, Carlo. *Letters from the Desert*. London: Darton, Longman & Todd, 1972.

Casey, Maurice. *An Aramaic Approach to Q: Sources for the Gospels of Matthew and Luke*. Society for New Testament Studies, Monograph Series 122. Cambridge: Cambridge University Press, 2002.

Chadwick, Henry F. *The Early Church*. The Pelican History of the Church 1. Harmondsworth, UK: Penguin Books, 1967.

Cornford, Francis MacDonald. *The Republic of Plato*. Oxford: Oxford University Press, 1979.

Cronk, Sandra. *Dark Night Journey: Inward Re-patterning Toward a Life Centred in God*. Wallingford, PA: Pendle Hill Publications, 1991.

Cronk, Sandra L. *Gospel Order: A Quaker Understanding of Faithful Church Community*. Pendle Hill Pamphlet # 297. Wallingford, PA: Pendle Hill Publications, 1991.

Dodd, C. H. *The Interpretation of the Fourth Gospel*. Cambridge: Cambridge University Press, 1953.

Ellis, George. *Faith, Hope and Doubt in Times of Uncertainty*, The James Backhouse Lecture 2008. [Kenmore, Queensland]: The Religious Society of Friends (Quakers) in Australia, 2008.

Fager, Chuck. "From Detoxification to Godwrestling: Three Stages of Bible Study." In *Reclaiming a Resource: Papers from the Friends Bible Conference*, edited by Chuck Fager, 55–64. Falls Church, VA: Kimo Press, 1990.

Fox, George. *A Collection of Many Select and Christian Epistles, Letters and Testimonies . . .* Philadelphia: Marcus T. C. Gould, 1831.

———. *The Journal of George Fox*. Edited by John L. Nickalls. London: Religious Society of Friends, 1975.

———. *The Works of George Fox*. State College, PA: New Foundation Publications, George Fox Fund, 1991.

Gibran, Kahlil. *Jesus, the Son of Man*. London: Heinemann, 1954.

Goldsmith, Joel S. *The Mystical 'I'*. Longboat Key, FL: Acropolis Books, 1971.

Gregory the Great. *Forty Gospel Homilies*. Translated by David Hurst. Cistercian Studies 123. Kalamazoo, MI: Cistercian Publications, 1990.

Guiton, Gerard. *The Early Quakers and the 'Kingdom of God': Peace, Testimony and Revolution*. San Francisco: Inner Light Books, 2012.

Gwyn, Douglas. *Apocalypse of the Word: The Life and Message of George Fox*. Richmond, IN: Friends United Press, 1991.

———. *Seekers Found: Atonement in Early Quaker Experience*. Wallingford, PA: Pendle Hill Publications, 2000.

Harvey, Nicholas Peter. *Morals and the Meaning of Jesus: Reflections on the Hard Sayings*. Cleveland, OH: The Pilgrim Press, 1993.

Hewitson, Gerald. *Journey into Life: Inheriting the Story of Early Friends*. Swarthmore Lecture 2013. London: Quaker Books, 2013.

Hughes, Gerard W. *God of Surprises*. London: Darton, Longman & Todd, 1985.

Ingle, H. Larry. *First Among Friends: George Fox and the Creation of Quakerism*. New York: Oxford University Press, 1995.

Johnson, David. *A Quaker Prayer Life*. San Francisco: Inner Light Books, 2013.

Kearney, Peter. "To See the Light." On *Make Me a Song*. Crossover Music, Mittagong, NSW, Australia, 1986. CD.

Keiser, R. Melvin, and Rosemary Moore, eds. *Knowing the Mystery of Life Within: Selected Writings of Isaac Penington in Their Historical and Theological Context*. London: Quaker Books, 2005.

Keith, George. *The Woman-Preacher of Samaria* . . . 1674. http://quod.lib.umich.edu/e/eebo/A47200.0001.001?rgn=main;view=fulltext.

Kelly, Thomas R. *A Testament of Devotion*. New York: Harper & Row, 1941.

Kübler-Ross, Elisabeth. *On Death and Dying*. London: Tavistock Publications, 1970.

Marrow, Norman. *The Four Gospels: Newly Translated from the Greek*. Luton, UK: White Crescent Press, 1977.

Martin, Marcelle. *Invitation to a Deeper Communion*. Pendle Hill Pamphlet # 366. Wallingford, PA: Pendle Hill Publications, 2003.

———. *Our Life Is Love: The Quaker Spiritual Journey*. San Francisco: Inner Light Books, 2016.

Martyn, J. Louis. *The Gospel of John in Christian History*. New York: Paulist Press, 1978.

Merton, Thomas. *Conjectures of a Guilty Bystander*. London: Burns & Oates, 1968.

———. *Contemplative Prayer*. London: Darton, Longman and Todd, 1973.

———. *Life and Holiness*. New York: Image Books, 1964.

———. *Thoughts in Solitude*. New York: Farrar, Strauss and Giroux, 1999.

Myers, Ched. *Binding the Strong Man: A Political Reading of Mark's Story of Jesus*. Maryknoll, NY: Orbis Books, 2008.

Nhat Hanh, Thich. *The Heart of the Buddha's Teaching: Transforming Suffering into Peace, Joy and Liberation*. London: Rider, 1998.

Ostler, Nicholas. *Empires of the Word: A Language History of the World*. New York: Harper Perennial, 2005.

Penn, William. *No Cross, No Crown* [1668]. Philadelphia: Friends' Bookstore, 1845.

———. *Some Fruits of Solitude* [1693]. Richmond, IN: Friends United Press, 1978.

Pfeiffer, Charles F. *Between the Testaments*. Grand Rapids, MI: Baker Book House, 1983.

Pickvance, Joseph. *George Fox on the Light of Christ Within*. New Foundation Publications No. 3. State College, PA: George Fox Fund, 1989.

Priests for Equality. *The Inclusive Bible*. Lanham, MD: Rowman & Littlefield Publishers, 2007.

Rinpoche, Sogyal. *The Tibetan Book of Living and Dying*. Rev. ed. London: Rider & Co., 2002.

Saint Augustine. *Confessions*, Translated by R. S. Pine-Coffin. Penguin Classics. West Drayton, UK: Penguin Books, 1961.

Saint Bonaventure. *The Works of Bonaventure: The Mystical Vine—Treatise on the Passion of the Lord*. Translated by Jose de Vinck. Quincy, IL: St Anthony Guild Press, 1960.

Sawyer, John F. A. *Sacred Languages and Sacred Texts*. Abingdon, UK: Routledge, 1999.

Shewen, William. *Counsel to the Christian-Traveller: Also Meditations & Experiences* [1683]. San Francisco: Inner Light Books, 2008.

———. *The True Christian's Faith and Experience* [1675]. San Francisco: Inner Light Books, 2007.

Strauss, Mark L. *Four Portraits, One Jesus: A Survey of Jesus and the Gospels*. Grand Rapids, MI: Zondervan, 2007.

Temple, William. *Readings in St. John's Gospel*. Wilton, CT: Morehouse Barlow Co., 1985.

ten Boom, Corrie, with John and Elizabeth Sherrill. *The Hiding Place*. Old Tappan, NJ: Spire Books, 1971.

Thomas à Kempis. *The Imitation of Christ*. Translated by Br. Benet Tvedten. Brewster, MA: Paraclete Press, 2008.

Tolstoy, Leo. *The Kingdom of God Is Within You*. Mineola, NY: Dover Publications, 2006.

Vermes, Geza. *The Authentic Gospel of Jesus*. London: Penguin Books, 2004.

Wallace, Terry H., Susan S. Smith, John C. Smith, and Arthur Berk, eds. *Traditional Quaker Christianity*. Barnesville, OH: Ohio Yearly Meeting, 2014.

Whitacre, Rodney A. *John*. IVP New Testament Commentary Series. Downers Grove, IL: InterVarsity Press, 1999.

Wink, Walter. *The Powers That Be: Theology for a New Millenium*. New York: Galilee Doubleday, 1999.

Yearly Meeting of the Religious Society of Friends (Quakers) in Britain. *Quaker Faith and Practice*. 2nd ed. London: Religious Society of Friends, 1999.

ENDNOTES

[1] Whitacre, *John*, 24-26. The Gospel According to John may or may not have been derived from written records, yet it is a consistent record of the ministry of Jesus and presumably summarises decades of oral teaching. In early Christian times there was a strong oral tradition of authoritative people who could speak the words of Jesus, as is apparent in the Letter of Clement to the Corinthians, a tradition that predated and even continued after the writings of the early gospels. It is thought that the Letters of Peter may be of similar origin, with better educated writers recording the words and teachings of Peter since the original Greek text of these letters is more sophisticated than would be expected of a fisherman whose primary language was Aramaic. See also Barnett, *Bethlehem to Patmos*, especially p. 183. Appendices 1 and 2 have brief overviews of the historical background of the early Christians and appendices 3 and 4 contain a discussion of the origins and style of the Gospel According to John.

[2] There are many excellent scholarly works on John's gospel. See, for example, Brown, *The Gospel and Epistles of John*. Another book by Brown, *The Community of the Beloved Disciple* (Mahwah, NJ: Paulist Press, 1979), deciphers what the gospel tells us about the church situation in which it was written. John is explicit in terms of why the gospel was written and hence why he selected and arranged the material as he did. I have also benefited from the stimulation provided by the notes in the 2011 *NIV Study Bible*, by much of William Temple's *Readings in St. John's Gospel*, by C. H. Dodd's *The Interpretation of the Fourth Gospel*, and by David Hurst's rendering of *Forty Gospel Homilies of Gregory the Great*.

[3] Fager, *Reclaiming a Resource*, 55-64.

[4] For example, see Dodd, *The Interpretation of the Fourth Gospel*; Whitacre, *John*, 24-26.

[5] Johnson, *A Quaker Prayer Life*, 4.

[6] Shewen, *The True Christian's Faith and Experience*, 25-26.

[7] The radical worship and life of the early Quakers is explored in such works as Braithwaite, *The Beginnings of Quakerism*; Braithwaite, *The Second Period of Quakerism*; Ingle, *First Among Friends*; Gwyn, *Apocalypse of the Word*; Gwyn, *Seekers Found*; Birkel, *Silence and Witness*; and Guiton, *The Early Quakers and the 'Kingdom of God'*. George Fox's *Journal* is a classic account of the difficulties of the early parts of a spiritual journey, and it records the primary witnesses of Quakers.

[8] See appendices 1-2, 4.

⁹ The nonviolence of Christ was reasserted in Tolstoy, *The Kingdom of God Is Within You* (1894) and recently by, for example, the Baptist and Quaker Walter Wink in *The Powers That Be* (1999).

¹⁰ The Roman prefect or procurator was a manager, overseer, or administrative superintendent who had the responsibility for procuring tax revenue, managing mines and construction projects, acting as paymaster for public servants, and legally keeping the peace. In contrast, a proconsul was a military governor. Tacitus and others refer to Pilate as prefect or procurator. Matthew 27:2 refers to Pilate as governor.

¹¹ See Mark 10:45 and Matthew 20:28. In Luke 9:48, Jesus says *Whoever welcomes this little child in my name welcomes me; and whoever welcomes me welcomes the one who sent me* (NIV).

¹² See, for example, Matthew 10:40, 11:27; Mark 9:37, 10:18; Luke 22:42.

¹³ The other gospels certainly mention this focus on God, though it is often glossed over given their emphasis on Jesus' teachings and healings. For example, the *only* words recorded as spoken by Jesus in his first thirty years, before his public ministry, are those in Luke when Jesus was reunited with his parents after being lost for three days: *Didn't you know I had to be in my Father's house?* (Luke 2:49 NIV). During his temptation in the wilderness, Jesus repeatedly rebuts the tempter with Old Testament quotations that require acknowledgement of God (Luke 4:1–12) rather than relying on his own authority. Jesus is 'meek', that is, God-fearing, humble, and gentle (Matthew 11:29). Early in his ministry, Jesus is clear that God is greater than himself, such as when he replies to a rich man and seeker who had addressed him as "good master": *Why callest thou me good? there is none good but one, that is, God* (Mark 10:18). Similarly, he instructs the Hebrew teachers of the law that the first great commandment involves total focus on God, not on himself (Matthew 22:34–40; Mark 12:28–34).

The most central example is the Lord's Prayer (Matthew 6:5-13; Luke 11:1-4). Jesus does not institute a prayer to himself; he institutes a prayer to his God, Father, *Abba*. Later Christians developed prayers to Jesus, but Jesus himself clearly prayed to God in reverence and holy obedience.

It is also worthwhile noting that even in Old Testament predictions of the coming of a saviour (Isaiah 7:13–14, 9:1–7, 11:1–5), Isaiah is clear the saviour will carry the spirit of the Lord and that faithfulness will be his belt. Isaiah had known the saviour would be a servant of God.

¹⁴ Paul writes to the Philippians what may have been an early Christian hymn, and the words make Jesus' humility very clear:

> In your relationships with one another, have the same mindset as Christ Jesus:
>
>> Who, being in very nature God,
>> did not consider equality with God something to be used to his own advantage;
>> rather, he made himself nothing
>> by taking the very nature of a servant,
>> being made in human likeness.
>> And being found in appearance as a man,
>> he humbled himself
>> by becoming obedient to death—
>> even death on a cross! (Philippians 2:5-8 NIV)

[15] Abba is used three times in the KJV New Testament. The other two instances are in the Letters of Paul: *For ye have not received the spirit of bondage again to fear; but ye have received the spirit of adoption, whereby we cry, Abba, Father* (Romans 8:15) and *And because ye are sons, God hath sent forth the Spirit of his Son into your hearts crying, Abba, Father* (Galatians 4:6). For the dimensions of 'pater', see The KJV New Testament Greek Lexicon, www.biblestudytools.com/lexicons/greek/kjv/pater.html. The word for 'Hebrew' (referring to the language) in the KJV New Testament is commonly translated as 'Aramaic' in the NIV and TIB, e.g., John 5:2 referring to the pool of Bethesda, John 19:13 explaining the Pavement of the judgment seat, and John 19:20 referring to languages in the title on the cross. In Paul's witness of the vision on the road to Damascus (Acts 26:14), the KJV mentions Hebrew, but both the NIV and TIB state that Jesus spoke in Aramaic. See also appendix 1. Endnote 209 gives examples in the Old Testament where the word translated as 'Syrian' in the KJV is translated as 'Aramaic' in the NIV.

[16] Jesus' words are from Psalm 31:5.

[17] This equivalence is argued by Joseph Pickvance, *George Fox on the Light of Christ Within*, 2–3. The intimate connection between Light and Life is also made in Psalm 36:9: *For with thee is the fountain of life: in thy light shall we see light.* See also Psalm 27:1 and Isaiah 2:5. Paul refers to this understanding: *ye shine as lights in the world; Holding forth the word of life* (Philippians 2:15-16).

[18] The assertions of Jesus as the Word and Light and Life were lived experiences of the disciples and early Christians. They became doctrine later.

[19] Hughes, *God of Surprises*, 113. See also Matthew 13:44.

[20] *The Bhagavad Gita*, 51.

[21] Micah 6:8.

[22] Harvey, *Morals and the Meaning of Jesus*, 84–85.

[23] Fox, *The Journal of George Fox*, 665. Fox fully accepted the argument in Romans 5:18 that if one couple's sin (that of Adam and Eve) had led to the continuing damnation of humans, then one man's obedience and sacrifice (that of Jesus) had led to salvation.

[24] Dewsbury. *A True Prophecy of the Mighty Day of the Lord* (1655), in Barbour and Roberts, *Early Quaker Writings, 1650–1700*, 100.

[25] My sense is that the masculine pronouns used in the KJV refer to the Word, as Pickvance argues in *George Fox on the Light of Christ Within*. Others, including Conservative Friends, read them as referring directly to Jesus (see Wallace, Smith, Smith, and Berk, *Traditional Quaker Christianity*, 3–4). John 1:14 has such impact because it specifically and clearly identifies the Word as Jesus. This understanding is evident in the wording of *The Inclusive Bible* (John 1:1–5). The belief in Christ containing the fullness of the image of God is also clear in John 1:16 and Colossians 1:15-20.

[26] The Word must have been an important concept in Jesus' teachings because it is also emphasised by Mark, though Mark does not elaborate on its meaning or significance: *And straightway many were gathered together . . . and he preached the word unto them* (2:2). Similarly, Luke writes about those early disciples who were *eyewitnesses and servants of the word* (1:2 NIV). In Mark's rendering of the parable of the sower (Mark 4:14–20), Jesus identifies the seed with the word: *The sower soweth the word* or *The farmer sows the word* (NIV). James in his general letter emphasises it is the word which is to be listened to and obeyed: *But be ye doers of the word, and not hearers only, deceiving your own selves* (KJV); *Do not merely listen to the word, and so deceive yourselves. Do what it says* (James 1:22 NIV). Those who knew the Old Testament would recall the words of Moses in Deuteronomy 30:11–14 and elsewhere, for example, 1 Samuel 15:22.

[27] John 1:4–9 is the principal biblical description of this Light, but it is also referred to in Matthew 6:22. The presence of this Light, as a sign of divine presence and a Guide, was also referred to in the Old Testament, e.g., Isaiah 58:8 and Isaiah 60:1-3, 19–20.

[28] Merton, *Conjectures of a Guilty Bystander*, 142.

[29] The theme of Jesus as the bringer and source of Light is not limited to John's gospel, though it is John who is most explicit. See also Matthew 4:16, 5:14–16, 6:22-23.

[30] Fox, *The Journal of George Fox*, 152.

[31] Abbott, *Everyday Prophets*, 1.

[32] Fox, *The Journal of George Fox*, 29 (1648 entry).

[33] Fox, *The Journal of George Fox*, 19 (1647 entry).

[34] See also 1 John 3:2; Romans 8:16; Galatians 3:26; Ephesians 5:8; 1 Thessalonians 5:5.

[35] This possibility is also attested by John (17:21-23) and later by Paul (2 Corinthians 3:18; Colossians 1:25-27, 2:9-10).

[36] The Levites, the Pharisees, and the Sadducees were particular groups within the Hebrew religious structure and community. The Levites were the priestly class of the tribe of Levi, established by Moses and responsible for maintaining the temple and the ancient law. The Pharisees, although committed to equality and strict adherence to the laws and regulations of the traditional Hebrew Scriptures, were commonly accused of seeking public recognition and finding loopholes in the law for their own benefit. The Sadducees were a hereditary line of high priests established during the Hasmonean rule (see appendix 1) and were wealthy aristocratic landowners. Jesus criticised all three as hypocrites for following the letter but not the spirit of the law.

[37] The passages 1:6-9, 1:15-33, and then 3:25-36 have been interpreted as John refuting claims by the followers of John the Baptist that the Baptist was indeed the Messiah. The same point of John the Baptist being the forerunner is made by Mark (1:1-8) and Luke (3:15-18). Communities did exist that followed John the Baptist (Acts 19:1-5), and the apostles worked to convince them that Jesus is the Christ.

[38] As in many other gospel narratives, this quote echoes the Old Testament prophets, in this case Isaiah 40:3: *The voice of him that crieth in the wilderness, Prepare ye the way of the Lord, make straight in the desert a highway for our God.*

[39] See also Mark 1:10-11 and Luke 3:21-22.

[40] See the quotes from and commentary on the letters of the Quaker Elias Hicks (1748-1830) in Paul Buckley, *The Essential Elias Hicks*, 65.

[41] See Myers, *Binding the Strong Man*; Wink, *The Powers That Be*.

[42] This belief and great hope in the coming of an all-powerful 'Messiah' derives from ancient writings of Judaism in Numbers 24:17-19; Deuteronomy 18:15, 18; Isaiah 9:1-7, 11:1-5, 42:1-7, 35:3-10, 61:1-2; Jeremiah 23:5-6; and Daniel 9:25-26. Micah 5:2-5 had prophesised that this ruler and the shepherd of his people would be born in Bethlehem of Judah. That belief and hope was current at the time of Jesus' birth (Luke 2:25-38). Isaiah 9:7 could well have encouraged the Hebrews to anticipate a worldly Messiah who would establish an earthly kingdom. In contrast, Jesus' work was oriented towards a spiritual kingdom of God.

Messiah is a Greek transliteration of a Hebrew or Aramaic word whose Greek translation is Christos; it originally meant 'the anointed one'. Anointing was the ritual marking priestly appointments (Exodus 40:13-15; Leviticus 4:3) and royal kingship (1 Samuel 16:1, 13; 26:11), yet the Messiah, the Christ, was not just one of these regular anointings but *the* one anointed by God.

John's gospel is the only place in the KJV New Testament that uses the term 'Messiah', and then just twice: first by Andrew when he announces he has found the Messiah, the Christ (John 1:41), and second when Jesus is recognised as the Messiah by the Samaritan woman (John 4:25, 29). In both dialogues, the use of Messiah fits the language we might expect to have been used by both Andrew and the Samaritan woman. Each of these passages also explains that the Greek term is 'Christ', which is the term used elsewhere throughout the gospel, for the latter would have been more familiar to most of John's readers. However, in Mark 1:1 the NIV includes Messiah even though the KJV uses only Christ in that verse. This confirms that the term Jesus Christ indicates that 'Jesus is the Christ' and 'Jesus is the Messiah'.

[43] For example, see Deuteronomy 12:11; Psalms 4:8, 23:6, 27:4, 90:1; John 14:10, 17; Colossians 2:9; 1 Timothy 6:16; 2 Peter 3:13; and 1 John 3:17, 4:12. Note that the NIV normally uses 'lives' instead of 'dwells', which does not have the same connotations in modern English as dwell does in the traditional biblical context.

[44] The other gospels place the clearing of the temple during the passion week at the end of Jesus' ministry. Temple, in *Readings in St. John's Gospel*, argues that John is most likely correct since Mark was artificially arranging the teachings of Peter to fit into the span of one year leading up to the final Passover when Jesus was crucified. The gospels of Matthew and Luke tend to follow Mark's pattern of writing. It is also quite possible that Jesus performed this act more than once, as presumably many of his teachings were articulated in many places at different times.

[45] Wisdom of Solomon 8:1-4 (KJV Apocrypha): *Wisdom reacheth from one end to another mightily: and sweetly doth she order all things. I loved her, and sought her out from my youth, I desired to make her my spouse, and I was a lover of her beauty. . . . For she is privy to the mysteries of the knowledge of God, and a lover of his works.* See also Sirach (Ecclesiasticus) 1:1-18; Wisdom of Solomon 7:25-26; Proverbs 1:20-21, 3:13-18, 4:5-13, 8:1-3, 9:1-6; Matthew 11:19.

[46] See especially Proverbs 2:2-13. The early Christian distinction between worldly and spiritual wisdom is emphasised by Paul in 1 Corinthians 2:1-16 and in James 1:5 and 3:13-17. This spiritual wisdom is a gift from God and was given to some in Old Testament times (2 Chronicles 1:7-12; Proverbs 1:7; Job 28:28; Daniel 1:17, 2:21),

and also to Jesus (Mark 6:2; Luke 2:40, 52), and it is possible for us (Ephesians 1:17).

[47] 2 Kings 4:1-7. The concept that Elijah would return is based on the tradition that he was taken up into the sky rather than buried in the earth (2 Kings 2:11). His reappearance is mentioned in Malachi 4:5. The Jews were actually asking if Jesus was Elijah come back to life on earth (Matthew 16:14, Mark 6:15, Luke 9:8). The New Testament uses the name Elias, which is the English equivalent of a Hellenized Hebrew name for Elijah in the early Greek gospel texts.

[48] From William Penn's preface to Fox's 1694 *Journal*, issued also as "*A brief account of the rise and progress . . . of the Quakers*". Quoted in Yearly Meeting of the Religious Society of Friends (Quakers) in Britain, *The Quaker Faith and Practice*, #19.48.

[49] In John 2:20, the Jews confirm that the temple has been under construction for forty-six years. Reconstruction started in 19 BCE, placing the events in John 2 at around 28 CE.

[50] Zechariah 14:21 is prophetic justification for this clearing of traders from the temple.

[51] The sacking and burning of the temple at Jerusalem in 70 CE also effectively ended ritual slaughter, as the necessary Jewish holy place had been destroyed. Friend Marelle Aumend has pointed out that it was Jesus who terminated the practice of ritual slaughter that had been part of Jewish culture for thousands of years. When Christians travelled to other lands such as Rome, such killing was also stopped in these foreign communities.

Donations to the temple were only accepted in the Hebrew currency (shekels), so money changers were needed to handle other coinage such as the Greek drachmas and Roman denarii that were also widely used in local business and trade.

[52] Genesis 14:18; Psalm 110:4; Numbers 1:50; Hebrews 5:6. The same point is made by Paul in Romans 3:20-21. The early Quakers recognised this new covenant.

[53] Guiton, *The Early Quakers and the 'Kingdom of God'*. See especially pp. 9, 188, 298-99.

[54] An early Christian letter (Hebrews 9:11-12, 10:9) recalls the words in Jeremiah 31:31-34 saying that God will write the laws in our hearts.

[55] Fox, *The Journal of George Fox*, 107. See also pp. 125-26.

[56] Merton, *Life and Holiness*, 55.

[57] See Braithwaite, *The Beginnings of Quakerism*, 489–90. The original story was recorded in Thomas Ellwood's *The History of the Life of Thos. Ellwood*, published in 1714.

[58] Braithwaite, *The Beginnings of Quakerism*, 490.

[59] Penington, "The Axe Laid to the Root of the Old Corrupt Tree . . .", 1659, http://www.qhpress.org/texts/penington/axe.html.

[60] Penington, "Where is the Wise? Where is the Scribe?" (1660), in Keiser and Moore, *Knowing the Mystery of Life Within*, 151.

[61] Fox, Epistle 265 (1669), http://esr.earlham.edu/qbi/gfe/e265-273.htm. The initial quote is from Proverbs 4:18–19: *But the path of the just is as the shining light, that shineth more and more unto the perfect day. The way of the wicked is as darkness: they know not at what they stumble.*

[62] Kearney, "To See the Light", verse 1.

[63] John 1:19–28; Mark 1:1–8; Matthew 3:11–12; Luke 3:15–18.

[64] Quoted in Buckley, *The Essential Elias Hicks*, epigram in front matter.

[65] Dewsbury, "There Is No Way For People To Come To Salvation, But They Must Know Christ Revealed In All Their Hearts" (1688), in Burns and Wallace, *The Concurrence and Unanimity of The People Called Quakers*, 22, 28.

[66] Luke also notes especially the gratitude of an outsider, a Samaritan, after the healing of the ten lepers (Luke 17:11–17); Jesus asks about the other nine after only one, a Samaritan, returns to praise God and give thanks. The other nine, presumably Jews, had followed the letter of Jesus' instructions under the law and gone to show themselves to the priests.

[67] Recent scholarship has corrected the historical bias against the Jewish people derived from the New Testament. See, for example, Amy-Jill Levine, *The Misunderstood Jew: The Church and the Scandal of the Jewish Jesus* (New York, NY: Harper One, 2006).

[68] Fell, *The Testimony of Margaret Fox Concerning her Late Husband George Fox . . .* (1652), as quoted in Yearly Meeting of the Religious Society of Friends (Quakers) in Britain, *Quaker Faith and Practice*, #19.07. The Scripture quoted is Romans 2:28–29.

[69] Genesis 33:18–19; 48:21–22.

[70] For more on this new covenant, see the Letter to the Hebrews, chapters 7–9.

[71] Penn, *No Cross No Crown*, chapter 5, section 4.

⁷² Penn, *No Cross No Crown*, chapter 6, sections 3 and 6.

⁷³ Keith, *The Woman-Preacher of Samaria*, 2, 7, 11.

⁷⁴ Fox, Epistle 260 (1668), http://esr.earlham.edu/qbi/gfe/e260-262.htm.

⁷⁵ The day of visitation often comes when we are being tested, and have to choose between being a witness or denying the Light. It generally can also be a time of great spiritual strengthening. See Isaiah 10:3 and 1 Peter 2:12.

⁷⁶ John uses the term 'Son of man' ten times. Jesus is quoted in all the gospels as referring to himself in this way in three contexts: (1) describing what would happen to him on earth (e.g., Matthew 20:18, Mark 10:33, Luke 9:58, John 3:14), (2) giving the reasons he, as Christ, came to earth (e.g., Matthew 20:28; Mark 8:19-34, 10:45; Luke 19:10; John 6:27), and (3) describing visions of things to come (e.g., Matthew 26:64, Mark 14:62, Luke 21:27, John 1:51).

There are three other uses of the term Son of man in the New Testament, each of which post-date the life of Jesus: (1) Stephen uses it in his vision of heaven opening just before he is stoned to death: *Behold, I see the heavens opened, and the Son of man standing on the right hand of God* (Acts 7:56, (2) John in the first vision in the Revelation: *And in the midst of the seven candlesticks one like unto the Son of man, clothed with a garment down to the foot* (Revelation 1:13), and (3) also in John's first vision: *And I looked, and behold a white cloud, and upon the cloud one sat like unto the Son of man, having on his head a golden crown* (Revelation 14:14).

The term is also used widely in the Old Testament as a description of a human being as 'son' (e.g., Numbers 23:19, Job 25:6, Isaiah 51:12, Psalm 146:3); as a term of address to a human being by God when talking in a vision to a prophet as 'son' or 'Son' (e.g., Daniel 8:17, Ezekiel 2:1, and another ninety times in Ezekiel); and once describing the personage of the Christ in human form as 'Son' (Daniel 7:13-14).

The uses by Jesus, himself both an earthly and a heavenly man, are mainly referring to the earthly form. When he says the 'Son of man' has nowhere to lay his head or is being delivered up and crucified, he is referring to his earthly form that experiences fatigue and will be tortured and put to death while acknowledging the Christ that inhabits that body. The heavenly man can never be killed. The allusion is also there to the use by Ezekiel, for Jesus acknowledges that he too is a servant of God. Jesus may have been well aware of the nuances of this term referring to himself.

Jesus' role as the Christ (referred to with the capitalized 'Son' in the phrase 'Son of man') follows Daniel 7:13-14 and is recapitulated in the Revelation to John. That Jesus saw himself as the Messiah is clear in the discussion recorded in Mark 8:29-38. In answer to Peter's statement that Jesus is the Christ (Messiah), Jesus refers to himself as 'Son of man' and then outlines the suffering he will endure and predicts his final coming in glory.

In referring to himself as 'Son of man', Jesus refers to his presence on earth as a human being in contrast to his spiritual being as the Son of God. On earth, in his role as Son of man, he has to go through suffering, as was prophesied by Isaiah (53:1-11).

John 5:27 appears to refer to Jesus' role as the Christ manifested on earth with the authority to pass judgment, as foreshadowed in Daniel and recapitulated in the book of Revelation.

[77] See, for example, John 1:12-13; Galatians 3:26-28.

[78] Mark and Matthew, having recording the miracles of the feeding, write that Jesus dismissed the crowd and the disciples so as to be alone and pray (Mark 6:45 and Matthew 14:23).

[79] A furlong is the length of a medieval open field, the area of which was one acre (one furlong long by 0.1 furlong wide). Medieval communal fields were divided into strips. The system of long furrows arose because turning a team of oxen pulling a heavy plough was difficult. This offset the drainage advantages of short furrows and meant furrows were made as long as possible. An acre was the expected area a person with a pair of oxen could plough in one day. In modern terms, a furlong equals 660 feet or 220 yards and is therefore equal to 201.168 meters. 'Furlong' was used as the translation of the Latin word *stadia*, of which there were eight to the Roman mile (*mille passum* = 1000 paces).

[80] Fox, Letter to Lady Claypole (1658), in Fox, *The Journal of George Fox*, 346-48.

[81] Other references and allusions to the Way are in Acts 16:17; 18:25-26; 19:9, 23; 22:4; 24:14, 22; and 2 Peter 2:2.

[82] Dodd, *The Interpretation of the Fourth Gospel*, 337.

[83] The Christian Eucharist or Communion is modelled on the Kiddush, a weekly Jewish sacramental observance in which the host at the meal on the eve of the Sabbath or of a festival recites a benediction and prayer over a cup of wine. The host sips from the cup and then passes it to his wife and to the others at the table; then all wash their hands and the master of the house blesses the bread, cuts it, and passes a morsel to each person at the table. Jesus would have done this regularly, and he gives this ceremony added significance in terms of his own spiritual being.

Douglas Gwyn discusses Quaker rejection of the physical Eucharist. See Gwyn, *Apocalypse of the Word*, 166–68.

[84] Luke 4:4; Deuteronomy 8:3.

[85] Fox, Epistle 31 (1653), http://esr.earlham.edu/qbi/gfe/e021-034.htm. See also John 6:51 and 1 Corinthians 12:13.

[86] See also John 7:13, 19, 25, 30, 32, 44; 8:37, 40, 59.

[87] Brown, *The Gospel and Epistles of John*, 48–49.

[88] A detailed discussion is given in Dodd, *The Interpretation of the Fourth Gospel*, 88–91.

[89] Dewsbury, *A True Prophecy of the Mighty Day of the Lord* (1655), as quoted in Barbour and Roberts, *Early Quaker Writings, 1650–1700*, 95.

[90] Hughes, *God of Surprises*, 112–13.

[91] Marrow, *The Four Gospels*, 64.

[92] Harvey, *Morals and the Meaning of Jesus*, 27–28.

[93] Fox, Epistle 10 (1652), http://esr.earlham.edu/qbi/gfe/e001-020.htm#e1.

[94] This regular alternation of prayer at night and ministry during the day is attested by Luke: *And in the day time he was teaching in the temple; and at night he went out, and abode in the mount that is called the mount of Olives. And all the people came early in the morning to him in the temple, for to hear him* (Luke 21:37-38).

[95] Jesus' time away in prayer, often alone or with a couple of close disciples, especially at night, is abundantly documented in the gospels. See also, for example, John 6:3, 6:15, 11:54; Mark 1:35, 1:45-2:1, 3:13; Luke 4:1-13, 4:42, 5:16, 9:28, 21:37-38.

[96] Fox, *The Journal of George Fox*, 98.

[97] Plato's *Republic*, written about 360 BCE, contains an allegory of the cave wherein men, in a state of unwisdom, are chained for the whole of their existence so they only see the shadows of others moving behind them as flickering images from the firelight upon the cave wall. One man is taken out to the cave entrance and into the sunlight, where he realises the truth that the world really is maintained by the light of the sun and sees the wonderful beauty of this world. When he returns, the others in the cave cannot believe him, and it is likely they will kill him. See Cornford, *The Republic of Plato*, chap. 25.

[98] Brinton, *Guide to Quaker Practice*, 15.

[99] Fox, *The Journal of George Fox*, 14.

[100] This usage of "I Am" is explored more fully in chapter 23.

[101] Thomas à Kempis, *The Imitation of Christ*, 27.

[102] Brother Lawrence, *The Practice of the Presence of God*, 25.

[103] Merton, *Thoughts in Solitude*, 79.

[104] Other examples of 'convince' being used to mean to convict, to prove wrong or guilty, are in Job 32:12, Acts 18:28, 1 Corinthians 14:24, Titus 1:9, James 2:9, and Jude 1:15.

[105] Quoted in Yearly Meeting of the Religious Society of Friends (Quakers) in Britain, *The Quaker Faith and Practice*, #11.08.

[106] John Banks, *A Journal of the Life, Labours, Travels, and Sufferings* . . . (ca. 1696), as quoted in Barbour and Roberts, *Early Quaker Writings, 1650–1700*, 183–84.

[107] Exodus 3:13–14; Revelation 22:13.

[108] Matthew 5:38–48; Romans 12:9–21.

[109] The same point is made by Jesus in Luke 13: 4-5.

[110] Psalm 51:10.

[111] 2 Corinthians 3:6.

[112] The same charge was given by Joshua (7:19) that Achan tell the truth and not hide evidence of his having looted a captured city.

[113] Isaiah 40:11, 63:11; Jeremiah 23:1–6; Ezekiel 34:1–31; Micah 2:12–13.

[114] Fox, *The Journal of George Fox*, 109.

[115] Burrough, *The Epistle To The Reader* (1658), introduction to George Fox, *The Great Mystery of the Great Whore of Babylon Unfolded*. . . ., www.strecorsoc.org/docs/burrough1.html. The text is reminiscent of Psalm 23 and Ezekiel 34:1–18.

[116] The festival was a commemoration of the dedication by Judas Maccabeus in December 165 BCE, after the temple had been earlier profaned by the Hasmonean king Antiochus IV Epiphanes. See also Brown, *The Gospel and Epistles of John*, 60.

[117] The full quotation is: "You will say, Christ saith this, and the apostles say this; but what canst thou say? Art thou a child of Light and hast walked in the Light, and what thou speakest is it inwardly from God?" Yearly Meeting of the Religious Society of Friends (Quakers) in Britain, *The Quaker Faith and Practice*, #19.07.

[118] See, in this gospel alone, John 7:1, 32; 10:39; 11:8, 57; 12:10.

[119] Kübler-Ross, *On Death and Dying*.

[120] Rinpoche, *The Tibetan Book of Living and Dying*. This book makes the case for what I have written from the Buddhist perspective, with wonderful clarity and the wisdom of an ancient tradition.

[121] Martin, *Our Life Is Love*, 39.

[122] That Jesus is the Christ is explicitly stated by Andrew (John 1:41), Peter (Matthew 16:16; Mark 8:29; Luke 9:20), the woman of Samaria (John 4:25, 29), and Martha (John 11:27) and is implied by Philip (John 1:45). Nathanael felt the same (John 1:49).

[123] Thomas à Kempis. *The Imitation of Christ*, 172. This was written prior to 1427.

[124] See also Matthew 16:24, Mark 8:34, and Luke 9:23.

[125] The practice of washing the feet of travelers and guests was customary in ancient civilizations, especially in places where sandals were the chief footwear. A host would provide water for guests to wash their feet and perhaps wash their feet himself, though most likely assigning a servant to the task. This is mentioned in several places in the Old Testament (e.g., Genesis 18:4, 19:2, 24:32, 43:24; 1 Samuel 25:41), as well as in other religious and historical documents. It is rooted in the Old Testament practice of foot washing in preparation for the marital embrace (Song of Songs 5:3) and in the ritual ablutions performed by the high priest of the old covenant (compare Exodus 30:19-21 and Leviticus 16:23-24 to John 13:3-5).

[126] Gibran, *Jesus, the Son of Man*, 166.

[127] In Latin, *Mandatum novum do vobis ut diligatis invicem sicut dilexi vos*. This is the Latin translation of John 13:34: *A new commandment I give unto you, That ye love one another; as I have loved you.*

[128] Matthew 27:3; Acts 1:18, 25.

[129] See Deuteronomy 6:4-6 and Leviticus 19:18. Leviticus 19:18 reads, *Thou shalt not avenge, nor bear any grudge against the children of thy people, but thou shalt love thy neighbour as thyself: I am the LORD.* The two requirements of forgiveness and love are clearly to be met together.

[130] See also 1 Peter 1:22-23, 1 John 4:11-12, and 1 Corinthians 13:1-13. Also, see Tolstoy's book *Walk in the Light While Ye Have Light*.

[131] Carretto, *Letters from the Desert*, chaps. 1-4.

[132] Carretto, *Letters from the Desert*, 25.

[133] Brown (*The Gospel and Epistles of John*) notes that the 'other disciple' may have been another way for John to refer to himself, as he also used the phrase 'the disciple whom Jesus loved' and the early Christian tradition was that John was himself a priest and hence was 'known to the high priest'. Temple (*Readings in St. John's Gospel*) is sure the 'other disciple' is John the son of Zebedee, Jesus' cousin, the beloved disciple. Could it have been Judas or one of the other disciples? This is unlikely, in my thinking, for John is normally very clear on facts and sequences of events and would have said so.

[134] For example, see Matthew 14:27, 17:7; Mark 6:50; Luke 8:24-25, 12:24; John 14:27. Jesus may also be recalling the words of Moses to Joshua when he was about to lead the Israelites into Canaan (Deuteronomy 31:6-8). See 1 John 4:18: *Love casteth out fear.*

[135] Merton, *Contemplative Prayer*, 26.

[136] Jesus' frustration was apparent periodically during his ministry. For example, in John 7:37-38 he cried out during the water rituals that he is the real source of 'living water'. My sense is there is some frustration in his upbraiding of the Pharisees (e.g., Luke 11:37-52) and also in his words to the crowds who asked for more and more miracles, almost like entertainment, rather than seeking a transformed life (e.g., Matthew 17:17; Luke 4:24-27, 9:41, 11:29-32).

[137] 'Paraclete' is the English transliteration of a Greek word (in Latin, *paracletus*), which meant an advocate in law, with meanings of supporting, uplifting, consoling, encouraging, and comforting.

[138] Kelly, *A Testament of Devotion*, 51.

[139] Homily 30, in Gregory the Great, *Forty Gospel Homilies*, 236.

[140] See, for example, Leviticus 7:37; Numbers 6:14, 7:1-89; Joshua 8:31; 2 Kings 16:13; Ezekiel 45:17.

[141] Saint Bonaventure, *The Works of St Bonaventure*, 147-89.

[142] From a sermon given in York in 1721. Yearly Meeting of the Religious Society of Friends (Quakers) in Britain, *The Quaker Faith and Practice*, #20.22.

[143] This is the scriptural text underlying the formal name of the Quakers: the Religious Society of Friends

[144] John Macmurray, *Ye Are My Friends* (London: Quaker Home Service, 1979).

[145] John Greenleaf Whittier, "Andrew Rykman's Prayer" (1863).

[146] Shewen, *Counsel to the Christian-Traveller*, 78-79. Matthew 11:3.

[147] Hicks, Letter (1819), as quoted in Buckley, *The Essential Elias Hicks*, 60.

[148] For instance, see Abba Isaac, Ninth Conference on Prayer, in *John Cassian: The Conferences*, ed. Boniface Ramsay (New York: Newman Press, 1997). This was recorded in the early fifth century and was based on the instructions in John 17 as well as some of the writings of St Paul.

[149] Fox, Epistle 139, http://esr.earlham.edu/qbi/gfe/e131-152.htm.

[150] From a 1654 paper in *Doctrinals*, in *The Works of George Fox*, 4:43, as quoted in Rex Ambler, *Truth of the Heart*, 62–64.

[151] Harvey, *Morals and the Meaning of Jesus*, 92–94.

[152] The brutality of crucifixion is hard to exaggerate. Luke (22:44) records that Jesus' *sweat was as it were great drops of blood*. Hematidrosis is a very rare condition in which the epidermal skin cells are ruptured, causing blood to leak from ruptured capillaries into the sweat glands. A human being literally sweats blood, and in Jesus' case it is stated the drops did not just accumulate like perspiration on the skin but dripped onto the ground. Medical evidence shows this may occur when a person is suffering extreme levels of stress and anxiety, for example, when facing his or her own death; acute fear and intense mental contemplation are the most frequent causes. Jesus was no doubt a 'sensitive soul' and would have been well aware of the ordeal in front of him. The scourging and humiliations were designed also to weaken the prisoner before the actual hanging on the cross, where the victim died of heart failure and lung collapse after many hours of agonizing pain. For a while the victim could support his weight with his feet and so use his chest and abdominal muscles to breathe. But when his legs were broken, this could not happen; breathing became increasingly arduous and then impossible, and cardiopulmonary collapse ensued.

Although the date of Good Friday varies in our calendar, the best estimates place the date of Jesus' crucifixion as Friday, April 7, 30 CE, or April 3, 33 CE. Paul Barnett (*Bethlehem to Patmos*, 51) opts for either 30 or 33 CE after a three- or four-year ministry. Pilate was governor 26–36 CE, so this must be the time frame. Jesus' ministry started in the fifteenth year of the reign of Tiberius Caesar (Luke 3:1), i.e., 29 CE. John's gospel makes it clear there were at least three Passovers during Jesus' ministry, meaning that his crucifixion occurred most likely in 32 or 33 CE.

The start of the seven-day Passover period occurs on the Hebrew calendar day of the 15th of Nisan, which can fall on several days of the week in the modern Gregorian calendar. The gospels refer to the preparation for the Passover being on a Friday, with the Passover starting on a Saturday at the time of Jesus' crucifixion. The preparation was done a day early because no work was to be done on the Saturday, the Sabbath. Two dates are possible for a Friday Passover preparation day: 4 April 30 CE and 3 April 33 CE. Luke 23:45 implies a solar eclipse, which is impossible close to the full moon, so the mention of the darkened sun seems to be poetic licence. Similarly, Acts 2:14-21 and a manuscript referred to as 'Report of Pilate' indicate that the resurrection happened when the sun was darkened and the moon turned to blood, i.e., a solar and a lunar eclipse. Humphreys and Waddington argue there was only one lunar eclipse, a time of darkness and red moon, during Pilate's governorship, and it was Friday, 3 April 33 CE. This date was the 14th of Nisan, not the Passover meal day of the 15th of Nisan. Hence Friday, 3 April 33 CE is the most likely day of the crucifixion, and the 'ninth hour' is equivalent to 3 pm.

One issue here is that 33 CE would make Jesus' age thirty-seven or thirty-eight when he was crucified. In comparison, Luke 3:23 notes he was about thirty when he started his ministry, so he would have been thirty-three or thirty-four when he died.

Detailed studies of the time frame of Jesus' death may be found in works such as H. Hoehner, *Chronological Aspects of the Life of Christ* (Grand Rapids, MI: Zondervan, 1977); Colin J. Humphreys and W. G. Waddington, "The Jewish Calendar, a Lunar Eclipse and the Date of Christ's Crucifixion", *Tyndale Bulletin* 43, no. 2 (1992): 331 51.

[153] Dewsbury, *"The discovery of the great enmity of the serpent"* (1655), abridged and slightly reordered from the original text. As quoted in Yearly Meeting of the Religious Society of Friends (Quakers) in Britain, *The Quaker Faith and Practice*, #19.45.

[154] Temple, *Readings in St John's Gospel*, as quoted in Ellis, *Faith, Hope and Doubt in Times of Uncertainty*, 30–31. Temple draws on Jesus' responses to the tempter while in the wilderness (Luke 4:1-13).

[155] See John 8:14-16; 12:23-27, 32-33; 15:18-25. See also Psalm 35:19.

[156] Martin, *Our Life Is Love*, 127-28.

[157] That Jesus came to save people from their sins is made clear in Matthew 1:21, and indeed this forgiveness and salvation happened many times in the healings during his ministry (e.g., Matthew 9:2, Mark 2:5, Luke 5:20). Jesus himself is clear he came to save, not to condemn. The only direct gospel reference to Jesus dying for the sins of all is Matthew 26:28, when Jesus says of the wine, *Drink ye all of it; For this is my blood of the new testament, which is shed for many for the remission of sins.*

Paul was visited by Jesus in a vision (Acts 9:3-9, 22:6-17), experienced the forgiveness of his sins, and was then empowered to become fully obedient as a missionary spreading the gospel. Paul is one of the main advocates of the doctrine of Jesus being sent to die for the sins of all, given his statements in Romans 3:25, 1 Corinthians 15:3, and Colossians 1:14. The First Letter of John also argues that Jesus was sent as the 'propitiation for our sins (1 John 2:2, 4:10), and the same concept is found in Revelation 1:5.

[158] Hicks, Letter (1823), as quoted in Buckley, *The Essential Elias Hicks*, 67.

[159] See also Hebrews 4:15: *For we have not a high priest which cannot be touched with the feeling of our infirmities; but was in all points tempted like as we are, yet without sin.*

[160] See, for example, Lamentations 1:14, Isaiah 47:6, and Jeremiah 28:10-14.

[161] Nhat Hanh, *The Heart of the Buddha's Teaching*, 5. Other works that illustrate the parallel teachings and presence of the inner Christ/Buddha/Krishna are Thich Nhat Hanh, *Living Buddha, Living Christ* (New York: Riverhead Books, 2007); Paramahansa Yogananda, *The Second Coming of Christ*, 2 vols. (Los Angeles: Self-Realization Fellowship, 2007); William Johnstone, *The Mirror Mind: Spirituality and Transformation* (London: Harpercollins, 1981).

[162] See also Acts 1:3-5 and 1 Corinthians 15:4-8.

[163] I note in *A Quaker Prayer Life* that the Quaker experience is that each person is given a measure of the Light, of faith, and of connectedness with God (Romans 12:3, Ephesians 4:7) and that our measure can be increased by following the Light. We are not to boast or go beyond our measure (Romans 12:3; 2 Corinthians 10:13, 15; 2 Corinthians 12:7). Careful discernment is required to know our own measure and to live obediently within that measure. In comparison, Jesus was accorded fullness of the Light, not just a measure (Luke 4:1; John 1:14, 3:34; Colossians 1:19).

[164] Fox, *The Journal of George Fox*, 11 (1647 entry).

[165] Howgill, *The Inheritance of Jacob Discovered, After His Return out of Egypt* (1656), in Barbour and Roberts, *Early Quaker Writings, 1650-1700*, 177.

[166] The same admonition to begin ministry with the gifts received from the Spirit is made in a different format in Mark 16:14-20.

[167] Much had happened in this time, with many events contributing to a widening split between Rabbinic Judaism and the early Christian church. It is easy to understand antipathy to the Jewish leaders. Stephen had been stoned in the winter of ca. 35-37 CE after a trial by the Jewish Sanhedrin. John's brother James had been killed by Herod Agrippa I in 44 CE, also the time when Peter was first

taken into prison, and both acts were apparently done to please the Jewish authorities. Andrew was crucified in 60 CE by order of the Roman governor Aegeas at Patras in Greece, and he was bound, not nailed, to the cross in order to prolong his sufferings. James (the 'brother', i.e., cousin, of Jesus) and leader of the early church in Jerusalem, had been stoned to death on the orders of the Jewish high priest Annan in 62 CE. The Romans laid siege to Jerusalem at the Passover in 70 CE, capturing it in August–September that year and burning the temple. Paul's missionary journeys following his conversion after the stoning of Stephen took place mainly between ca. 45 CE, his imprisonment in Rome 61–63 CE, and his death in perhaps 67 or 68 CE.

How long would John last? William Temple considers John 21:23 may have been included to "explain and dissipate the rumour that St. John would survive until the Second Coming". Temple, *Readings in St. John's Gospel*, 389. John himself died in Ephesus ca. 100 CE at the start of the reign of the Roman emperor Trajan.

[168] Thomas à Kempis, *The Imitation of Christ*, 89, with allusion to John 21:22.

[169] Jesus makes similar assertions of God's overwhelming goodness and of God as the source of his life and power in Matthew 11:25–27 and in Mark 9:37 and 10:18.

[170] *The Bhagavad Gita*, 85.

[171] Early Church historians (Irenaeus, Eusebius, and Jerome) listed the second pope as Linus (mentioned in 2 Timothy 4:21), though other writings listed Clement and even Paul. John's emphasis on the Holy Spirit as an inner Guide may have been a warning against concentrating spiritual authority in the hands of one individual.

[172] Romans 1:21–22.

[173] Fox, *The Journal of George Fox*, 235 (1655 entry).

[174] Fox, *The Journal of George Fox*, 143 (1652 entry).

[175] Nayler, *His last testimony* (1660), as quoted in Yearly Meeting of the Religious Society of Friends (Quakers) in Britain, *The Quaker Faith and Practice*, #19.12.

[176] Martin, *Invitation to a Deeper Communion*, 4.

[177] See Luke 16:8; John 12:36; Ephesians 5:8; 1 Thessalonians 5:5.

[178] Matthew 5:43–48.

[179] Andrews, *The Sermon on the Mount*, 149. Charles Freer Andrews was an English priest who lived a Christ-like life in India in the

service of the poor and was close to both Mohandas Gandhi and Rabindranath Tagore.

[180] Exodus 3:13-14. The meaning of YHWH is given as "I AM WHO I AM". Crowford Howell Toy and Ludwig Blau, "Tetragrammaton", *Jewish Encyclopedia*, http://www.jewishencyclopedia.com/articles/14346-tetragrammaton.

[181] *The Bhagavad Gita*, 87 (10:32).

[182] See Verse 15:49 in "The Koran", University of Michigan, www://quod.lib.umich.edu/cgi/k/koran.

[183] The difference between the 'I' as the personal ego and the mystical 'I' of the eternal divine presence is addressed by Joel Goldsmith in *The Mystical 'I'*. The difference between the two meanings can be seen in Isaiah 47:10-11, where the *I am* is self-centred, compared to Isaiah 48:12, where the divine *I am* is acknowledged as the creator from the beginning to the end.

[184] Goldsmith, *The Mystical 'I'*, 64. The texts referenced are John 14:6 and Zechariah 4:6.

[185] Jesus never says he is God. In fact, he says just the opposite; he says he can do nothing without God. Thus, we can see God at work in Jesus' actions.

[186] See Exodus 16:1-35. The word 'manna' means 'What is this?'

[187] Deuteronomy 8:2-3: *And thou shalt remember all the way which the LORD thy God led thee these forty years in the wilderness, to humble thee, and to prove thee, to know what was in thine heart, whether thou wouldest keep his commandments, or no. And he humbled thee, and suffered thee to hunger, and fed thee with manna, which thou knewest not, neither did thy fathers know; that he might make thee know that man doth not live by bread only, but by every word that proceedeth out of the mouth of the LORD doth man live.*

[188] The early Christian pastoral letter of James, the brother of Jesus, is clear: *Do not err, my beloved brethren. Every good gift and every perfect gift is from above, and cometh down from the Father of lights, with whom is no variableness, neither shadow of turning* (James 1:16-17).

[189] Ambler, *Light to Live By*, 9. The original is from Fox, *To all that would know the way to the kingdom* (1653), in *The Works of George Fox*, 4:17. This experience is also described in Isaiah 26:3.

[190] Penington, "Some Questions and Answers for the Opening of the Eyes of the Jews Natural" (1661), as quoted in Keiser and Moore, *Knowing the Mystery of the Life Within*, 153.

[191] Hicks, *Journal* (1819 entry), as quoted in Buckley, *The Essential Elias Hicks*, 30.

[192] Penington, *Babylon the Great Described* (1659), 1.187, as quoted in Keiser and Moore, *Knowing the Mystery of Life Within*, 199. Penington is referencing Ephesians 5:8: *For ye were sometimes darkness, but now are ye light in the Lord: walk as children of light.*

[193] Fox, Epistle 61 (1654), http://esr.earlham.edu/qbi/gfe/e058-078.htm. Fox's sixteenth-century language can be strange, yet the meaning is clear. See also Romans 5:18.

[194] See Gwyn, *Apocalypse of the Word*, 82–91, and George Fox, *Journal*, 33.

[195] Maxim 519 in Penn, *Some Fruits of Solitude*, 73.

[196] Ali, *The Meaning of the Holy Qur'an*, Surah 66:8. See also 24:35-36.

[197] *The Bhagavad Gita*, 78–79 (8:9, 10, 22, 26).

[198] Hewitson, *Journey into Life*, 7.

[199] See various early Quaker writings quoted in Johnson, *A Quaker Prayer Life*.

[200] For example, see Isaiah 35, Jeremiah 31:31–34, and Ezekiel 36:26-27.

[201] Gregory the Great, Homily 16 (ca. 591), in *Forty Gospel Homilies*, 114. Augustine used the phrase 'sweet Truth' (*Confessions*, 87).

[202] Cronk, *Gospel Order*, 5.

[203] See Deuteronomy 31:6–8, Psalm 23, and Isaiah 41:10. Also note the specific reassurance not to be daunted by those who revile you in Isaiah 51:7 and Matthew 5:11.

[204] Bodily resurrection in the sense of being reborn in a new and perfect world formed in the future 'at the end of time' was a recurring theme in many religions, with records dating back to some cults of the ancient Egyptians. Resurrection in the existing world of a dead person brought back to life was also documented elsewhere, for example, Jesus' raising of Lazarus. See also the Old Testament examples of Elijah (1 Kings 17:17–24) and Elisha (2 Kings 4:18–37) and the New Testament examples of the raising of Jairus's daughter (Luke 8:41–56) and the raising of Dorcas by Peter (Acts 9:36–41). See "Olam Ha-Ba: The Afterlife", *Judaism 101*, http://www.jewfaq.org/olamhaba.htm.

[205] Vermes, *The Authentic Gospel of Jesus*, 59–61. The Essenes were a Judaic sect at the time of Jesus who lived in monastic communities and may have been the authors of the Dead Sea Scrolls.

[206] Paul explains the resurrection as coming alive in Christ in 1 Corinthians 15:20-23.

[207] There are many, many examples of this in written personal histories. Here is the experience of the Dutch resistance worker Corrie ten Boom after the war upon meeting the Nazi S.S. guard who had guarded her shower room door in the Nazi concentration camp at Ravensbruck:

> His hand was thrust out to shake mine. And I, who had preached so often . . . the need to forgive, kept my hand at my side. Even as the angry, vengeful thoughts boiled through me, I saw the sin of them. Jesus Christ had died for this man; was I going to ask for more? Lord Jesus, I prayed, forgive me and help me to forgive him. I tried to smile, I struggled to raise my hand. I could not. I felt nothing, not the slightest spark of warmth or charity. And so again I breathed a silent prayer, Jesus I cannot forgive him. Give me Your forgiveness.
>
> As I took his hand the most incredible thing happened. From my shoulder along my arm and through my hand a current seemed to pass from me to him, while into my heart sprang a love for this stranger that almost overwhelmed me.
>
> And so I discovered that it is not on our forgiveness any more than on our goodness that the world's healing hinges, but on His. When he tells us to love our enemies, He gives, along with the command, the love itself. (ten Boom, *The Hiding Place*, 238)

[208] Recorded are the reigns and conquests of Joshua (Joshua), Gideon (Judges), David ca. 1000-962 BCE (1 Samuel and 2 Samuel, 1 Chronicles), and Solomon and subsequent kings (Kings and Chronicles).

[209] Ostler, *Empires of the Word*, 47, 78-84. See also Casey, *An Aramaic Approach to Q*, and Sawyer, *Sacred Languages and Sacred Texts*. References to the Syrians (KJV) as Arameans occurs in the NIV in several places, including 2 Samuel 8:5 and 10:6-19, 2 Kings 5:2 and 18:26, and Isaiah 9:12.

[210] See, for example, John J. Parsons, "Did Jesus Speak Hebrew?", Hebrew for Christians, http://www.hebrew4christians.com/Articles/Jesus_Hebrew/jesus_hebrew.html. The words transliterated as Christos and Messiah are from earlier Aramaic words (Dodd, *The Interpretation of the Fourth Gospel*, 87-88).The words *Eloi, Eloi* (Matthew 27:46-49) or *Eli, Eli* (Mark 15:34-36) *lama sabachthani* that Jesus spoke on the cross are Greek transliterations of either Aramaic or Hebrew.

[211] 1 and 2 Maccabees chronicle the Hasmonean revolt.

[212] The Synoptic Gospels are parallel texts, each a bit different as the writer addresses his audience in his own way, though in many cases the verses are word for word. Mark, the first account written down, is based on the teachings of Peter in Rome, and his version recurs in the other two Synoptics. Mark provides a solid framework with authentic geographic and social information on Jesus' movements in Galilee and his travels to Jerusalem. The gospel intermixes comprehensive accounts of the miracles to attest Jesus' divine nature with parables and other sayings to teach us how to behave and so stay on the Way to the 'Kingdom of God'. Matthew was writing to the Hebrews, and so his gospel starts with a lengthy justification of Jesus as an inheritor of the Hebrew tradition and a direct descendent of David, and many times he draws on Old Testament texts to show Jesus is the one expected, the Christ who does the deeds prophesied by Isaiah. Luke's gospel is a summary, and he is clear in his opening that it is written as a comprehensive, factual document. Luke, as might be expected of a doctor, is especially concerned with the poor and the suffering. The gospel of Luke may have been written as early as 58–60 CE since it does not mention the murder of James in 62 CE.

[213] Barnett, *Bethlehem to Patmos*, 34–37.

[214] See Acts 11:26; by 40 CE the message of Christ had been preached in Antioch, a major Roman city in northern Syria.

[215] Chadwick, *The Early Church*, 20; Martyn, *The Gospel of John in Christian History*. See also Acts 24:5.

[216] Acts 6:8–7:60.

[217] Peter and the brothers James and John (sons of Zebedee and Salome) had a deeper and closer relationship with Jesus than the other disciples did (Mark 9:2, 14:33; Luke 8:51).

[218] See *The NIV Study Bible* (2011), 9644.

[219] Barclay, *The Gospels and Acts*, xxv, xxxi–xxxiv; Temple, *Readings in St. John's Gospel*; Brown, *The Gospel and Epistles of John*, 9–10; Whitacre, *John*.

www.ingramcontent.com/pod-product-compliance
Lightning Source LLC
Chambersburg PA
CBHW022054160426
43198CB00008B/223